THIS TOO IS INDIA

Githa Hariharan has written novels, short fiction and essays over the last three and a half decades. Her highly acclaimed work includes the novels *The Thousand Faces of Night*, which won the Commonwealth Writers' Prize for Best First Book in 1993, *The Ghosts of Vasu Master*, *When Dreams Travel*, *In Times of Siege*, *Fugitive Histories* and *I Have Become the Tide*. She is the author of the short-story collection *The Art of Dying* and the essay collection *Almost Home: Cities and Other Places*. She has written children's stories and edited a collection of translated short fiction, *A Southern Harvest*, and the essay collection *From India to Palestine: Essays in Solidarity*. She has also co-edited *Battling for India: A Citizen's Reader*. For more on this Delhi-based author and her work, visit www.githahariharan.com.

EDITED BY
GITHA HARIHARAN

THIS TOO IS INDIA

CONVERSATIONS ON DIVERSITY AND DISSENT

cntxt

Published by Context, an imprint of Westland Books, a division of Nasadiya Technologies Private Limited, in 2024

No. 269/2B, First Floor, 'Irai Arul', Vimalraj Street, Nethaji Nagar, Alapakkam Main Road, Maduravoyal, Chennai 600095

ISBN: 9789360452926

10 9 8 7 6 5 4 3 2 1

Typeset by Jojy Philip, New Delhi

Printed at Manipal Technologies Limited, Manipal

In tribute to all those who came together to build
the Indian Cultural Forum, 2015–2022

Contents

Holding Up Many Skies

Diversity and Dissent: The Body and Soul of Culture

Words have already been said
much before us and
much after us.
Cut off every tongue of ours
If you can,
But words have already been said.

Lal Singh Dil, 'Words', translated from the Punjabi by Chaman Lal

When it is genuine, when it is born of the need to speak, no one can stop the human voice. When denied a mouth, it speaks with the hands or the eyes, or the pores, or anything at all. Because every single one of us has something to say to the others, something that deserves to be celebrated or forgiven by others.

Eduardo Galeano, *The Book of Embraces*

Not everything that is faced can be changed; but nothing can be changed until it is faced.

James Baldwin, 'As Much Truth as One Can Bear'

Introduction

India. The idea of India. The ideas of India. These are words that we speak and hear and think every day—almost, it seems sometimes, as often as we breathe. What images, what ideas, what intimately related words do they summon? Like many readers, writers and citizens, I too could respond instantly: plurality, multiplicity. Diversity, sometimes in unity, often not.

There comes a time when words, even words that mean something to you, take on a new life. Or so they did with me.

Between 2015 and 2022, I was part of the Indian Writers Forum, set up as a platform for individuals and groups in the cultural and academic communities. Our activities included sharing ideas and work, debate and discussion, on the two sites we set up, the *Indian Cultural Forum* and *Guftugu*. The *Indian Cultural Forum* was to address, more directly, 'cultural politics'. And *Guftugu*, the online journal which smartly declared our conviction—'Culture Matters'—was to showcase diverse cultural and artistic practice, as well as debate on such practice, through multiple forms and languages. Both online and offline, the Forum provided a safe and friendly space for an astonishing variety of people—from young students and 'invisiblised' writers, to internationally recognised artists and professors. They spoke to all of us, they spoke to each other.

I thought I had a fair idea of what 'cultural politics' may be when I helped set up the Forum. Like many of my colleagues, young and old, I found I had quite a lot to learn before I could navigate this slippery terrain. There were the multiple languages of cultural politics, almost all available to me only through translation. There were the various locations to map: where artists, writers or academics came from, whether in terms of class, caste, community, gender, sexuality, region, age, expressed or latent ideology. This was not a list; it was a maze. But it is a journey in a maze I strongly recommend to all writers, artists and academics if they want to go beyond the self and discover, or rediscover, what it is to read and write and teach and learn in the real world. It certainly forced me to get out of my room, away from my writing table, to explore; and not just the familiar and visible, but more than a few nooks and crannies of the bewildering, exciting, challenging mosaic called India. Every bit of theory, whether well-baked or half-baked, was tested in this process of exploration. And every lesson—and every mistake—assured me that there was much left to cover in this vast subcontinent-sized syllabus.

But what gains there were for me personally! A sampler: I discovered writers, translators and texts in many languages. I got a real sense, as reader, writer and citizen, of what it means to be part of a multilingual country. I received a few hard knocks about learning to be open, even vulnerable, about my privilege and my particular mix of identities. Most of all, despite a life that has been connected to social and political movements, I was learning afresh how to be part of a 'broad front'. How to enlarge, every day, the individualistic life of a writer to a 'front'; then a broad front, where consensus is part of the struggle as much as the fight against the enemy. In short, I was learning how to *live* a broad front.

Each encounter opened a door, or at least a window. It invited me to talk more, read more, write more, think more and go in search of more people with more knowledge. I was no longer a mere writer. Once you are part of a broad front which involves conversations with writers, translators, artists, filmmakers, theatre persons, musicians and dancers, teachers, activists, all from a place like India, how do you go back to being just a writer?

My own gains from the Forum comprised this wealth of learning, because in such a forum, it was possible to hear multiple voices. I could learn, in greater depth, what it means to live in a diverse country; I saw, up close, multiple riches but also multiple axes of inequality. This collection is my tribute to that sense of engagement—that process of constantly *becoming* that accompanied every conversation. The sense of belonging that underlies the words spoken; the solidarity that is given and received through an idea or a poem or play or song or novel. And all this give-and-take despite oceans of distance between one person's life and the other's.

These conversations also told me something useful about the self. I know the starting point is always the backstory of the self, the unforgettable backstory all of us need to acknowledge but not be hemmed in by. This core self, this starting point, can be a burden we carry all our lives, to be shed again and again like moulting skin. It is also the wealth we carry all our lives, malleable—thank goodness—so we can grow. The self is the deepest layer in our heads, even as we grow beyond it, even as we learn to become citizens of a bigger world.

These citizens of the larger world: each one *is* a citizen, whether acknowledged as such or not. These citizens—the self and the other—are all located within our own world, what the writer Nayantara Sahgal calls 'that glittering aspiration called India'. What are the facets of this glittering diamond? The myriad facets give voice to that old, rich word we need to learn afresh every day: diversity. Then, the fault lines, old and new, manifest themselves as divisions and exclusions. The diamond is a jewel for some, a blood diamond for others; for far too many. And, always, there are also the facets that guide us like perpetual lamps, the struggles to resist these divisions, to work for inclusion.

As this cluster of aspirations, this cluster of ideas we call India, translates into practice, how do diversity and divisions manifest themselves in the work of writers, historians, dramatists, musicians, activists? This question draws together the conversations in this collection.

I began putting together this collection with what seemed a simple purpose: to share some conversations which widened and deepened my knowledge and understanding of ideas, history, and artistic and literary practice. In short, the mosaic in which I, like my fellow citizens, have very high stakes.

The word *some* is important here. Like all stories and conversations, these are incomplete. They invite another conversation, sometimes conversations with someone else altogether on the same subject. Those I had the opportunity to talk to, sometimes over the years, are not representative in any way. Perhaps the attempt to be representative is best left to official policies and documents.

All the same, it is good to be aware of the limiting borders of the collection. For instance, 'Holding Up Many Skies' speaks mainly of women of my generation. Of course this is important to me in a personal way. But someone younger will, I know, do (or has already done) the work of compiling newer texts, views and experiences of struggles to do with gender and sexuality. The section on caste seemed to me to present multiple approaches to personal and collective experiences of discrimination and inequality. But it would be absurd to think that five conversations could be more than a quick and pale view of the subject.

These caveats aside, it is important to say that the conversations that happened, and later, the conversations that were selected for this volume, do come together as a patchwork chronicle of the times. Certain themes recur: education, the idea of a university in particular; multilingualism; the dream of a living democracy, a secular republic that upholds reason and knowledge. And, throughout, cutting across theme and language and region and community, the yearning, the aspiration, for less discrimination, less muzzling of voices and stories, less inequality. More inclusion.

It is equally important to say that there was a question that sat somewhere in the background, waiting like a sphinx as I had these conversations; and later too, as I edited them. How do you speak of and to those whose work you may admire, but who have produced that from a life very different, perhaps far less privileged than yours? Meaningful conversations call for honesty with yourself, an attempt to recognise how much of an insider or outsider (or a combination of the two) you are in the conversation.

Filmmaker, writer and teacher Trinh T. Minh-ha suggests putting into practice the formula of 'speaking nearby' rather than 'speaking about'. In an interview in 2018, she is asked, *'In your first film, Reassemblage, the voice-over declares: "I do not intend to speak about; just speak nearby." What does this mean?'* Min-ha says,

> When you decide to speak nearby, rather than speak about, the first thing you need to do is to acknowledge the possible gap between you and those who populate your film: in other words, to leave the space of representation open so that, although you're very close to your subject, you're also committed to not speaking on their behalf, in their place or on top of them. You can only speak nearby, in proximity ...[1]

Though I did not know the phrase 'speaking nearby' when I had these conversations, I hope I was aware of the 'distance' between me and the person or text—the part of the Indian mosaic that I was in conversation with. Yet the point of the conversation, its driving impulse, was a desire to understand, so as to move towards a more intelligent and meaningful solidarity. It is not that I agree with everything everyone in this volume says, or even necessarily understand every nuance of the various views expressed. But all of us in this collection do share a framework: a real-life understanding of what that weather-beaten phrase, 'unity in diversity', may be made to mean.

Having spoken with and near the people in these conversations, having met their texts, got an overview of their views on the divisions in India, as well as their dreams for India, what are some tentative conclusions I can reach? Or if conclusions are too ambitious, what are some questions I can raise?

First, what we hear; then, the questions that follow naturally. We hear, in the case of those affected by the day-to-day inequities of the caste system, that the autobiography of an individual and a community serves as the meeting point of artistic and

[1] Erika Balsom, 'Reality is Delicate', An Interview with Trinh T. Minh-ha, *Frieze*, Issue 199, November–December 2018 (https://www.frieze.com/article/there-no-such-thing-documentary-interview-trinh-t-minh-ha).

political expression. We hear women claim the right to write their own histories, whether those of the past or those that are still unfolding. We hear teachers describing their idea of a real education, and the importance of questions in the day-to-day quest for knowledge. We hear poets and playwrights, musicians and translators puzzling over layered ideas such as tradition and community, but also insisting on diversity and dissent as the body and soul of cultural and artistic practice.

In response to what we hear, we can raise a question or two. Is it possible to be a writer or an artist, a reader or a student or teacher, or indeed a citizen, in a political vacuum? If not, can we conclude that we have to view each one of us as a political being who should have access to public space?

A few words about the making of this book. Many of these conversations were originally videotaped. What is spontaneous and chatty in an oral conversation has, obviously, to be tightened and made to 'behave better' for it to work as the printed word. But I had to do this in such a way that the printed conversation remains 'true' to the voice of each of the speakers. The conversations cover a wide range of subjects, and I discovered that certain details need explanation, or need to be put in context. All the notes were added to the conversations during the process of editing.

In sum: the conversations have begun, they go on. They must go on. Words have been spoken, and they must not be forgotten. Words must be spoken, more conversations had, more arguments exchanged like gifts that travel both ways, many ways.

Githa Hariharan
New Delhi, 2024

That Glittering Aspiration Called India

NAYANTARA SAHGAL

Making and Unmaking India

Autobiography, novels, short fiction, history, political commentary, edited letters: over the decades since India's independence, Nayantara Sahgal's rich body of work has to be read in the context of Indian political life. To some extent, this is because of the family she comes from—she is the niece of Jawaharlal Nehru and the daughter of Vijayalakshmi Pandit. But mostly it is because her literary career, as her biographer Ritu Menon points out, '... spans from the 1950s to the present, a chronology that moves from the high idealism of the freedom movement to the disillusionment and cynicism that prevail today.'[2]

I had read several of Nayantara Sahgal's books over the years from the time I was a teenager. Much later, I met her at a 'literary festival' or two. But our friendship grew firm because of something bigger than us. In 2015, a large number of Indian writers from different parts of the country, writing in different languages, came together—although most of them did not even

---

[2] Ritu Menon, *Out of Line: A Literary and Political Biography of Nayantara Sahgal*, Fourth Estate, HarperCollins, 2014, p. ix.

know each other. In protest against the growing attacks on free speech, and on the practice of rationalism and diversity, these writers returned their state awards. This powerful statement of protest then spread to other communities, from scientists to filmmakers, theatre persons and artists.

Among the earliest of the writers to return their Sahitya Akademi awards, Nayantara Sahgal wrote in a statement, 'Unmaking India', on 6 October 2015:[3]

> India's culture of diversity and debate is now under vicious assault. Rationalists who question superstition, anyone who questions any aspect of the ugly and dangerous distortion of Hinduism known as Hindutva—whether in the intellectual or artistic sphere, or whether in terms of food habits and lifestyle—are being marginalised, persecuted, or murdered. A distinguished Kannada writer and Sahitya Akademi Award winner, M.M. Kalburgi,[4] and two Maharashtrians, Narendra Dabholkar[5] and Govind Pansare,[6] both anti-superstition activists, have all been killed by gun-toting motor-cyclists.

---

[3] 'Nayantara Sahgal returns her Sahitya Akademi award', *Indian Cultural Forum*, 6 October 2015 (https://indianculturalforum.in/2015/10/06/nayantara-sahgal-returns-her-sahitya-akademi-award/).

[4] M.M. Kalburgi (1938–2015), Kannada writer, noted scholar of vachana literature, and former vice-chancellor of Kannada University, Hampi, Karnataka, was outspoken in his criticism of superstition and right-wing groups. He was assassinated by two unidentified persons at his home in Dharwad on 30 August 2015.

[5] Narendra Dabholkar (1945–2013) was a physician, an activist and a rationalist who founded and led the anti-superstition movement, the Maharashtra Andhashraddha Nirmoolan Samiti (MANS). He was assassinated in Pune on 20 August 2013.

[6] Govind Pansare (1933–2015) was a communist lawyer and writer, and an activist against caste and superstition. He and his wife were out on a morning walk near their home in Kolhapur when they were shot at. While his wife, Uma, was saved with medical treatment, Govind Pansare died of his injuries on 20 February 2015.

> Other dissenters have been warned they are next in line. Most recently, a village blacksmith, Mohammed Akhlaq, was dragged out of his home in Bisada Village outside Delhi, and brutally lynched, on the supposed suspicion that beef was cooked in his home …[7]

Like many thoughtful writers who ask themselves exactly what they are doing in the public space, or why they need to take a political stand, Nayantara says, in an essay called 'We All Belong to the Country of Imagination':

> What, you might ask, has all this political-sounding activity to do with literature? Writing is a political activity in the sense that imagination reacts and responds to—for or against—the atmosphere of its time. Plays and poems and novels are not about politics, but they are the products of their times, and often of politically conscious imaginations … It is the engagement of writers with their times that has made for unforgettable fiction.[8]

Such engagement has meant, for instance, Nayantara's public stand against her cousin Indira Gandhi's Emergency; or her protest against the ongoing 'unmaking of India' with the rise of the right-wing ideology of Hindutva, whether in government, in public institutions, or in the day-to-day lives of a diverse citizenry. Nayantara has spoken in public events, written in newspapers and anthologies; she has signed statements. She has

---

[7] On 28 September 2015, Muhammad Akhlaq, fifty-five, was kicked and stoned to death after being dragged out of his house in the village of Bisada, at Dadri, Uttar Pradesh, fifty kilometres from Delhi. The lynching took place because the mob suspected there was beef in his house.

[8] Nayantara Sahgal, 'We All Belong to the Country of Imagination', Keynote speech delivered at the Dhaka Literary Festival, 18 November 2015, and published in K. Satchidanandan (ed.), *Words Matter, Writings against Silence*, Viking, Penguin Books India, 2016, p. 247.

also made choices in her personal life that express her belief in equality and in the freedom to love and live as she thinks right. The word 'political' can hold a great deal. It can, and should, encompass our view of, and challenge to, every aspect of our individual and collective lives that is affected by existing power structures. Perhaps it is this awareness that has made Nayantara Sahgal say: 'I cannot write if I do not write politically.' In other words, politics serves as her emotional mainspring even when she is writing fiction.

In 2017, Nayantara Sahgal published a dystopian satire, *When the Moon Shines by Day*. Like much of her work, this is a sharp, almost brutal political take on contemporary India. In a review in the magazine *Biblio,* I wrote that

> There used to be an India, an India that was idea, ideal and reality, what Nayantara Sahgal has described as 'a glittering aspiration'. This idea dared to imagine a nation built on its diversity. This idea recognised that living such diversity would only work if it was rooted in a democracy … Yes, there is an India now, this India in the present. And that old glittering aspiration—is it languishing in memory, dream or hope? When will it turn this hope into act, take its demand to the streets?[9]

Both past and present make up the layered background of *When the Moon Shines by Day*. The novel situates 'ideas, politics and cultural contests … in people's daily lives … and quietly, without fanfare, fuses the non-fictional quality of the day's news with the narrative demands of fiction.'[10]

---

[9] Githa Hariharan, 'When India Is No Longer Home'. Review of *When the Moon Shines by Day* by Nayantara Sahgal. *Biblio: A Review of Books* 22 (10–12), 2017.

[10] Ibid.

Soon after this book was published, Nayantara spoke to me about the making of India—her own experience of the Indian freedom struggle, and the two different ideas of India espoused by Gandhi and the Hindu Mahasabha. Moving to the present, she spoke of how the nation is being unmade—transformed in the name of Hindutva—through violence, exclusion, the suppression of dissent, and the growth of an ideology that parades as religion and distorts Hinduism.

18 September 2017

Githa Hariharan (GH): Let's begin by recalling the idea of India you were witness to in your own family—your parents, and in particular, your uncle Nehru—and then Gandhi. You actually describe this idea as the 'glittering aspiration called India'. Would you start with that so we have a context for our conversation?

Nayantara Sahgal (NS): What I meant by the 'glittering aspiration' was the struggle for freedom led by Mahatma Gandhi, a struggle in which my parents were involved. In fact, my father died of his fourth imprisonment under British rule.[11] It was an amazing period in Indian history—Gandhi brought together people in a way that cut across all the divisions, be it religion, region, class, caste or gender. That is how he created what became the foundation of independent India. Bringing together this rich diversity into a strong political unity that overthrew the British Empire was an extraordinary achievement.

[11] Nayantara's father, Ranjit Sitaram Pandit, was a barrister, linguist and scholar who took part in the non-cooperation movement. He died in 1944, shortly after being released from jail.

GH: You describe the solidarity then as a rugged idealism. Since we also want to talk about what sort of solidarity we need today, shall we recall how solidarity, how a sense of inclusiveness, happened at that time?

NS: There was the star of freedom and all these people were invited to join the march towards this star. It was a long march of twenty-five or twenty-six years in which people of all classes joined. I have to emphasise that it was the first classless venture that took place in any country. This unique achievement took place because through Gandhi, people like us, who had perhaps never had any communication with rural India, became involved, and people began organising things together. My father and mother spent most of their time in rural areas and my uncle, Jawaharlal Nehru, much like Mahatma Gandhi, travelled the length and breadth of India, speaking to village audiences. It was the first time that an English-speaking class joined hands with those speaking regional languages. The confluence was evident in the slogans that were raised during that time—'Hindu-Muslim Ek Ho!' Or 'Bharat Mata Ki Jai!' Nehru always sought the definition of 'Bharat Mata' from the common people instead of defining it himself. Another slogan was 'Inquilab Zindabad!' Such slogans were radical and emotional at the same time and they united the young and old.

GH: Could you talk about the vision that held all the freedom fighters together, across the board?

NS: It was the call to freedom that was the unifying factor. And Gandhi-ji had shown that this could be done non-violently. If it had not been a non-violent struggle, it would not have been a popular struggle, in which thousands of people, especially women, participated. Gandhi-ji invited women to participate in the freedom struggle and in 1932, about 30,000 women who were part of the struggle were in jail. Women across classes and religions participated in the movement. One of Gandhi's leading followers, Rajkumari Amrit Kaur, was Christian. Many of his comrades in the struggle were Muslim, for example, Maulana Abul Kalam Azad or Badruddin Tyabji. Some were Parsi. India's freedom struggle was the very epitome of secularism in that it brought people from different classes, different religions, speaking different languages, together. This is also reflected in the fact that there are patriotic songs in nearly all the Indian languages. Gandhi-ji's favourite hymn was in Gujarati, '*Vaishnava Jana To*' by the fifteenth-century poet Narsinh Mehta. The hymn said that the Vaishnava is the man who can feel another's pain, and so projected what freedom meant to Gandhi.

Gandhi's prayer meetings had Muslim, Christian and Hindu prayers. One can hardly forget his famous prayer '*Ishwar Allah Tero Naam*'[12] which preached the unification of all religions to reach one transcendental God. As a child, I also remember seeing a frail and skinny Gandhi-ji whose voice didn't carry very far. But this voice shook an empire. Compare this with the way elections are fought today—in the last election [in 2014], our present prime minister [Narendra Modi] made sure there were life-size images of himself everywhere.

GH: Let's move on—sadly—from that point of aspiration to where we are today, and to your novel, *When the Moon Shines by Day*. When I began reading it, I thought it was going to be a dystopia set in the future. But soon I realised the story

[12] Gandhi's version of the Ramdhun bhajan brought together the Ishwar of the Hindus and Allah of the Muslims to emphasise the composite nature of Indian society. The song was sung during the 1930 Salt March and is still part of the Gandhian legacy.

was unfolding in the present. The 'Directorate of Cultural Transformation' in the novel was especially resonant, living in the times we do. What has happened to the 'glittering aspiration' that was India, not just in your novel, but also in today's reality?

NS: We must realise, that from a country that believed in an inclusive idea of India, we are being reduced to a monoculture which is called Hindu. But what is projected as Hinduism today is a travesty of Hinduism. Hindutva is a distortion of Hinduism for a true Hindu—not a Hindu just by accident of birth, but a believer like me. My religion matters to me. In the name of Hindutva, Hinduism is being changed, distorted.

Debate and dissent have been crushed and outlawed. We know what is happening to dissenters. There have been gunshot murders of writers and journalists by passing vigilantes.[13] There has been mob lynching of ordinary people—a poor blacksmith and a dairy farmer[14] who were doing their jobs have been lynched by mobs on public thoroughfares, within sight of the police, and the Hindutva lot is quiet about this. The killers have not been punished. Instead, the victims' families are, often, made out to be the guilty party. This is very much a

[13] On 5 September 2017, less than two weeks before this conversation, the journalist Gauri Lankesh was shot dead outside her home in Bengaluru by a pair of assassins on a motorbike. In previous years, the rationalist Dr Narendra Dabholkar (in 2013), communist leader Govind Pansare (2015) and Kannada scholar M.M. Kalburgi (2015) were killed in almost an identical manner. The killers, in nearly every case, were identified by eyewitnesses, and, in each instance, were found to have links to a Hindu extremist organisation called Sanatan Sanstha.

[14] Pehlu Khan, 55, was killed in April 2017—while six others with him at the time were beaten viciously—by a mob of some 200 gau rakshaks or 'cow protectors' in Alwar, Rajasthan. Khan, a dairy farmer, was on his way home from purchasing some cows and calves.

reality of the present times. We are all witnesses to these insane travesties of justice.

GH: If we look at the old fault lines in our country, of caste or community or gender—rather than seeing them erased, we see terrible new manifestations of these divisions. I am thinking, for example, of the public flogging of dalits in Una in 2016.[15] Would you say that the new distortions of what Indian culture is about will only deepen those old fault lines of caste and community?

NS: Hindutva, as I see it, maintains that India is Hindu and this is a country of Hindus. Christians, Buddhists and Sikhs are going to be tolerated. But Muslims are to be treated as our enemies. The Mussalman has to be shown his place if he wants to live here—he is here on sufferance. The other fault line that is growing deeper under Hindutva is the oppression of dalits. There is a kind of cow mania in India today, set in motion by the ruling party. There have been violent crimes committed by the gau rakshaks who are supposed to protect the holiness of the cow. But the dalits have recently protested against this development by refusing to lift cow carcasses.[16] This kind of uprising would have delighted the hearts of both Gandhi and Ambedkar.

GH: When we spoke about the 'political' earlier, another word I should have added is 'ideology' or 'ideological'. One of the

---

[15] In July that year, a mob of gau rakshaks accused seven men from the Sarvaiya family, dalits living in Una, Gujarat, of cow-slaughter. Four of the victims were undressed by the mob, tied to a car and dragged by it, beaten with iron pipes and rods, and flogged in public. A video recording of the abuse was widely circulated.

[16] The public protest took this form in a number of villages, culminating in a meeting at Mota Samdhiyala, near Una.

very strong threads running through your novel is something many of us recall these days—the Nazi example. There is a German character in your novel who says 'Our past is your future.' Your novel suggests that it is already here. And you also suggest that this ideology implies eugenics and ethnic cleansing. Can you elaborate on this parallel?

NS: The reason I have brought in the German comparison is partly based on fact. One must recall that the Hindu Mahasabha was the ancestor of the Rashtriya Swayamsevak Sangh (RSS).[17] The Hindu Mahasabha was greatly enamoured of the rising dictatorship in Europe. In the 1920s, Hitler was not yet in the saddle, but Mussolini was. So a representative of the Hindu Mahasabha called B.S. Moonje (whom I have included in my novel) went to Italy to meet Mussolini.[18] The dictator advised Moonje that the mind must be trained for war from childhood. The Hindu Mahasabha had always believed that the Mahatma was bad for India because he emasculated the Indians through his policy of non-violence. That is why they wanted to obliterate him—and want to obliterate our memory of him. That is why Nathuram Godse killed Mahatma Gandhi. So the connection between European dictatorship and the Hindu Mahasabha was very strong. The European dictators were their icons; they felt we

[17] The Mahasabha was founded in 1916, and the RSS in September 1925.

[18] Moonje was in Rome from 15 to 24 March 1931, and recorded his (highly favourable) impressions of the fascist state in thirteen pages of diary entries. These include his account of a meeting with Mussolini on 19 March, at which Moonje praised Mussolini's militarisation of Italian schooling and society, while Mussolini wanted to hear more about Gandhi (https://frontline.thehindu.com/cover-story/moonje-amp-mussolini/article6756630.ece).

had to become a militant nation. And that is why I included the German character in my novel.

GH: Although there are variations in India—their discrimination was based on race, ours is based on caste—one must emphasise that the comparison certainly rings true even for those who might claim that there is a lack of parallel in a literal way.

NS: You will remember that 'the director of cultural transformation' in the novel says that caste is a beautiful thing because we have developed skills through caste. According to him, we have refined skills because of caste being carried from generation to generation. There are four castes and there are four outcastes and the untouchables must remain so.

As far as eugenics is concerned, there was an experiment under the Nazis to produce a superhuman race who would rule the world. When Hitler began invading Czechoslovakia, Austria and other places, his slogan was 'Today Europe, Tomorrow the World'; and this world would be ruled by superhumans, by Europe's 'master race', the Aryans. There was no such race, so it had to be produced through experiments, a race that had white skin, blonde hair, blue eyes ... Those children had to be kept in Nazi homes. I was amazed to discover very recently that a similar experiment has also begun in India.[19]

GH: At a time when writers, filmmakers, artists—the cultural community in general—are at risk, it's important to revisit

---

[19] See, for instance, Radhika Iyengar, 'RSS Custom Babies and Hindutva Theory of Aryans as the "Original Hindus"', *The Indian Express*, 12 May 2017 (https://indianexpress.com/article/opinion/web-edits/rss-custom-babies-and-their-theory-of-aryans-as-the-original-hindus/) and *Newsclick*, 10 May 2017 (https://www.newsclick.in/rss-marketing-illegal-mumbo-jumbo-science-making-superbabies).

what you've written in the book, as well as what you have done in your own life. Let me take up one specific intervention in recent times. You returned your Sahitya Akademi award in 2015 in protest against the 'unmaking of India'. Your act implied that art has to be political, that it has to take a stand in public space.

NS: We are all political because we live in a political environment. Just as the human race grows in a natural environment, so we have different kinds of political environments. Growing up, we are shaped and affected by these environments. But writers, especially, have not been able to avoid the political. Writers like Harold Pinter, Arthur Miller, and several Latin American writers have written politically, and their works have lasted because they were political. Their work reflects a universal theme within a specific context; they wrote about the human cost of living in a political environment. To the feminist movement, even the personal has often been regarded as political. So there is no avoiding the political.

GH: It occurs to me that there is an undercurrent of 'women's narrative' throughout the book. You come up with examples of discrimination, but also of active physical oppression of women throughout history. This oppression is exacerbated during times like ours because of the prevailing ideology. Was this planned?

NS: Nothing in this book was planned, everything flowed spontaneously. There are two women's narratives in the book. One depicts oppression—how women are controlled. The other is about four women, a sisterhood of women. And one of the remarkable things about their bond is that they have never been taught to efface themselves. We have two kinds of women in the book—the determinedly independent woman who knows her mind; and women who respond to a baba's call that Hindu women must have at least five children. The wife of an important businessman close to the ruling party decides to make pregnancy fashionable to influence her friends. Instead of a sari which is a lot of bunched cloth around the protruded belly, she wants a separate wardrobe so this will inspire Hindu women to get pregnant and have more children.

GH: This is actually the reverse of the propaganda that Hindus have two children and Muslims have five and so they might outnumber us.

NS: Yes, this is done in the novel to make the Hindu population grow.

GH: Caste divides spatially in India, especially in the rural areas. But increasingly we are seeing this in the cities as well and along community lines. So a Muslim may find it hard to rent a place in certain localities. In your novel, there is complete ghettoisation, something that we hope will not happen in the future. If Muslims have to come to a mainstream area, they have to change their names. Is this some kind of warning?

NS: This is, of course, my imagination at work. But the fact is that enough division has already happened, and more of it is happening every day. During the Emergency of 1975, we knew we were living in a dictatorship because the opposition had been put in jail and all debate had been crushed. The situation today is much more dangerous because everything is happening under the guise of democracy, whether it is mob lynchings or public murders, with the killers not being apprehended or convicted.

GH: I want to ask you to speak to our young people about the way forward. What should we do, not just as writers, or lawyers, or parliamentarians, but as citizens? Where do you see cause for hope?

NS: We now see protests by different groups of Indian citizens. Women, dalits, scientists, historians, filmmakers and movie stars—all kinds of people are reacting to this situation. We now have civil servants who are taking part in something called the 'Karwaan-e-Mohabbat' from the Northeast to Gandhi-ji's ashram in Gujarat,[20] making common cause with people who have suffered horribly in the past and the present. These are signs of hope—signs of giving courage to people who have suffered.

The class we call writers is an obstinate bunch of people. We will keep raising our voices. Three rationalists and a very fine journalist have been killed. Other writers have been hounded; one writer was told his fingers would be cut off. But we are not going to keep quiet and give up. This society has, since Independence, been given freedom of expression, of religion. We are free to choose what we eat, how we live, how we dress or how we love. And we are not giving up these rights, these freedoms.

GH: Let's revisit 2015 when all of us were talking every day. I recall it because it was a moment when writers, academics, filmmakers and even scientists came together and, as a gesture of protest, returned their state awards. This was just after the murder of M.M. Kalburgi, but also immediately after the murder of Akhlaq. Since then, there have been several other murders. What is the way to defeat the parivar of hate this

[20] Founded in Assam in September 2017, the Karwaan was led by volunteers from civil society, most prominently Harsh Mander. Since his resignation from the Indian Administrative Service after the Gujarat riots of 2002, Mander has taken up a number of critical issues of social activism.

time? How can we reinvent that fervour and courage to fight the ruling dispensation like we did in 2015?

NS: All these movements by various people give me hope. Teesta Setalvad, for example, is still fighting for the victims of the Gujarat riots.[21] More of us need to take on the existing horrors that confront us and try to do something about them—so people will be convinced that we can create a climate of love in a vitriolic climate of hate.

GH: And this, of course, restores—or remakes—the vision with which the country was created.

NS: We cannot recreate this vision as dramatically as Gandhi did. You know he went naked because that that is how the rest of India lived, in abject poverty, without clothes to cover themselves. What we can do is prove our solidarity with our neighbour, a Muslim or a Christian neighbour. Or anybody who is in trouble for not being an advocate of Hindutva. We must help them.

GH: In other words, we need to struggle to make India inclusive …

---

[21] On 24 June 2022, a three-judge bench of the Supreme Court issued an unsigned judgment dismissing Zakia Jafri's appeal that Narendra Modi, along with 62 others, be held accountable as part of a larger conspiracy behind the riots in Gujarat that also took the life of her husband, Ehsan Jafri, on 28 February 2002. The court made denigrating references to those who had supported Zakia Jafri during her struggle for justice, and made it clear they could now be prosecuted. The very next day Jafri's co-petitioner, Teesta Setalvad, was arrested at her home in Mumbai by the Gujarat Anti-Terror Squad. The squad arrived without a warrant and took her back to Gujarat with them. She was held at the Sabarmati Central Jail, Ahmedabad, for 63 days, till 3 September.

NS: We must heed the warning that we are not a Hindu Rashtra yet. We are very much a secular nation, and we must remain that way.

AYESHA KIDWAI

Revisiting Freedom's Shade with Anis Kidwai

It is October 1947 in the hill town of Mussoorie. Indian independence is just two months old; the tragedy of the Partition is unfolding. Shafi Ahmad Kidwai is a freedom fighter like several members of his family. As the administrator of the municipality, he has been working hard to keep the peace in Mussoorie. But the atmosphere is charged: a riot, or any sort of violence, can break out any moment. And it does. Shafi Ahmad Kidwai is murdered. His widow, Anis Kidwai, goes to Delhi, distraught. She meets Gandhi there; it seems almost natural for all kinds of people to go to Gandhi, hoping for solace.

Gandhi, pragmatic as always, advises Anis to work among those suffering the worst of the upheaval—the displaced, those who crowd squalid refugee camps, those whose families are broken, those who have lost the lives they knew.

And indeed, Gandhi's advice works. Anis's days are filled. Her life is taken over by her work in the refugee camps. The Purana Qila Muslim camp is full of the ill, the wounded and the old, of women and children; at one point, there are as many as 80,000. Not far away is the better camp at Humayun's Tomb, established by the Indian government and managed by Jamia volunteers.

The work, too often heartbreaking, continues, as every old and new fault line of prejudice and hatred turns people into beasts. But there are heroes and heroines of humanity too, managing to live out a brave moment amid the desolation. These are sometimes individuals; mostly they are dedicated volunteer groups like the 'Jamia boys', or the Shanti Dal that tries to recover abducted women.

Anis writes it all, what she sees and feels and thinks, one word following the other, right to left in her diary. The diary entries continue as Independence turns a year old, then two. In 1949, she draws on this diary—she brings together her words, memories, observations, dreams and hopes for the new nation—and writes a memoir, *Azadi ki Chhaon Mein*. The grey and darker shadows of freedom, yes; but really, the generous shade and shelter that freedom, azadi, can give people, everyone, for the new nation to actually taste Independence.

It is 2002. In the wake of the horror of events in Gujarat, Anis's granddaughter, Ayesha, reads *Azadi ki Chhaon Mein* closely. She sees the link between the present—the hatred and violence that can diminish citizens, *people*, to Muslim and Hindu—and the terrible borders that were drawn on the land and people's lives and hearts in the past her grandmother writes of. But Anis's clear voice articulates more than the horrors of Partition. She writes of ways of surviving, of coping, of carrying on to build a hardwon free India.

This is, perhaps, what moves Ayesha to begin her translation from Urdu to English:

> *Azadi* is a gift of memory that both inspires and liberates. To every story of atrocities committed in the name of religion, one of organised resistance by citizens is added—when Harijans are evicted from a Delhi village, Subhadra Joshi and Anis Kidwai restore them to their homes; when the city is rife with tension between refugees and the remaining few Muslims, students and teachers of Jamia Millia open a school for Hindu and Muslim children to study and play together; when rumours of a fresh wave of rioting on 15 June 1948 course through the province of Delhi, the frenetic efforts by Shanti Dal activists ensure that the date passes by without incident.[22]

Ayesha adds: '… *Azadi* also points us to many important lessons that we should have learnt.' Anis's voice, her balanced account of inhumanity and humanity, atrocity and resistance, tells Ayesha that the past speaks to us, if only we would listen to it. If she listens to her grandmother's words, she may find insight into the present (and the horrors of 2002) that she is searching for:

> Translating *Azadi Ki Chhaon Mein* has had a profound impact on my life and thinking, not the least because it turned me into a translator … In my academic life, Anis's account of the role of Mridula Sarabhai and her band of women social workers in the rescue of abducted women have led me to research and publish about them, as well as on Muslim women's life writing and the Hindustani vs. Hindi–Urdu–Hindustani debate. In my personal life, translating *Azadi Ki Chhaon Mein* has given me the unique opportunity to really know my grandmother, … whose candour, hopefulness,

[22] Translator's Introduction, *In Freedom's Shade*, Penguin Books, 2011, p. viii.

> generosity and belief in women's autonomy form the bedrock of the values held dear by my family.[23]

As Ayesha translates, she shares her work with a few friends. I am one of them. As I read chapter after chapter that Ayesha sends me, critical moments in our collective history become vivid, real, peopled. They tell us of the *then*, but also the *now*, they show us the awful and brave links between past and present. They tell us of real lives, of real people from diverse communities, struggling to come together to make an inclusive nation.

24 February 2012

Githa Hariharan (GH): Ayesha, a chapter or two into the book, I was completely engaged, and not just as a witness to our history. I was drawn in by this woman, Anis, full of fears and disappointments, but also full of desires for her friends and the community around her. Most of all, so full of hopes for this new nation, India. What struck me was how alive and relevant her memoir is. Would you begin with a context—how did you come to translate *Azadi Ki Chhaon Mein*?

Ayesha Kidwai (AK): I first came to this book, really came to it as an adult, around 2002, after the Gujarat riots.[24] We were all impacted by what happened in Gujarat, and earlier,

---

[23] Ayesha Kidwai, 'My arduous yet rewarding journey as a translator', *The New India Foundation* (https://newindiafoundation.stck.me/post/2216/In-Freedom-s-Shade?fbclid=IwAR3fsAp9RKtVdw9WpqGWKDc76cRWpmXHpbEPc7B443H1uIH4GaI2efEcMlA).

[24] Considered the worst 'riot' in India since Partition, there were state-wide attacks against Muslims in Gujarat, leaving behind horrific stories of death, rape, suffering and displacement. Justice continues to evade the survivors, especially because the state government then—belonging to the

by what had happened in 1984.[25] So I came to the book to try and understand what Partition was like and how this new eruption of violence was different. I saw the reaction of people like Kuldeep Nayyar[26] who said that sixty years after India's independence, this was the first time he had wept. After Partition, when he had crossed the border over to India, he had resolved to himself that this [violence] would never happen again. But it did—and when he went to Gujarat, he wept.

So I came to the book very much like you, expecting to find tears, to find visions of horror. But instead I found a perspective which could be that of a friend, of somebody who is a witness but not complicit; and who is painfully conscious of the fact that if you are a witness and you remain mute, you are complicit.

As I began the process of translation, I discovered that the book was not intended as a memoir. It was published in Urdu in 1974, but it was known earlier. When Anis Kidwai wrote it in 1949, she was a political witness. She was competing to create memory. And the means by which she created memory was by peopling this universe of Delhi in 1947-48, not only with victims, but with the people who fought against hate and violence. In some sense, this book is a 'dual memoir' now, when we receive it as a memory. There is a restorative aspect

---

same party that is now in power at the Centre—is accused of looking the other way, if not actively conniving in the violence.

[25] Following the assassination of Prime Minister Indira Gandhi by her Sikh bodyguards on 31 October 1984, there were planned attacks on Sikhs in Delhi and other parts of the country. Thousands were massacred, and thousands were displaced. Armed mobs attacked the homes and businesses of Sikhs, and gurudwaras.

[26] Kuldeep Nayyar (1923–2018) was a veteran Indian journalist and human rights activist. He was a strong advocate of peace between India and Pakistan.

to it, putting into the picture all the people who had fought at that time.

We've had a kind of collective silence about Partition and its afterlife: it is taken as something that just happened. It lasted two years, maybe it went on a long time in terms of migration, but it is sort of secluded. It has become encrypted, it has no history. All the secularism, along with everything that goes with it organically, would seem to have either sprung from our generation, or the generation before Independence. Looking at the time before Independence would then mean returning to a past that was more secular than what followed. For me, this book is tremendously important because it restores Partition in the life of this city into a historicity.

GH: It also restores Partition to human stories that are still true today in both positive and negative ways. There's the anguish, the abducted women, the feeling that you are being pulled out by the root from what you've thought of as your home, and being sent somewhere else. There are these stories of anguish. And then there are the stories of your man and woman and child on the streets doing something extraordinarily brave, helping someone quite spontaneously. Perhaps you could talk about an example of each of these aspects?

AK: I think the first example of this bravery is Anis Kidwai herself, because this book begins with her husband, Shafi Ahmad Kidwai, getting murdered in Mussoorie in October 1947. The first chapter, in which she describes what Mussoorie had been like and how the place slowly empties out, is extraordinarily moving. Muslims were sent to the camps. Shafi Ahmad was the only person preventing the land owned by Muslims from being taken over. That story then ended in his ghastly murder.

And Anis Kidwai couldn't understand what had happened for a week, she couldn't gather herself.

Then, giving truth to the song that we all sing in demonstrations, '*Tu zinda hai, tu zindagi ki jeet pe yaqeen kar*', Anis Kidwai came to Delhi. She did not want to pursue the matter of who murdered her husband—why would she make the murderer's mother lose her son? Why would she make his wife a widow? That's what she said. And so when she came to Delhi, she went to Gandhi—again someone whose individual connection with people is lost to us because of the way his saintliness has been portrayed.

Gandhi sent her to work. So here was a woman in terrible circumstances, working in the Purana Qila camp. First of all, to give relief to all the people who had been evicted from their homes, the Muslims who didn't want to go, but were forced out. This is a story of Partition which has not been told.

I think the real tragedy of Partition is that the stories don't travel in their specificity. The people who came across each border told the stories of the terrible things that happened to them on the other side. So there's an exemption that we have managed to grant ourselves: it happened elsewhere. Anis Kidwai's stories about the Purana Qila and Humayun's Tomb camps are not stories about Muslims, but about the internal displacement that violence produces.

The first three chapters of the book are about trying to stop these camps from coming into being. My favourite story in the first half of the book is about these two women, Anis Kidwai and Subhadra Joshi, deciding that the only way to stop this enforced eviction was to stop people from coming to the camp. Once people came to the camp, hordes of other poor, destitute, displaced people took over their homes. There was no way you could persuade somebody to go back. So these two women decided to go to Kasabpura—this was when Gandhi-ji was on his fast in 1948. And as they were driving by, Anis Kidwai and Subhadra Joshi saw the Muslims loading their belongings onto a lorry. They managed to persuade them not to go. But on the opposite side of the road, there was a line of Hindu refugees waiting, and they surrounded the women. I think the women got their point across through the force of empathy and reason, saying, 'We will get you homes but don't make the others leave.' It is stories like this we find in the book, and they are told with great delicacy. It is not an orgy of death and it is not an orgy of blaming, both of which we have come to expect in Partition literature. And the only thing that enables Anis Kidwai to escape from the prison of recrimination is a sense of who her friends are. To her, they are not Hindu or Muslim. So she completely changes the perspective you can have on Partition.

GH: And this is written about a time when India, as we know it today, was a baby. The first two years must have been so full of hope, along with the disappointment that Independence was beginning with bloodshed and division. You knew Anis Kidwai as a grandmother and then as somebody writing this memoir—if she were talking to young people today, what do you think she would say about those first two years? There are some very moving moments when she sees the birth of the nation. And some of those comments, some of those thoughts, some of those worries of hers, resonate with us today.

AK: I think she would want to get across the way she viewed the world. There was the specificity of being a Muslim woman, a fairly elite Muslim woman, part of the political elite. And that person was out on the streets every day, working in the camps, or taking her young daughters to play with Hindu children at school.

More directly, I think Anis Kidwai would say, 'Don't let people form your memories because those memories are partial. You must form your memories yourself.' Though (like Anis), we may actually fail to make sense of why Partition happened, we need to understand that we will find an answer in the fight against communal divisions, separation and hatred. This fight is an antidote to the madness that engulfed society then, and the madness we have seen in more recent times.

All of us who have been activists since the late seventies—when citizens' groups wrote reports and tried to tell the truth about riots and communal violence—have been trying to say that only truth can be the basis of reconciliation, so look at the truth. Understand that this was the complexity of the problem, and move forward, knowing that if you're going to work with the categories of just Muslim and Hindu, you're not going to make much headway. Instead, if you ask the question of a Muslim woman or a HIndu woman, there are connections that can be established between the two. And that connection during Partition was first established by victimhood, and then by fighting back. If you can do that, then each victim can be a person who says, 'Now with me, the cycle stops. It ends.'

GH: That ties up with your story of Anis Kidwai and Subhadra Joshi coming together and *doing something*, not just being victims. I also want to get a sense of what Anis was like as a woman. We have so many clichés in our head, not only about historic events such as Partition, but also about the women of those times, even more so if they were Muslim women. What sort of education they had, for instance. So if you could share some stories.

AK: Anis Kidwai's father wrote humorous pieces in English in satirical magazines. So she was placed in that segue that you had in the early twentieth century for families in, let's say, Uttar Pradesh—that of a zamindari turning into a professional elite. Her father was trained as a lawyer, but made his name in the pan-Islamic fervour and the nationalist fervour that swept Awadh in the first twenty years of the twentieth century. He died when she was about eleven years old. Until then she had a very rigorous education. And after that, she had to move to the village of Masauli and live a hemmed-in life. She was put in purdah, which she struggled to get out of for the next sixteen years. But around her, the world was politicised. Her husband, Shafi, and her brother-in-law, Rafi Ahmad Kidwai, were Congress activists, and she was consumed with a passion to join them, but the public space was not hers.

But ironically, Partition made the public space available to women. The nature of the public space in a place like Delhi was completely altered by Partition. Women who had never stepped out were in the kafilas and caravans of the displaced; women and children were all over the place as victims. For many women, going out was legitimate at that point, because there were other people out there, other women in the public space. Certainly Anis Kidwai's life was transformed by those two years of Partition.

As for knowing her, I am extremely fortunate that I have got to know my grandmother in the non-kinship sense because this memoir sets her up as a person … With any act of witness-writing, you have to get to know the woman who is writing and like her; you cannot know her through kinship. Initially, it was a shock to be able to see Anis as a real woman, not just my grandmother. But in the process of translation, I understood many things about her. I didn't have a grandmother who cooked. I didn't have a grandmother who was at home for even ten days at a stretch. I had a grandmother who raced across the lawn and into the arms of some bearded gentlemen. I had a grandmother who could tell me what I should read in English, a language she didn't speak, because she read these books in translation. I had a grandmother whose friends were all single women. A grandmother who said you have to be fearless. It's only through this book that I came to understand many things. My favourite memory of her—I must have been eight then—is of the time I refused to learn to read the Quran, mostly because I knew I could impress her with a smart comment. I said, 'I can't learn by rote. I'll learn Arabic when I grow up and then learn to read the Quran.' And she bought it completely. I thought she would be angry, but she said, 'Oh, that makes sense.'

GH: She's a reader and writer, you can make that out. And I think this is important to call attention to, because after all, she's writing a narrative. It's not a diary. She uses her diary perhaps, draws on her memories as a witness, but she thinks back to events, contemplates them. And she quotes poetry most knowingly. Was she particularly interested in poetry, because she uses it so much in the memoir?

AK: She was a great fan of Iqbal, and her first article was published in a women's magazine in Urdu at the age of thirteen, I think. She was also a literary critic. Anis was given an education, since there was also a cultural milieu in which art and literature were signifiers of being elite or advanced … The relationship between art and life for all Urdu speakers of that generation was that art can interpret life.

GH: I want to bring our conversation back to present times. I wonder if you have had any reactions from your readers.

AK: I've had amazing reactions from both young and old readers. The young reacted the way many of us have when reading this book, saying, 'There was a temporal depth to partition, there were real people in it, not just victims.' I've also had more specific reactions from the young. Somebody who lives in Karol Bagh said to me, 'This book is a gift.' She had never understood [till she read the book] why the place she lives in, which has refugees from West Pakistan, has the culture and demography it does.

The older generation's reactions have been moving. In this desire to contain Partition because we do not want to be revisited by any communal act, we have sealed off this place as if law and criminality do not apply. This deprives us of the gift of history.

Let me give you a couple of examples. In all the writings about the occupation of Babri Masjid, there has been no reference to the fact that this also happened in 1949. Through 1947–48, particularly 1948–49 onwards, mosques and religious places of Muslims were either razed to the ground, or occupied. Refugees were sent to live there. Idols were planted in many religious places. It happened in Delhi, and is described in the chapters of *Azadi*. When we saw it happen at the Babri Masjid, we thought of it as a random communal act, but it wasn't random. It was, as Anis Kidwai hints, a sustained attack by certain forces in society to erase and defile mosques. The Babri Masjid attack harks back to that. Anis Kidwai tried to raise this issue in a meeting, saying that we have to have one policy about religious places, but nobody except Mridula Sarabhai listened to her. There is no law, no notion, of the criminality of such acts.

Another example is about government officials—police officers in particular—and their role in sexually harassing young women. There is a historical connection between this strange conjuncture of being an official, and the feeling that you can harass, molest or rape. Let me tell you about one of the reactions I got. In a public meeting, I pointed out a character, Rathod, whom Anis Kidwai mentions. He was found guilty but he didn't get punished. Women activists spoke about this for ten years after Partition—they pointed out that many of the women who had been abducted ended up in the houses of government officials, and the entire machinery did everything to prevent that from being recognised as a crime.

When I said this, and added that there is a historicity there, a gentleman who was a retired officer of the Indian Administrative Services choked and nearly started crying. He said that when he came to Delhi in 1947 as a government official, he was told by a colleague of his that because of people like Mridula Sarabhai and Anis Kidwai, the police were raiding homes to find the women who were abducted. His colleague told him that they had an abducted woman in their house and when they heard the police were coming, they made her drink kerosene. And in the shocked silence that followed, the retired IAS officer added, 'This is the first time I've been able to say it.'

GH: So the book served to open up certain memories for various people, memories of the violence they were part of, either at the receiving end or at the perpetrating end, or somewhere in between. What about the years after Partition? What about the aftermath?

AK: People like Anis Kidwai made it to the Rajya Sabha because of the good auspices of people like Nehru. That's one kind of person. And a lot of other women got access to public space because of Partition. And the stories of both sorts are about the afterlife of Partition.

Anis Kidwai was a member of the Rajya Sabha from 1956 onwards, for twelve years. Parliament in those years was peopled with women who had fought in the freedom struggle, either intellectually or as social activists. These women generated a wave of bills in Parliament. The woman who moved the largest number of bills from 1952 onwards was called Sita Parmanand. She was a DPhil from Oxford, a barrister. She did everything possible to try and bring the experiences of working women and mothers during Partition into the legislative domain. One of the first bills was to set up orphanages. They were all private members' bills, but they never became law. One exception was Subhadra Joshi's bill on bigamy, which was directly related to what happened during Partition.[27]

In 1956, Anis Kidwai and Savitri Nigam—who worked with the Hindu refugee camps in Kalka and that area—moved a bill to prevent the molestation of women. This bill represents a really important moment because we don't have a bill on sexual harassment in the Indian Parliament yet. We don't have an act.[28] We have bills that are repeatedly floated and nothing happens.[29] Well, this was the first such attempt,

---

[27] Subhadra Joshi's bill to amend the code of criminal procedure was passed in 1957, and was the sixth private member's bill to become law in India. Only fourteen such bills have passed in Parliament since Independence. The last one was over fifty years ago, in August 1970 (https://timesofindia.indiatimes.com/india/just-14-private-members-bills-passed-by-parliament-till-date-the-last-was-in-1970/articleshow/47046338.cms).

[28] In the case of *Vishaka vs The State of Rajasthan and Others*, the Supreme Court's judgement of 1997 laid down guidelines against sexual harassment in the workplace. In 2013, these were buttressed by the passage of the Sexual Harassment of Women at Workplace (Prevention, Prohibition and Redressal) Act. But the ambit of these initiatives remained limited to a woman's place of employment and the employer's responsibility to her. On the whole, women's protection in public spaces is confined to the provisions of the Indian Penal Code of 1860, Sections 354 (A) and 509, against 'outraging the modesty' of a woman.

[29] Between 2015 and 2020, some 1,800 private member's bills were proposed before Parliament, a mere sixty of which came to be considered on the floor, and none was passed (https://www.thehindu.com/podcast/50-

and three women spoke on the bill. Savitri Devi introduced it, Anis Kidwai spoke second, and Sita Parmanand spoke third. Those of us who are in institutions where we've served on anti-sexual harassment committees, would recognise that debate immediately. Two of the three women lost their cool—Savitri Devi and Anis Kidwai—and both of them raised the spectre of the abducted woman. They said, 'But what about abducted women? There are government officials today who have abducted women in their homes. Why are you not proceeding against them?' They were heckled from the government benches, there was laughter, and there were snide remarks. Sita Parmanand chided the hecklers and made some reasoned proposals.

So that's one kind of afterlife in which people who were activists continued to be activists. There were also all the people who wrote their autobiographies. Many women who got education or jobs because of Independence, wrote their stories. That is also part of the afterlife of Partition.

So if we use Anis Kidwai's memoirs, as in my case, you begin with the quest for personal antecedents, and you end up with a completely different vision. These people wanted to inscribe themselves into the history that we write of modern India, but we have failed to follow up on these leads. But it's never too late to start. So all the people who fought—they are the legacies of Partition we can work with, in terms of what they fought for. They are better placed to tell us who we are than the people who raped and killed each other.

---

years-since-the-last-private-members-bill-was-enacted-into-law-are-they-still-relevant-the-hindu-in-focus-podcast/article32311242.ece).

Postscript: In 2023, the National Council of Educational Research and Training (NCERT) announced a 'rationalised syllabus' to be taught to high school students. From the 2023–24 academic session, the plan is that Class 12 textbooks will drop entire chapters and 'topics'—ranging from the favourite historical victims of the right-wing: the Mughals of the sixteenth and seventeenth centuries, to the Industrial Revolution, to social movements.[30] Theme 14 of 'Themes in Indian History' has also been dropped, namely, 'Understanding Partition (Politics, Memories, Experiences)'.[31]

This can only be described as an irrational interruption in our collective process of imagining the India we want. How do we continue this process without understanding the many truths of Partition, the horrors and hopes it spawned, and its urgent lessons for the present?

---

[30] 'No Mughal Courts, Industrial Revolution, Partition in Revised UP Board Syllabus', *The New Indian Express*, 4 April 2023 (https://www.newindianexpress.com/nation/2023/apr/04/no-mughal-courts-industrial-revolution-partition-in-revised-up-board-syllabus-2562571.html).

[31] *National Council of Educational Research and Training* (NCERT) (https://ncert.nic.in/pdf/BookletClass12.pdf).

ROMILA THAPAR

Battling for the Future

The first time I met Romila Thapar was at a book fair in Delhi, in the early eighties. I was at the stall of the publishing house I then worked for. Suddenly there was a bustle, a sense of anticipation. Several of my colleagues—and not just editors who read books—stood up, beaming. Romila Thapar and S. Gopal[32] were heading towards our stall. A young colleague whispered to me, 'It's Professor Thapar! She lets us call her Romila!' For the next half hour, even the ignorant or undeserving among us received the gifts of warmth, anecdotes about scholars and books, and stories about the past—all the pleasurable stuff of history.

Over the years since, I have continued to receive similar gifts of conversation about everything—from the Mahabharata

---

[32] Sarvepalli Gopal (1923–2002) was an eminent historian of modern India and a founding member of the Centre for Historical Studies at JNU. Gopal's highly acclaimed work includes a three-volume biography of Jawaharlal Nehru, whom he admired and was close to; as well as a biography of his own father, Sarvepalli Radhakrishnan, India's first Vice President and its second President.

to ways in which the right-wing crushes dissent, to Buddhist nuns, the writing of memoirs and negotiating old age. Perhaps the best part of these sessions at her home has been the very believable illusion that it is a dialogue; that we are equals, not informal teacher and student.

Romila is a historian; indeed, she is truly what we Indians like to call an *eminent* historian. But for many students and scholars, for friends and interested strangers, she is first and foremost a teacher. The kind of teacher who is accessible, who listens; and who knows the value of both reason and imagination. The kind of scholar and citizen who asks questions, and encourages others to question. In short, the kind of person who can tell us—and put into practice—what education really might be, and what should make a university.

Romila taught briefly in Kurukshetra University (1961–62) and longer in Delhi University (1963–70). But it is Delhi's Jawaharlal Nehru University (JNU) she will always be closely identified with—she began teaching there in 1970, as part of the group that honed the vision of a new, open-minded, inclusive university. She taught at JNU's Centre for Historical Studies for a little over two decades and continued to be associated with the university—whether officially or in the minds of students and teachers—even after retirement.

On 9 February 2016, students held a demonstration in JNU to mark the third anniversary of Afzal Guru's execution.[33]

[33] Mohammed Afzal Guru (1969–2013) was hanged for the attack on the Indian Parliament in 2001, despite the evidence against him being circumstantial at best. See Nandita Haksar, 'Afzal's Story', *Outlook Magazine*, 3 February 2022 (https://www.outlookindia.com/website/story/afzals-story/232712).

Citing videos of the event (later discovered to be doctored),[34] the Delhi police charged then JNU Students' Union president Kanhaiya Kumar and others with 'sedition, rioting and unlawful assembly'. The students were accused of chanting 'anti-India' slogans demanding azadi (freedom). A few days later, Kanhaiya Kumar and two other students were arrested. The vice-chancellor appointed by the government, M. Jagadesh Kumar, did not protest the incursion of the police on campus; but students at the university and across the country did. On campuses and outside, students, teachers and citizens raised their voices in solidarity.

In response to the situation in JNU as well as the protests, Romila Thapar spoke to me about JNU's vision for educating youth: a university where the point of education was teaching the young to become questioning citizens. Romila also traced the pattern of recent attacks against voices of dissent on Indian campuses. Her plain-spoken advice to students and teachers both in and outside the classroom: 'The thing is to question.' Our conversations over time reflect this in practice: answers are not always ready to hand. Still, it is the question—the intelligent, contextualised question—that sets us off on one possible road to knowledge.

15 February 2016

Githa Hariharan (GH): Over the last year, we have seen protests, on campuses and elsewhere, against the crushing of dissent.

---

[34] See 'Lack of Evidence Turns Spotlight Back on Doctored JNU Videos', *The Wire*, 3 March 2017 (https://thewire.in/politics/jnu-videos-doctored-shilpi-tewari) and Jahnavi Sen, 'Arrest "Anti India Elements" Says Rajnath, So Police Pin "Sedition" On JNUSU Head', *The Wire*, 13 February 2016 (https://thewire.in/education/arrest-anti-india-elements-says-rajnath-so-police-pin-sedition-on-jnusu-head).

Many questioning voices have been targeted in an attempt to muzzle them. We could say this attempt has peaked with what is happening in JNU now; after all, JNU is the predictable target for vilification as 'anti-national'. Would you comment on what we are witnessing—misinformation, students and teachers accused of being 'anti-national' or 'seditious', either because they are leftist or have spoken up, and the university allowing, if not inviting, the police into the campus?

Romila Thapar (RT): From its beginnings, JNU has had this kind of propaganda circulated about it. Let me talk a little about the faculty. It used to be said about JNU, 'Oh, unless you are a Marxist you can't get a job there.' This was and is absolute nonsense. If you did a head count of the number of people who declared themselves to be Marxist, you would end up with a fraction of the faculty, a tiny fraction.

In those days—I am talking about the 1970s—if you were in any other university, including Delhi University, you were very quiet about the fact that you were a Marxist, because people would take it out on you in different ways. In JNU, it did not matter. You were Marxist or you were not. It was taken as something that was part of your philosophical explanation. I attribute this to the fact that in many other universities, you had to be a member of a communist party to be a Marxist. But in JNU, we emphasised reading the texts and reading widely, so you could be a philosophical Marxist without going anywhere near a communist party. The thing was to question. What was important was the historical method: you begin with saying you question a particular aspect of, or topic in, existing knowledge.

GH: I could add that you question, and then you act. Often, questioning and dissent could take the form of action.

RT: Yes. Yes, indeed.

GH: I also want to refer to JNU's passionate engagement with issues outside the campus. In 2012, when a young physiotherapy intern was raped in Southwest Delhi,[35] the JNU students were immediately out on the streets.

RT: Oh yes. This kind of engagement goes back much earlier, right into the early years of JNU. In fact, it takes on the whole business of what a democratic society is. I think ours was among the first universities to say, 'We will have student-faculty committees, we will have students sitting on the board of studies, we will have students sitting in the academic council.' The university consists of faculty, students, and the administration, and all three wings have to be represented in the bodies that control the university. This principle was very strong in JNU.

Again, a lot of problems that arose in the early years were sorted out within the university. I recall people like Bipan Chandra[36] and myself, and two or three others, being gheraoed (encircled) because there was some problem over admissions

---

[35] In December 2012, Jyoti Singh Pandey, a twenty-two-year-old trainee in physiotherapy, was gangraped on a bus, and died of her grave injuries thirteen days later. There were mass protests across the country. A judicial committee (headed by Justice J.S. Verma) was set up to suggest amendments to the criminal law. The Committee produced a comprehensive report on rape, sexual assault, trafficking, child sexual abuse and honour killings. As always, the recommendations of the Committee have not been implemented as envisioned (https://sabrangindia.in/article/revisiting-justice-verma-committee-report-2013-justiceforrapevictims). Six men were arrested in connection with the fatal assault. Of the six, one was found hanging in prison; another, a juvenile, could not be tried as an adult. The remaining four were executed in 2020.

[36] Bipan Chandra (1928–2014) specialised in the economic and political history of modern India.

or something. Even the vice-chancellor was gheraoed. But as I said, it was all resolved by the university community.

GH: You are describing the tradition of the university looking after itself. This is why we find the fact of the police being called into the campus a few days back so shocking. I suspect everyone in JNU is, at the moment, remembering 1975 and Mrs Gandhi's Emergency.

RT: The Emergency was the first time the police came into the campus. But even as the police entered the campus, the university team came together to protect the people the police wanted to pick up. The vice-chancellor was actually on the spot to meet whoever was in charge, to say, 'You know, you can't pick up students like this.'

GH: The attack on JNU this time, in 2016, also seems to erode the vital link the university students and faculty have established with the neighbourhood. There are people standing at the gates of the university—people who have nothing to do with the university—demanding it be closed. This seems tragic because the university students have always taken up issues beyond the university—from the neighbourhood to the city and the country.

RT: This is a case of striking at the heart of an institution that should be a viable institution in a society. After all, institutions do not exist in a vacuum. They have a social context. If you create a situation in which an institution is attacked *by* the social context, then you destroy both the context and the institution. And this is really why what is happening today is horrific. There is no other word for it.

GH: As a teacher of many years, Romila, what would you say to students in JNU today, given the situation? And to your colleagues in JNU, the teachers?

RT: I am delighted with the reaction of both categories of people. I thought the protests were really remarkable—the university came together to defend the student who had been arrested,[37] as well as to defend itself.

I think there was a real sense in which teachers and students felt this was *their* institution. That is extremely encouraging. I am very pleased about it, because I have spent much of my working life there, trying to create academic qualifications superior to those in many other places, *as well* as trying to create an ambience in which teachers and students are comfortable with each other.

More conversation followed on the intellectual vision with which JNU was set up in 1969. The idea of the new university was to explore Indian society through interdisciplinary studies and discussion. In 1971, the Centre for Historical Studies, one of the oldest centres in the School of Social Sciences in JNU, launched its postgraduate studies programme guided by a team that included Romila, S. Gopal and Bipan Chandra. The programme was a departure from the usual conventional takes on the study of history. Simply put, it did not view the past as 'another country'; instead, the past was the subject of study because it shaped the present. The Centre also pioneered a course of study of contemporary history.

GH: To continue with the idea of the university in general, but also JNU in particular … you have been associated with JNU from the beginning—would you give us an idea of what this vision was? Would you call it Nehru's vision?

---

[37] On 12 February 2016, Kanhaiya Kumar, president of the JNU students' union, was arrested and slapped with charges of sedition and criminal conspiracy.

RT: The vision really was not so much Nehru's—we must remember that the university came into existence after he died. It was originally supposed to be called Raisina University, after the village where the Viceregal Lodge was built. Then somebody had a bright idea: 'Why not name it after the first prime minister?' So it was called the Nehru University.

The JNU vision actually developed through the 1960s among academics and intellectuals in India. They thought, 'We are an independent country, we have an identity.' And they asked themselves, 'What kind of society do we want to build?' The response was this vision—the university had to help in understanding both the identity of India, and the kind of society we wanted.

When I joined JNU at the end of 1970, I think I may have been just the third professor to join. We did not really start functioning until 1971, actually late 1971. The vice-chancellor then was not an academic but he was a man of much vision, now that I look back on it.[38] He told us, 'I want a university which is not a replica of any of the existing Indian universities. I want a university that will tackle new ideas, and explore knowledge. And I want it to be interdisciplinary.' This was the mandate we were given. I remember how we worked on this mandate in the History Centre since we too agreed with it and wanted to make it possible. There were three of us first, then we recruited a few people about three or four months down the line, so that we were about ten of us. And we brainstormed day and night, day and night, thinking of new courses; the kinds of courses that would help us explore Indian society.

---

[38] Gopalaswamy Parthasarathy (1912–1995) was a national-level cricketer, journalist and diplomat before being appointed to the vice-chancellorship of JNU (1969–74) at the founding of the university.

GH: Academics was not something disconnected from the rest of teaching and learning.

RT: Precisely. Academics was not disconnected. What we were doing had a context. It was not as if I was dealing with something abstract in ancient Indian history. I had to tell myself that the past is not another country. The past is still with us. And what is it that we are doing with the past? How are we relating it to the present? This was a major aspect of our exercise.

The other aspect we were very conscious of was the fact that since we were doing new courses, they had to be extremely analytical. And so we began with one of the courses that we had invented, 'Historical Method', which did not exist in any university at that time. The course was intended to explain to students that there is a *method*, that the social sciences have a method. History is not just a story, it is not a narrative for which you read six books, string the events together and say, 'This happened, then this, then that.' There is an explanation for why things happened, why people became the kind of people they were, and the kinds of roles they played. So the basics of social sciences involve some questions: What is your evidence? How reliable is your evidence? What causal links are you making between your bits of evidence? What is this leading you to? Is your eventual argument based on logic and reasoning? These were fundamental issues.

GH: Romila, you have given us a clear idea of the academic, scholarly, intellectual base of what a university project is. I want to ask you about the extension of this base. Surely, a young person goes to college or university for academic study, but also life in general, including life as a citizen. Learning to be a citizen is intimately tied up with the vision you have for how academics will be conducted. I refer to this because I want us to talk about JNU's 'tradition' of questioning both within the classroom, within the context of academics, as well as within the context of society.

RT: That was a remarkable thing. It was remarkable both for me and the students who came to us. I had taught in Delhi University, and I had taught a bit in London University before that. On the whole, my experience was that the teacher came into the class and gave you whatever lecture they wanted to. You took your notes and you went off, and did a little bit of reading. That was it.

What we began doing in JNU was quite different. For example, in my first lecture I said to the students, 'A lecture is not a monologue. It is a dialogue between you and me. I will say things that you may not understand very fully, or that you may disagree with. In which case, please stop me, and we can have a discussion.'

For the first three weeks, there was dead silence. I would talk; they would listen and take notes. Then suddenly one day, a student raised her hand and said, 'I don't think I quite agree with that. Could you explain it?' And we had a lovely discussion. After that the class changed. The best thing about a lot of the JNU lectures was that there were really 'discussion lectures'.

Inevitably, Romila and I came back to the present, where we had to confront right-wing antipathy to an open university. Ever the historian, Romila summed up the situation. 'Though the Indian anti-colonial struggle was largely secular,' she said, 'we have now regressed: the battle in India today is between religious nationalism and secular nationalism.'

GH: Let me move over to the ideological divide. Would you say there is antipathy among the right-wing, in general, to the idea of an open university? To the idea of education as we have been discussing it?

RT: Generally I would say the right-wing tends to be a little opposed to an open university. In India, the situation is such that it's not just the right-wing, it's also religious extremism of a certain kind. And let's face it, we have been through this process in trying to discover our identity and the kind of society we want.

There were many people who were with us, and many people whom we supported and worked with. And there were the others for whom the kind of society we wanted was anathema. I mean, groups like the Sangh Parivar did not approve of the kinds of societies that we were talking about.

GH: Yes, they were very unhappy.

RT: The RSS would be very unhappy. And this really goes back to the period of nationalism, in that anti-colonial nationalism was relatively secular. I would underline the word 'relatively', because not everybody was a Nehru. Many of the leaders were, quietly, one way or the other, Hindu nationalists or Islamic nationalists, Muslim nationalists.

But with the anti-colonial nationalism, you had what some people call sub-nationalisms, and others refuse to call them nationalisms at all. You had the Hindu Mahasabha and the Muslim League. The Muslim League went from strength to strength, and finally ended up getting Pakistan. So the teleology of their nationalism was met in the creation of Pakistan. The Hindu Mahasabha, which then became the RSS, was left facing a secular country.

I think the nationalism question has shifted somewhat; the battle today is between Hindu extremism as Hindu nationalism, and other forms of extremism and nationalism based on religions, versus what we like to think is a more secular nationalism. That is where the battle is being fought at the moment.

The RSS and the BJP regard JNU as a kind of fountainhead of free thinking. It's a place where people imagine the kind of society in which the Hindu citizen will not be the primary citizen. There will be equal citizenship for everybody. And of course, there is the whole swell of the 'lower' castes, and the dalit movements, and the tribal movements, and feminist movements. All that is growing as well. So there is a certain kind of desperation on the part of those who thought that come Independence, we will have a Hindu Rashtra. That is not happening. And I see over the last eighteen months [roughly mid-2014 to February 2016] or so, a growing sense of frustration that this is not happening. This is part of the reason why there has been incident after incident of the sort we have seen in JNU. Almost every week there is an incident of some kind, giving rise to protest and confrontation. We are a society thick with confrontation. We are not a harmonious society at the moment.

—∞—

In 2020, Romila and I had a long four-part conversation beginning, as usual, with the university; and, as always, the university as a space for free thinking. We moved on to the evolution of citizenship. Then, quite naturally, our discussion shifted to the National Register of Citizens (NRC), and its threat to citizens' rights, in addition to the tragedies already unfolding in Assam in the course of the NRC exercise there. We rounded it off with the grim scenario of the present, but also the thought that a plan of action—or the semblance of one—may bring us hope. In the face of exclusionary laws and practices, what options do different constituencies of citizens have?

7 March 2020

GH: As always, Romila, let's talk first about the university campuses. You've been associated with so many universities, and with JNU in particular, where we've seen courage on the part of students, but also brutality in the crushing of dissent.[39] Could you talk to us, once again, about this new low for freedom of speech on the campus, and what education is meant to be? What the university space is meant to be?

RT: Let me begin with stating that the relationship embedded in the idea of the citizen and the state is a new one. We have to understand that this new relationship requires institutions; they emerge with this relationship between the state and citizenship. And one of these institutions, an institution of fundamental importance, is the university. Not everyone understands that the university is very different from the institutions of learning and scholarship that existed earlier. You had gurukuls, you

[39] On 28 January 2016, Mamidala Jagadesh Kumar was appointed as the vice-chancellor of JNU. His tenure, which lasted till 2022, saw frequent outbreaks of one-sided violence on the university campus: by the Delhi police, the Akhil Bharatiya Vidyarthi Parishad (founded by the RSS), and, on 5 January 2020, by a masked mob of fifty intruders armed with rods who were never prosecuted, even though some of them had been identified from CCTV footage as members of the ABVP. Unchallenged by the Delhi police, they entered the campus and attacked students and teachers for three hours, leaving at least forty people with serious injuries. Mamidala Jagadesh Kumar was appointed chairman of the University Grants Commission in 2022, and remains in office to this day.

had mutts, you had madrasas for instance. In all these places, learning meant being familiar with certain texts, knowing the language, and reciting those texts, and being familiar with the ideas in them. Philosophical discussions took place, but very often they took place on the margins of these institutions.

The fundamental difference between those institutions and today's university is that the university is the only institution in which there is absolutely free thinking. There has to be free thinking, otherwise it's not a university.

What is the point of a university? It is to teach people to think. Together with thinking, it is to teach people to ask questions. Because, as everybody knows, the only way in which knowledge advances is if people ask questions of that knowledge. If they start challenging and questioning existing knowledge, that's when new knowledge emerges.

GH: The authority figure has to earn that authority every single day. And with every single response to a question.

RT: Absolutely. Now, if you have a system that says, 'Don't ask questions', or 'What I am teaching you is all that you need to know', then you're really annulling the whole university system. The university system must challenge knowledge, it must ask questions. In most societies, this period, when young minds are in universities, is when the questioning happens. After that, you get jobs, your life is taken up with other things. And there are very few who have the luxury of continuing to ask questions and adding to knowledge. That is really a small fraction of society. Nevertheless, the experience of asking questions, learning how to ask questions, is very important for everyone. And you don't ask just any old question. You ask a question which can, implicitly, draw forth information, knowledge, and evidence of connections. That ability to ask questions remains very important in any profession. Whether you're going to be a school teacher, or a doctor, a lawyer, an engineer, or a computer expert, the ability to ask questions is fundamental. Now, when you begin destroying that ability in the institution that is meant to teach you how to do it, then you've destroyed the institution, *and* you have destroyed the intellectual potential of your next generation.

GH: And when you have people saying, 'Students are meant to study', what they really mean is study their textbooks, seek information and answers from figures of authority. But not to question authority. Is it possible to ask the kind of questions you are referring to without asking questions of the world around them outside the campus—political questions?

RT: Yes. Political in its widest sense. You know, by political one isn't referring only to left politics, as is very often ...

GH: Or political parties.

RT: Or political parties, yes. It is political in the widest sense, about the world we're living in, about the world that surrounds us. Yes, this is what I meant, that the awareness of asking questions refers to absolutely everything that we're living with and in. That is absolutely essential. Indeed, it's not just asking questions about the world you're living in, but also about the texts, the books you're reading. After all, 1968 did take place almost uniformly around the world, with students saying, 'We don't think we're reading and studying the kinds of things we should be.' And then there was a change in courses and syllabi in many universities. That kind of dialogue between those who are teaching and those who are studying is essential. It is what we were aiming at in JNU. We wanted students to be able to stop a teacher in the middle of a lecture and say, I'm sorry, I don't understand, or, I don't agree. And then you had a discussion, which meant that there was much more clarity on the subject, both from the point of view of the person who was teaching, and the person listening to the lecture. That is what I meant by questioning with a purpose, questioning with the intention of understanding the problem much better than one does normally. It is crucial in a university. But it also means that if you're going to question what you're being taught, or how you're being taught, and you're questioning the world around you, then you're also questioning the system that's governing you. And that's where the problem comes in. When you start questioning the system that's governing you, those who are doing the governing start getting anxious and want to stop it.

GH: But the questions also lead to certain commitments. For instance, if your questions have led you to an understanding that everyone must have access to education, especially in a diverse country, you emphasise public education and maybe say, 'Let's lower fees.' That becomes an issue you take up. Or when you see that caste flourishes all around you, in all kinds of new guises, the questions you're asking will again lead you to make a commitment—and not everybody's necessarily in agreement. Maybe we should also clarify that we are not referring to students as a kind of homogeneous voice.

RT: No, no, not at all. In fact, diversity is very important here too. Once you say, 'No, I'm not in agreement', and the next person says, 'Well, so what is your opinion?'—you start questioning the first opinion. This is age-old. I have often said that the foundational procedure in Indian philosophy is so similar to the Socratic method. You first put across the view of your opponent, then your own; then you suggest a debate between the two and see if there can be a solution. What is referred to as purvapaksha–pratipaksha–siddhanta, which everybody who does any kind of philosophical study has to go through—this process of debate, discussion, and then finding a solution, or not finding a solution and saying, 'Well, the debate continues to be open.'

GH: So questioning, debate, these are the essentials in the educational process and on the site of the university. Let's move on to what is happening on campuses right now with the protests against the Citizenship Amendment Act (CAA), the National Population Register (NPR) and the National Register of Citizens (NRC) ...[40] At the heart of what has been going on is the notion of citizenship. When did this notion come into being?

RT: The thing we forget is that citizenship is actually a very modern notion. Everybody goes back to ancient Athens and Greece. But let's not forget that citizenship in Athens was extremely limited. Only about a third of the people living in the city of Athens were citizens. The rest were slaves and other

---

[40] The Citizenship (Amendment) Act, passed by Parliament in December 2019, offers immigrants from religious minorities in India's neighbourhood a fast-track path to Indian citizenship; but the offer pointedly excludes Muslim immigrants. The National Register of Citizens was mandated in 2003 by the BJP government's amendment of the Citizenship Act, 1955. Meant to identify 'illegal aliens' and separate them from the general body of citizens, the NRC was implemented first in Assam, where a complete draft of 'illegal aliens' was published in 2018. The following year, the BJP government announced plans to extend it to the rest of the country in 2021, but that could not happen owing to massive countrywide protests, a legal challenge (joined by the UNHRC) in the Supreme Court, and the outbreak of COVID. The National Population Register is defined as a database of all the 'usual residents' at their place of residence. It was first prepared in 2010, updated in 2015, and the plan is to combine it with the NRC process.

categories of people who didn't have the freedom of citizenship. That's a different story altogether. That's an older society with its own background of tribal structures and what have you.

Modern citizenship is something that comes very specifically at a historical moment. And what is this historical moment at which it comes? In the eighteenth century, you find a change as various things happen. Industrialisation begins; capitalism comes in, providing the economic base of this new form of society. The middle class emerges. And the middle class is very aware of the fact that the older authorities, the feudal aristocracy, basing themselves on the labour of the subject people, are in decline. The middle class is taking over. So you get a historical change, a very fundamental historical change. The old relationship of the lord and the subject, the king and the subject, gradually changes to a new relationship between the state and the citizen. Now, both the 'state' and the 'citizen' are new because the state under this kind of system is very different from the monarchy of earlier times. And the citizen is no longer a subject. The citizen has rights, and that is the meaning of the rights of citizenship. The citizen has rights and duties, and it is these rights and duties, obligations, that the Constitution speaks of.

GH: Before we get to the Constitution, suppose I introduce the Indian context here. Yes, there is a new contract between the institution of the state and the individual citizen and the citizenry as a collective. But in the case of India and many other countries, this is the result of a struggle for freedom from colonialism. So there is an additional edge there, in the sense that a certain contract has been envisioned. When we speak of the idea of India, is that what we're talking about?

RT: Let's not forget that citizenship didn't really exist under colonialism. The Indian was still the subject of the British rule, the British monarch. So that old idea of the king and the subject continued under colonialism in India. The real change only comes about when India ceases to be a colony and becomes a nation.

Now, my point is that the change in the relationship and the understanding of what is meant by citizenship, or by the citizen, was not fully discussed, explored and understood in these years of Independence. There's been a little hangover of the older idea of the subject. And the realisation that the citizen is the independent, thinking Indian who has views and has the right to express those views—that didn't quite establish itself.

So one of the problems we have today is making those in authority, anyone who's in authority, understand that in the change to what we call the nation, if you're going to use the notion of the citizen, you have to understand that it's a changed relationship. And you have to concede that the contract of the change, which is the Indian Constitution, has to be respected.

GH: And then the setting of this particular contract, which is why I refer to the idea of India during the freedom struggle, is taking cognisance of the fact that this is, and will always be, an extremely diverse citizenry.

RT: Absolutely, absolutely, that is understood. What is very, very clear is that if you are going to continue with democracy and the notion of citizenship, you have to understand that you cannot define a citizen by indicating one item of identity. You have to include multiple items of identity. The definition must take in all citizens, no matter what their thinking may be and what their pattern of culture may be. It does have to include everybody. And that's something that is causing a lot of problems because of majoritarianism coming into the picture. You can't have democracy if you're going to base your citizenship on majoritarianism.

GH: The Chief Justice has made special mention recently of the duties of the citizen.[41] And of course, you immediately want to ask about the relationship between the rights of citizens and their duties. So if you were to sum up some of these rights on the one hand, and some of the duties on the other, what would you say?

RT: Beginning with the basics and going up, the rights would be to at least a minimum reasonable livelihood, which means food, water, housing, etc. Employment, education, healthcare, and very important, along with these, is the freedom to say what you wish to say. So free speech, free thinking, and social justice. Unless every citizen has these rights, equality is not possible.

GH: We were talking about this process of reducing the citizen to a subject, which is distorting the relationship we have with the state in a constitutional democracy. We're no longer allowed to speak up. I know that freedom of speech is qualified, we're forever being referred to the qualification that free speech should not interfere with national security and so forth ... But look at the way sedition is being used, for example.[42]

---

[41] Addressing delegates at the International Judicial Conference, Delhi, on 22 February 2020, Sharad Arvind Bobde, then Chief Justice of India, said that so long as every citizen performs 'his' duty the rights are taken care of (https://www.youtube.com/watch?v=SKjNjLT1o6M).

[42] Writing in *The Wire* on 23 January 2022, Abhishek Hari noted that, since 2010, 405 people were charged with sedition after criticising a political leader. Of them, 95 per cent were booked after Narendra Modi became prime minister. Between 2014 and 2020, there was a 28 per cent

RT: There have been so many seditious citizens before, in our history … Perhaps sedition is something we should have got rid of immediately after Independence, because it's a very dicey situation when people can use it as …

GH: Part of recolonising ourselves.

RT: As part of recolonising ourselves. But even if we got rid of it, determined authority will bring back something of that kind. Talking about law, we have to also consider things like the judiciary, which in some cases, in many cases, has made judgements we are not very proud of as free citizens.

GH: In the case of the Assam NRC process, they did not cover themselves in glory.[43]

RT: They didn't. There should be a much greater consciousness on the part of those in the judiciary about the responsibility they have, not just to the authority of the moment, but to

---

rise in sedition cases each year (https://thewire.in/law/explainer-how-the-sedition-law-has-been-used-in-the-modi-era).

[43] The 2005 judgement of the Supreme Court in the Sarbananda Sonowal case blamed the central government for failing to stem the 'external aggression' and 'internal disturbance' caused by illegal migration from Bangladesh to Assam. The court also struck down a law, the Illegal Migrants (Determination by Tribunal) Act of 1983, which had so far provided those accused of being aliens with a small measure of protection against vigilantism. Admitting a petition from an NGO called Assam Public Works in 2009, the Supreme Court directed the central and state governments to update the NRC for Assam. From 2014 onwards, once Ranjan Gogoi became the senior judge on the bench hearing the Assam Public Works case, the Supreme Court increasingly took over the NRC process, hurrying it along by setting deadlines, demanding undertakings and receiving feedback in sealed covers from officials. In doing so, the Court effectively bypassed the central and state governments. People who complained of official arbitrariness, overreach and abuse found themselves in a spot, having to argue against the judiciary before the judiciary.

the future. What are the kinds of laws and legalities and judgements you're making, which will affect generations to come? And this is something that they do not seem to be conscious of. It is entirely a case of this moment—who's an authority, what is the issue, hence this is the judgment. This is very narrow, almost regressive behaviour on the part of those who should be thinking of judgements in terms of the kind of society we want, the kind of society that the future should bring.

GH: And is there a certain hesitation, even apathy, towards the urgent needs of the moment? For example, the courts have been dilly-dallying on coming up with a response to the various petitions against the CAA, NPR, NRC. What is stopping them?[44]

RT: It's worrisome. Responsible members of the judiciary should explain why all these urgent cases—to do with rape, or the CAA, or sedition—don't get settled as fast as they should be. Take the petition we've been involved with. It's over a year now, it's getting on to almost two years since these nine people are in jail.[45] There isn't even a series of trials going on, which

---

[44] Over 200 petitions against the CAA were pending before the Supreme Court since 2019. Listed several times for a hearing, the matter was repeatedly adjourned (https://www.telegraphindia.com/india/caa-hearing-in-supreme-court-put-off-again/cid/1902389. In March 2024, when the Home Ministry detailed the rules for the CAA, the number of petitions surged to over 230. On 19 March, a division bench led by Chief Justice D.Y. Chandrachud refused to put a stay on the Home Ministry's rules, but the petitions challenging the constitutionality of the CAA still await their day in court (https://www.scobserver.in/reports/citizenship-amendment-act-supreme-court-refuses-to-stay-the-caa-rules-directs-union-to-file-responses-to-interim-stay-applications/).

[45] On 28 September 2018, the Supreme Court dismissed a petition filed by Romila Thapar, Prabhat Patnaik, Devaki Jain, Satish Deshpande and

you would expect. And there they will sit for years to come, simply because the date has not been given. In some ways, this is making a mockery of a judicial system. Is this a deliberate strategy or is it because of a shortage of judges? Is it because there's a shortage of trained people who understand what the judiciary is? Do we need specialisation so you don't have one judge dealing with a range of cases, some of which he or she may not fully understand? One way or the other, something has to be done because it is beginning to become self-destructive in some ways.

GH: Romila, let me ask you about the way in which exclusionary laws—say in the form of the CAA and NRC—hem in citizens. As a historian, would you tell us how to view the movement of people, not only within the country as citizens, but also across borders? Surely this is how the history of the human race unfolds?

RT: Absolutely. Everyone is descended from settlers from elsewhere. The movement of people has now become much more intensive in the subcontinent. Every part of the country that you go to, the construction labour, building labour, whatever labour force it may be, is generally from UP, Bihar, Madhya Pradesh, places like that. I have just been to the Punjab

---

Maja Daruwala for the immediate release of five rights activists arrested three months earlier by the Maharashtra police, in the 'Elgar Parishad/ Bhima Koregaon' case. The number of those arrested went up to sixteen over the next two years. The eighty-four-year-old adivasi rights activist, Stan Swamy, died in police custody in July 2021, after repeated ill-treatment by the jail authorities and the National Investigation Agency, and being denied bail by the judiciary. As of June 2024, six years after the first arrests, the trial is yet to begin. The BK-16, as they have come to be collectively known, released a public statement on 6 June 2024, which may be read here: https://www.indiejournal.in/article/imprisoned-bk16-activists-release-statement.

where you couldn't see a single Punjabi labourer. They were all from these parts. And understandably so, because people go where they can get a livelihood. Now this is going to change the demography of the subcontinent. And the government does not understand that by bringing in these laws, they are interfering with the demography of the subcontinent as it would develop under normal circumstances, economic circumstances that lead people to travel. If you find a bunch of Assamese Muslims working in, let's say Karnataka, what are you going to do? How are you going to identify them? And the second generation will probably be Kannada-speaking children going to schools there.

But the bigger problem for me as a historian is that when you look at the history of any country, and particularly of areas that were, in the nineteenth century, specially earmarked as 'civilisations'—European, Islamic, Indian, Chinese, you name it—you find that civilisation, the process of civilisation, is possibly one of the most porous processes that can be imagined. People kept coming in, people kept going out. Ideas were exchanged, people were exchanged, so were customs and practices. For example, the entire Silk Route, Central Asia, has a mixture of people coming and going, including Indians. And so what are we going to do with this? How are we going to understand our own cultures if we put up barricades and say, 'No, nothing from there came in here, nor was it allowed to come in here', and this despite the actual evidence telling you that the situation was absolutely fluid.

The obsessive anxiety regarding migration today—whether it's us or the likes of Trump wanting to build a wall separating Mexico and the Americas—we have this obsession today, but it's an obsession denied by history. And it will be denied by history to come.

GH: To come back to India, and Delhi in the present. We've talked about ways in which the courts can actually engage with the situation as it is unfolding today. So in the case of Shaheen Bagh for instance, the Supreme Court has sent three mediators.[46] And there seems to be some dialogue being initiated. What do you make of it?

RT: I would certainly approve of more dialogue, both in the case of the Shaheen Bagh protests, and also the student protests. Responsible people, responsible citizens, must be sent to have conversations and debates with people who are protesting. This is the civilised way to proceed. Hopefully, something will come of the dialogue in Shaheen Bagh, and rather than take the extreme position of removing the protesters, they will be shifted, perhaps, to a particular area, so the protests as well as the dialogue can go on. People should go on talking, whether in Shaheen Bagh or in other protests.

I'm very impressed with the women at Shaheen Bagh and feel proud that these Indian women are taking such a clear-cut, firm position. In a sense, it is women in this particular protest [against the CAA and NRC] who would have to take on a central role, because whatever documentation you may have, eventually it is only the mother who knows who the father of the child is, and knows where the child was born, and when the child was born. That kind of documentation cannot come

[46] Sanjay Hegde, Sadhana Ramachandran and Wajahat Habibullah were the three interlocutors appointed by the Supreme Court on 17 February 2020, to meet with the women who had been sitting in protest at Shaheen Bagh ever since the passage of the Citizenship (Amendment) Act in December 2019. By February, the protest had spread to dozens of cities. It was finally ended in March by the nationwide lockdown announced at the start of the COVID pandemic.

from paper, it can only come from the mother. And I think it's significant that these protests are being taken up by women.

GH: And of course it's women who have suffered terribly in Assam because they have got married and moved to a place where they must show these documents.

RT: Look at the kind of confusion that's going on. There are women who have been declared to be 'foreigners', but not their children. When families are separated like this, the women are the fundamental sufferers. And so it's very impressive that those affected by these laws are the ones protesting against them.

GH: The unhappiness that so many have felt about the CAA boils down to one fact—that citizenship is being linked with religion. There is a question here of citizenship, but also the question of a rational refugee policy. Would you comment on a rational, egalitarian process for people to become citizens?

RT: Let me address the second question first. I think it's pretty obvious that a rational refugee policy means that we claim to be a society in which anyone who's persecuted in our neighbouring countries can seek asylum. The actual process of seeking asylum is a whole other matter as we know; but it should be open. There should be absolutely no conditions attached to the identity of the person who's seeking asylum. If they can prove that they have been persecuted, they have a claim.

GH: Regardless of religion or nationality.

RT: Absolutely. Once you start this identity business of religion and which country they're coming from, the next will be ethnicity, the next will be occupation. You can bring in all kinds of identities, but that has not worked anywhere else and it cannot work here. I have another problem with the CAA; in fact, I have many problems which I think need to be discussed and which haven't always been discussed in full detail. For instance: the way in which these new laws—CAA, NRC, NPR, the alphabetical laws—have been introduced, underlines and supports the idea of a Hindu Rashtra. What do I mean by this? The foundational principles of the Hindu Rashtra consist of Pitribhumi and Punyabhumi. Pitribhumi is the land of your ancestors which has to be within the boundaries of British India. We don't know which boundaries they're talking about, but we presume it's British India. Punyabhumi means that your religion has to have originated within those boundaries. You have to produce documents to prove where you were born, when you were born and who your parents were. This is Pitribhumi and Punyabhumi.

GH: This is what the NPR, the National Population Register, is attempting.

RT: The Pitribhumi refers to your ancestors, your parents, where they were born and who they were. Punyabhumi is your religion and the territory where it originated. So territory becomes a very important issue. I see this as a step towards establishing the ideology of those currently in power—establishing a Hindu Rashtra. They make no bones about it. So I see this not only as an attack on citizenship, but also as a subtle way of bringing in their own ideas about how to establish a Hindu Rashtra. This is one way of doing that.

GH: Romila, with all the protests that we've seen across India, women on the streets, students on the streets, all kinds of people on the streets, we've had a certain sort of response—an official response which again goes back to what you were talking about, the distortion of the relationship between the state and the citizen in present-day India. Would you like to talk about that? We have seen a response that's completely out of proportion and undemocratic, whether it's violence, detention, Section 144, sedition, or the National Security Act.

RT: Yes, in some ways I would say that this is almost predictable. When there is so much confusion on the part of the authority as to how to implement a particular set of laws, there will be differences of opinion on implementation and procedures, differences that might logically lead to rather high-handed actions of detaining and arresting people. What worries me is the way in which the situation is moving at the moment.

First, I think it's conducive to corruption. Suppose people who are impoverished, entire families with no documents, go to the presiding officer and say, 'We have no documents.' We know from the way in which administration functions that one of the easiest solutions is, 'Right, you pay me under the counter, I'll give you the documents.' And this could become a system, a lot of documents being forged for a price. This is worrying because in a sense you're not opposing the system of passing these kinds of laws, but you're introducing another element of corruption into the functioning of these laws. That's one possibility.

The second worry is particularly frightening. Look at the way in which protests are treated, and what has been going on in Delhi for example. Are we developing into a surveillance state? It's now got to the point when most people would say that the police no longer protect the citizen, which is what it's supposed to do. It is, in fact, on the side of authority, and it is challenging and threatening the citizen. So the ordinary citizen is not going to run to the police for protection, but will run away from the police. This is a critical situation. There will be nobody left in society whom the ordinary citizen can go to and say, 'Please protect me. I am being harassed. I'm being threatened.'

And then you have a system which has already started, which is that those in the law-and-order section of society will simply listen to those in authority and carry out their orders. The actual substance and the need for having people maintaining law and order will disappear, because there will be no law and order.

GH: But the claim of 'law and order' also gets used, very often, in all kinds of ways. So what you mean by law and order may not be what the person on the street is saying.

RT: People saying that the problem in the Delhi situation in the last few days—that it is one of law and order—is, frankly, unacceptable to me, because it's not about law and order.[47] It is very definitely one group of people wishing to attack another group of people for very obvious reasons. No, what I meant is that the people who are supposed to ensure law and order for your safety will no longer do so. And this we have seen repeatedly in the last few months. The police will attack universities as they did in Jamia and in Aligarh. The police will just sit by and watch a university being attacked, as happened

---

[47] Between 24 and 26 February 2020, there were many incidents of stone-pelting, arson, shooting and police brutality in Delhi, which left over fifty people dead and around 200 injured. On 22 February, a new site of anti-CAA protest was occupied by women in Jaffrabad, North East Delhi. The following day, the BJP leader Kapil Mishra issued a three-day ultimatum to the police to clear the protesters out from Jaffrabad and Chand Bagh (where another protest was underway). The violence began the next day and was concentrated in the areas of Chand Bagh, Madanpuri, Gokalpuri, Maujpur and Jaffrabad (https://thewire.in/communalism/delhi-riots-timeline).

in JNU. That's not maintaining law and order. And really the force with which people are attacked, even with lathis, makes one shudder—that these are the people supposed to be protecting the citizen. This disturbs me very much because I think that now as citizens, we are left with no protection.

There's been some talk about the boycott of the officers that come around getting information for the NRC. This, in a sense, is suggestive to me as it is to a couple of other people I've talked to. It recalls the civil disobedience movement of Gandhi. That if you wish to take a position against a particular law, be it the manufacture of salt, do it by saying 'As a citizen I have the right to do this. You can't stop me.'

Similarly, as a citizen I have the right to say that I will not give you this information if I choose not to. Do what you like. But then you must also ensure that detention centres are closed down and converted into schools and hospitals. It's another terrible blot on Indian society if you have detention centres for citizens.

In 2018, I was invited to conduct a conversation with Romila at the Kerala Literature Festival in Kozhikode.[48] *This was a truly public conversation. Not only did we have a sizeable audience and many questions at the end, but we had also to contend with the joys and miseries of an open-air setting on the beach. The ambient sounds kept us anchored to the present moment, and the place we were in: the distant lapping of waves, the calls of hawkers, and children blowing on plastic whistles or shrieking, hopefully*

[48] Founded in 2016, the Kerala Literature Festival (KLF) is an annual literary festival organised by the D.C. Kizhakemuri Foundation (DCKF), with poet and critic K. Satchidanandan as its director.

in enjoyment. But we managed to travel a great deal amid this clutter, all the way to the past, and, of course, the future. In a conversation titled 'Learning from the past, lessons for the future', Romila spoke of the contradiction between religious non-violence and political violence, and the bridge between ancient India and modern India.

8 February 2018

GH: It is a great pleasure for me to be in conversation with Romila, especially because she's a friend and a fellow traveller. And most important in these times, we value the historian who does not fabricate history, but questions those who are distorting it. I do want to preface our conversation by saying that I am here as an interested citizen and a writer. I am not an academic and not a scholar. What we are hoping to do is talk about the past insofar as it is used in the politics of the present.

Romila, we used to be told: 'Tell me what your classic is, and I'll tell you where you come from.' Suppose I twist that and say, 'Tell me what your way of looking at the past is, and I'll tell you where you come from in the present.' In other words, what are the different ways of looking at the past to use it in the present?

RT: First, let me say that Githa and I often have conversations in the privacy of her living room or mine. I think this is the first time that we are chatting with each other with an audience. So all of you are now part of something very private, which I hope will amuse and entertain you. And perhaps give you some understanding of what we are all about.

Now, Githa has asked me about history. I don't really know where to begin because it's a subject that I have read about and taught, and thought about so much. But let me clarify one thing. I often get people coming up to me and saying, 'You're a historian and there are so many controversies these days, where is the truth?' And I have to say, 'I'm very sorry, but we are not looking for the Truth (with a capital T), certainly not in my case as a historian. What I am looking for is how we understand the past, how we analyse it. And that's really as far as I'm willing to go. The past is past. It's over and done with. We cannot reconstruct it as it was, but we can try and understand it. And that is the important issue.

GH: Romila, hearing you frame the study of history, I think of my own school days when we had to study something called 'Oriental History'. Then and now, the official historians have always had an agenda.

RT: Indeed, they have always had an agenda, though that was not recognised early on. But that is the first question we ask today when we pick up a text. Whether it is a Sanskrit chronicle from the pre-Islamic period, or a Persian chronicle, the first question we ask as we read the text is, 'What is the agenda of the author?'

These are new questions. 'Who is the author? What is the agenda? What is the purpose of the text?' And very important, 'Who is the audience the author and the text are addressing?' This gives you some idea of the complications we face now when we look at texts as sources. You don't go to them and come back and say, 'In such and such a text it says this. This must have been what happened.' Not at all. Your next question is, 'If in such and such a text it says this, did it actually happen? And how do we test whether it happened?' This is very important. And here, yes, the agenda does govern the reading of a text. We originally had Orientalists and Indologists who did first-rate work in finding the texts, and analysing them up to a point —linguistically—and giving us the information of the texts.

Then the agenda changed. Just information was no longer enough. Now historians wanted to know what the approach of the author was. What the purpose of the text was. And so you had a tradition of colonial historians who wrote at great length about the purpose of these texts, and made certain statements. And the nationalists disapproved of some of these statements.

So a few of the nationalist historians, such as K.P. Jayaswal,[49] R.C. Majumdar[50] and others, questioned what the colonial historians had said. And then my generation came along and said: 'Wait a minute, both the colonialists and the nationalists have made mistakes. They are not reading the texts the way we should read them.' And so we gave a fresh reading to the text, putting it into context. And that has done something very interesting, which the general public is not really fully aware of. It has shifted history from being a subject in Indology, where you want information, to becoming a subject in what we call the social sciences, where you want more than information; you want to know the how and the why and wherefore of events. You want to analyse these events. You want to look at the context, and you want to look at causal relationships and logical reconstructions.

GH: Could you give us a specific example of the 'rational social science method' which does not pretend you can reveal

[49] K.P. Jayaswal (1881–1937) was a lawyer and historian who reconstructed Indian pre-colonial history in the context of the nationalist challenge to the prevailing colonial interpretation.

[50] R.C. Majumdar (1888–1980) was a historian who began his career studying ancient India, but is perhaps best known for his (often controversial) volumes on the history of the freedom movement in India.

the past, but you can sort of put in some pieces and say, 'This is possible'? Does any example come to mind?

RT: The example in which I explored this the most was my study of Somanatha,[51] the Mahmud of Ghazni raid in 1026 on the temple of Somanatha. The Persian chronicles were the only sources that were used for a long time, and they had descriptions of the temple and what was looted. It was very interesting that each chronicle changed the description of what was there. One said it was a Shiva lingam. Another said it was a pre-Islamic Arabian goddess, in a formless form. Somebody else said it was something else and so on. They couldn't quite make up their minds what it was that Mahmud of Ghazni had looted, except for the basic fact that the temple was very wealthy and that it had been raided for its wealth.

Then some of us came along and said, 'What about what happened after the raid?' So we started looking at Sanskrit texts, Jain texts, studies, histories, chronicles of the Chalukya dynasty of Gujarat [contemporaneous with Ghazni's raid], of individual rulers and Sanskrit inscriptions. A totally different story emerged: Somanatha had become a major commercial centre trading with the Arabs and the Persians. The temples were even richer than before and had a lot of land to their name. When the Arab traders came and wanted to build a mosque, the Somanatha temple actually donated some land to them. And this is in the century after the raid.

Now this was a revelation. And why did people not look at the Sanskrit text? Because the British colonial writers had divided Indian history into the Hindu period, the Muslim period and the British period. They said the Hindu period ends in 1200, then the Muslim period begins. And in the

---

[51] *Somanatha: The Many Voices of a History*, Penguin, 2004.

Hindu period you only read texts in Sanskrit because it's a Hindu period. And in the Muslim period you only read texts in Persian, not realising that the texts and the writing of the texts, and the writing of inscriptions, continued in Sanskrit and Persian—in Sanskrit right up to the nineteenth century.

So we had to use this kind of information. We had to stop talking about the Hindu-Muslim crisis and begin to look at the temple and commercial relations. We had to ask questions such as, 'What was the nature of these commercial relations? Who were the merchants who came and what was the nature of trade? Who did they mix with? Who did they marry?' And the Arabs, as we now know, set up as commercial settlers along the west coast. They set up a series of communities where they married locally and a new community emerged.

Then somebody said, 'What about the Hindu trauma?' The colonial writers had said a great deal about how Mahmud of Ghazni's raid had created such a strong Hindu trauma that it became the basis of Hindu-Muslim antagonism for centuries to come, from the eleventh century onwards. I went through the Sanskrit texts, but could find no reference to this trauma. There is no reference even to the raid, in fact. The texts described the destruction of the temple in various other ways. Then I chanced upon a debate in the House of Commons in 1842. A member in the House of Commons, the British Parliament, asks a question: 'Did this raid not create a trauma among the Hindus?'

The colonial writers picked this up and began talking about how the raid created a trauma among the Hindus. Then the nationalist historians picked it up, and they too said it created a trauma among the Hindus.

GH: And that brings us to present times. You have spoken of the colonial division of the Hindu period and the Muslim period. That has made today's politics possible—ironically the so-called nationalists today are actually using a colonial schema. That is one issue. And then this trauma you speak of also seems to have some link with the present narrative of Hindu victimisation, which calls for Hindus to become martial. Would you tell us more about these two strands of the right-wing narrative?

RT: Let me go back a bit. One thing to keep in mind is that nationalism emerges in the modern period. We cannot talk about nationalism in the Mauryan period or the Gupta period, or the Chola period, or the Mughal period. Absolutely not. Nationalism is a modern concept, and it is a way to bind people together and create a nation.

What existed before were kingdoms and states, not nations. Nations come into existence around the eighteenth century. Now, what happens with nationalism in our case is this: we had anti-colonial nationalism, which was a kind of secular nationalism. It was inclusive. It tried to bring all Indians together in a movement which was to try and get rid of colonial rule.

Now, side by side with that, and encouraged by colonial rule, there emerged what we call religious nationalism. It took root via the Muslim League in the case of Islamic nationalism, and the Hindu Mahasabha and suchlike with Hindu nationalism. Religious nationalism is very different from secular nationalism—anti-colonial nationalism—because anti-colonial nationalism is inclusive. It brings in everybody as much as possible, whereas religious nationalism caters to a particular religious community. It's confined, it's exclusive.

Now, history is an essential feature of all nationalism. The great European historian Eric Hobsbawm [1917–2012] has a lovely statement on this. He says, 'History is to nationalism what the poppy is to the opium addict.' It is the source of trying to give people a vision that can bring them together. And because of that, because of the centrality of history, very often what happens is that your religious or your linguistic—or in these days, caste nationalism—tends to create new histories, fantasy histories. These play havoc with genuine history—genuine in the sense of well-researched, well-thought-out history, based on hard evidence, as against histories which are more myth than history.

This is where history becomes a central issue in our kinds of societies. I have often thought about the fact that when I opted to study ancient Indian history—this was in the mid-1950s—everybody would say, 'Oh, you've taken the easy way out because nobody knows about that history. You can say what you like.'

Now I find it is the most contested history. It partakes of the nationalist tradition of having a golden age. All nationalist histories have a golden age. With Europe it is, of course, Greco-Roman. And so, in the Indian case too, there is a hunt for a golden age, and the Gupta period becomes the golden age.

The other contestation, or problem, emerges because those of us trying to bring in the importance of evidence—reliable evidence, evidence that has been analysed, evidence in which causal relationships have been examined deeply, evidence based on rational, logical connections—are regarded as 'anti-national' because we don't further the fantasy histories that are being put forward.

GH: Romila, let me complicate matters. It seems there are huge absences in our history. I know that all of us would like to say that the freedom movement was inclusive. We are talking of a written history in which large numbers of people are not visible, because of the caste system.

You remember we were talking about the first mention of caste in the golden period. So much for the golden period! Could you talk about that, and also about how we could express nationalism—in the good sense of the word—as citizens of India? Till dalits and other large sections of the population have a *visible* history of their own, we will have absences and contentions, such as the one about Bhima Koregaon.

RT: This is a very important point because a lot of nationalist history tended to go by what the texts were saying. So if the Dharmashastras describe society in a particular way and give much more visibility to the upper castes, there was a tendency for historians to say, 'Yes, that is how society functioned.'

Part of the reason for the absences is that those who were not literate didn't produce texts. And so we have to look for evidence of them in the texts of elite groups and upper castes who may mention them. Some do, but not at great length. So there is a certain amount of evidence that is missing in a direct way, and which needs to be discovered.

There are also other things we have to take into account. For example, the oral tradition was always dismissed by historians as being impossible, as inexact and indirect. 'Anybody can add anything they like.' And this became a little matter of debate when we discovered that there are many texts that we take for granted where bits and pieces have been added on, and we don't know who added them on, but we can suspect who did because of the message they carry.

The Mahabharata is a beautiful example of a text which has constantly been added on to in the past, gradually. In Africa, for example, it was said, 'Oh, there was no history south of the Sahara.' But they began studying the oral tradition more analytically and carefully; they began making a method for the study, and method is crucial in any kind of study. So just as we have a historical method we use, a method was also produced for the oral tradition. Now it is possible for us to go to non-elite sources, and even use the oral tradition to get some idea of what the history might have been.

GH: Romila, let's talk a little more about caste. What are the ways in which this completely extraordinary system of stratification—our negative contribution to the world—emerged, grew and lived? What were the strategies that actually allowed caste to become an institution that has lasted? Would you tell us how this fits in with the modern historian's paradigm?

RT: These questions are, perhaps, a little difficult because they are still being worked out. So I would make two points. One is that all societies have stratification. So it's not very unusual that Indian society also had stratification. The second point I would like to make is that all stratifications are subject to being changed. So the old idea that we had that caste as varna, as described in Dharmashastra, was something that made society static and was always observed, come rain or shine—this is completely untrue! We have enough historical evidence now to say that within each of the four varnas, for example, there were changes, movement up and down. So we have to relook at the whole caste stratification and see what these changes were.

The second point I would like to make is that there's always been this contention between jati and varna, and jati was always treated as a subcaste of varna. But now people are beginning to ask the question: 'If we say that the original stratification was jati, based on extended families, clan systems, or all these early forms by which society was divided, and varna then came in as a very deliberate design and strategy to demarcate groups of people from each other, are the two things not different?' They play along in a different way. Now, there is an interesting thing about what is called avarna. Savarna refers to the four castes that constitute varna. Avarna is a group that is not given a status in caste and which is outside society. We have very interesting references to the chandala who was the characteristic person regarded as the avarna, always living outside the society. But to begin with, the chandala was regarded as lower caste, and that was it.

For example, there's a very interesting dialogue in the Mahabharata[52] with the sage Vishwamitra, who's been performing tapasya like mad, because he is trying desperately to acquire so much merit that he becomes a major sage.

There's a famine in the land. Vishwamitra is desperately hungry. He comes to a chandala hamlet. In one of the houses he sees dog meat hanging, and he's just about to grab it and eat it, he's so hungry. The chandala comes out and says, 'Wait, what are you doing? If you eat that meat, you will lose all the punya you have been gathering with this intense tapasya.' And there's a dialogue in which the chandala explains to Vishwamitra, or tells him off, saying, 'This is not brahmin dharma. This is not how you are expected to behave.' And he explains to Vishwamitra why he's saying this is not the way he's expected to behave.

Finally, of course, Vishwamitra eats the dog meat and then says he will double down on the tapasya and get back his merit. This would be unheard of in the Gupta period, and

[52] In Book 12, Shanti Parva.

certainly unheard of today. But there is this dialogue in the Mahabharata, some kind of communication which indicates something interesting happening.

And coming to the situation of the chandala living outside the settlement. By the Gupta period, we have a description from Fa-Hien, a Chinese Buddhist pilgrim who visits India. And he says that they have here a category of people whom they regard as very polluted. Remember, the Mahabharata story is not talking about pollution. But now we have a category of people who are very polluted, therefore live outside the settlement. When they come into the settlement, they have to strike a clapper so that people will move away since they don't want to touch or be touched by the chandala. Again, it's in the Gupta period also that you begin to get references in the Dharmashastra to the asprishya, those not to be touched.

And that was the point that I was making, that this is your golden age, an age where lots of admirable things are happening, whether it is in literature or art or philosophy. Certainly all this makes it a remarkably brilliant age. But on the social side, it was different. And my question has always been, 'What kind of society was it that allowed the two things to co-exist?' This I haven't understood, I must confess.

GH: I remember your telling me that the asprishya couldn't leave their situation physically. Religious persecution has seen waves of people going elsewhere, but caste …

RT: They couldn't get up and go for the simple reason that they were regarded as genetically polluted. It is not just the individual who is polluted, but also the child born of asprishya parents is automatically polluted. So there's a genetic pollution. And the thing about the early period of Indian history was that there were no peasant revolts as such, unlike China that had lots of peasant revolts.

We had peasant migrations. The peasants were overtaxed, impoverished. They would move into the next kingdom. And this was something that was always feared by the kings because they would lose revenue if the peasants moved. But the untouchable, the chandala, could not move because no other kingdom would accept the polluted person. The other kingdoms didn't want to increase their population of polluted people.

So this category of people who were at the lowest occupational levels, both in terms of artisanal production and in terms of being agricultural labour, were forced to remain where they were. They couldn't get away because of the stigma of pollution. And in some ways, I suppose it is an astute method to keep available a permanent body of labour you can control completely.

GH: What about the medieval bhakti movements, limited but fairly powerful protest movements that experimented with fighting caste and this whole system of co-option? The perfect example is Basava [fl. twelfth century] and what happens to the movement he is part of, how it ends up creating one more caste, the Lingayat caste. So has that always been a kind of a strategy that you see in 'Hindu history'?

RT: You see it in all religions here because this category of polluted people is not restricted to the Hindu religion. It occurs among the Muslims, the Christians, also among the Sikhs. The first question we need to ask about the movements you refer to is, 'Was this a religious movement or a social movement, or a mixture of the two, one using the other, one giving strength to the other?' If you argue along these lines, you partly explain why even important religions not using this idea outside India use it here—they are continuing the social basis of what is going on in India. And I think that is an important thing to keep in mind, that there is this continuation.

GH: Coming to the present, could we talk about the role of the public intellectual today, and the role of university spaces, of educational spaces? Also, what sort of public discourse should we aspire to? That seems to be a huge problem today when we speak of history, literature or culture.

RT: After Independence, there was a strong feeling that we need to envision the kind of society we mean to build. There were two important issues involved. One was, 'Who are we as Indians? What is our identity?' And the other was, 'What is the kind of society we're going to build?' It was quite clear who we are as Indians: We are Indians on a larger scale because we are not divided into religious categories or caste categories or linguistic categories. We are Indian citizens.

The new thing at the point of Independence was that we now had a nation, we had a nation-state, and we had citizens. And the relationship had to be that of the citizen to the state, which in a sense cuts out all the other incisive categories that pull people apart. And, of course, despite attempts, we didn't achieve much in terms of forging this relationship between the citizen and the state, because we have arrived at a present point when nobody talks about *citizens* anymore. Everybody talks about majority communities and minority communities, which is entirely a colonial construct; it is entirely anti-democratic. Democracies don't have inherent permanent majorities and minorities separated by a single qualifying factor such as religion or language. The majority and the minority change with each issue under debate. So there is that distinction.

Perhaps the important thing is the question of how we make all our people learn to think. Because that's essential. And it is that critical aspect of education where we have failed. Yes, education may have spread literacy up to a limited degree, but …

GH: Education itself is a troubled site today. It's all very well for the powers that be to pay lip service to education, but they have also been saying things like, 'Drop the Mughal period altogether from the syllabus', or 'Darwin was wrong!' We seem to be grappling with new idiocies every day.

RT: But that is partly because in our educational system, we don't do the one basic thing that all good education systems require. And that is to teach the student to doubt accepted knowledge and to ask relevant questions. The student has to learn to argue that I will accept existing knowledge, but I have the right to advance this knowledge by questioning it. Once you do that, you have a different mindset.

If you don't do that, you have a mindset which says, 'It says so in the book, you learn it by heart and repeat it.' And the crisis today for students in school and in college is that they're not battling with ideas. They're battling with grades. 'What grades will I get?' That is the only question they ask. And I think that is tragic because, in a sense, it is the termination of a good educational system when you stop grappling with ideas.

GH: When I think of JNU with which you've been associated ever since it was founded, I can see that this kind of questioning was part of the vision for the University that all of you worked very hard to implement. Despite all odds, even today, you see that in the JNU campus, there are students who speak up and ask hard questions. But what do you do with those in authority who systematically suppress this natural desire to question?

What should writers and students and academics do in such a situation?

RT: We have to question the right of those who are trying to reduce us to silence. That is really necessary. I don't mean that we go out and indulge in violence and that kind of thing. But the central issue is the right of institutions to determine their goals. This right is not served by silencing institutions, or diverting them in such a way that they become ineffectual. This right has to be exercised within and outside the university—and this is where the question of the public intellectual becomes very important. The right to insist that institutions must not be silenced must have a social backing. And it will only have a social backing if the public understands what the issues are.

If people understand that you're converting your universities into non-entities, they can ask, 'Why are we paying all this money for university education? We want university education, which is an education that teaches us how to question, how to think, how to move knowledge ahead, whatever knowledge it may be.' But if there are institutions creating impediments to this kind of understanding and questioning, we have to question those institutions.

GH: I think that's a good point at which to draw this conversation to a close, since all your comments come together at the point of knowledge, the question of how we seek knowledge, and the understanding that knowledge is not something which is readymade, or something that belongs to a few people. It's something we are all working towards.

Annihilating Caste

BAMA

Cutting Through the System

Bama Faustina Soosairaj is better known as Bama. Her first book, the autobiographical *Karukku*, was published in Tamil in 1992, and in an English translation by Lakshmi Holmström in 2000.[53] I recall hearing from Lakshmi, even as she was translating the text, how searing a story it was, and how powerful and direct Bama's use of language. In her introduction to the published translation, Lakshmi writes:

> *Karukku* is the first autobiography of its kind to appear in Tamil, for dalit writing in this language has not produced the spate of autobiographies which have appeared, for example, in Marathi. It is also in many ways an unusual autobiography. It grows out of a particular moment: a personal crisis and watershed in the author's life which drives her to make sense of her life as woman, Christian, dalit …

And, summing up her take on the writer's purpose—the challenge, as well as promise it holds out to the reader—Lakshmi

---

[53] Bama, *Karukku*, translated by Lakshmi Holmström, Macmillan Dalit Writing in Translation, ed. Mini Krishnan, Macmillan India, 2000.

adds, '… Bama is writing in order to change hearts and minds. And as readers of her work, we are asked for nothing less than an imaginative entry into that different world of experience and its political struggle.'[54]

A different world of experience. Plain old struggle, individual and collective. Then, a lifetime of political struggle. And an invitation to extend a hand of solidarity. All this I read (and saw and heard) in *Karukku*. My learning deepened over the years with Bama's other work, as writer, teacher, thinker; and with her friendship.

Karukku describes the place where Bama grew up—Puthupatti in Tamil Nadu. The village has beautiful mountains, tanks, fields and woods. But this is not just 'nature'. It is part of the hard business of making a living. The fields are there to be worked in; the mountain woods have to be searched for firewood; the streams have to be coaxed into yielding their fish.

Moreover, the place, and every aspect of life in it, is sharply classified and divided—caste mapped. There is the settlement of the nadars who climb palmyra palms for a living; there are the koravars who sweep streets; the leatherworking chakkiliyars; the kusavars who make earthenware pots; the pallas, the thevars, the chettiyars, the aasaaris, the udaiyaars. And Bama's own community of agricultural labourers, the parayas.

Bama writes that the upper-caste communities

> … kept themselves to their part of the village, and we stayed in ours. We only went to their side if we had work to do there. But they never, ever, came to our parts. The post-office, the panchayat board, the milk depot, the big shops, the church,

[54] Lakshmi Holmström, Introduction, ibid., pp. xi and xii.

> the schools—all these stood in their streets. So why would they need to come to our area.[55]

Hemmed into such clear pockets of caste, Bama also describes the overwhelming sense, as she was growing up, that the village extended just up to the bus terminus, 'as if our entire world ended there'.

By the time Bama completed the eighth class in her village and went to high school in a neighbouring town, she knew, very well, what 'untouchability' was. It meant being the children of servants, of cheap labour. It meant her old grandmother calling a little boy 'ayya' and obeying his commands. It meant cupping hands to receive drinking water poured from a height of four feet. And it meant being taunted, on the streets or in school, as a paraya. Even a child knew what it was like to be thought of as contemptible—as a 'harijan'.

Bama studied hard. But no achievement in school or college would change what she was in the eyes of the teachers or the hostel warden or the people in the bus. Even if she got the best marks in class, even if she was determined to earn respect, she was only a paraya. Perhaps it was this growing realisation that she would never 'transcend' this identity that made her embrace it, not with resignation, but with a new zeal. She became a nun, hoping to teach dalit children in a village school. But the religious order had other plans for her.

After seven years in a world unlike the real world she grew up in, the real world she hoped to help change, Bama left the convent, only to find she did not know 'how to live'. It was this terrible period of isolation that forced her into doing something that would help her to survive. She began writing about her childhood, and about being dalit. She wrote about a

---

[55] *Karukku*, 2002, p. 6.

culture of survival—the hard work, and the sounds of songs or quarrels. She had the women speaking in the earthy language they actually spoke in—'the only armour' these women have against both landlords and husbands. She wrote in the dialect she had grown up speaking. She called this story of a dalit life *Karukku*, a double-edged reference to the stem of the palm leaf. The serrated edges of the leaf recalled for Bama not only the 'social cuts' people like her got every day, but also the more important fact that *they* had to cut through this stifling system.

Karukku is now something of a milestone in feminist literature, and in dalit feminist literature.

Many years after she wrote *Karukku*, the sharp-edged palmyra continues to cut her, but also inspire her to *cut through* an unjust and unequal system. 'There is no such thing as equality anywhere. We need to bring about a resistance. Resistance at an individual level is not enough, we need to set up mechanisms of resistance and other checks and balances at institutional levels.'[56]

Education, Bama says, is an essential means to build a better future. Bama was a school teacher for thirty-five years, from 1979 to 2015. They must have been years of hard work and frustration—she recalls only too well the ways in which inequalities persist in the education system: 'The education system does not care for an egalitarian society or social justice … Instead of changing the existing unequal system, it

[56]'There is no such thing as equality anywhere, we need to bring about resistance', *Indian Cultural Forum*, 10 September 2021 (https://indianculturalforum.in/2021/09/10/bama-interview-from-lifescapes/), extract published from *Lifescapes: Interviews with Contemporary Women Writers from Tamil Nadu* by K. Srilata and Swarnalatha Rangarajan, Women Unlimited, 2019.

justifies it …' But Bama also has a message of hope: Teachers can do wonders if they commit themselves to shaping the future generation.[57]

Bama and I have spoken over the years, and in early 2016, we retraced her journey, from writing autobiography and fiction to teaching dalit schoolchildren—all with one guiding purpose: to bring about change. In her own words, '… we must dare to stand up for change. We must crush all those institutions that use caste to bully us into submission, and demonstrate that among human beings there are none who are high or low.'[58]

29 January 2016

Githa Hariharan (GH): Bama, when we first met all those years back, we spoke of your autobiography, *Karukku.* Let's revisit that conversation.

Bama: Yes, the autobiography was published in 1992. You know that I had entered the convent to become a nun in 1985. I stayed there for seven years, but I couldn't continue there because of the caste discrimination in the convent.

GH: You'd actually joined the convent hoping to serve the dalit community.

Bama: I was a teacher for seven years. Then I resigned and went into the convent. My motive was to teach and to create an awareness in dalit girls. I chose that life because I knew that it carries power, and a lot of privileges also—I thought I

[57] '35 years of teaching: Writer Bama recollects inequalities in education', *Indian Cultural Forum*, 27 August 2021 (https://indianculturalforum.in/2021/08/27/bama_fearless_insightful_writer_of_dalit_lives/).

[58] *Karukku*, 2000, pp. 24–25.

would be able to meet and talk to girls, dalit girls. I entered the convent with that hope. But that hope was not realised. All I was supposed to do was teach English and mathematics. Since my dream of doing more than that could not be realised, I decided to leave. I left the convent in 1992. That was the time I suffered most in my life—I had no job, no place to go to, no money, no food. I used to worry about the next meal, where I would get it from …

GH: Bama, we have spoken earlier of the harsh reaction to your first book when it was published. The literary establishment criticised the language as not beautiful. And the paraiyar community in your village felt that you had exposed them in some way. Would you like to tell us about that? And how did the young people in the village manage to convince the others?

Bama: That was really unexpected actually, the reaction of my own people. I thought they would appreciate me, but they were upset. They told me I had shown them up to the outside world. That I had exposed the ugliness of their lives for all to see and hear. They felt betrayed. Of course, I had intended no such thing. But I was in the dock and I had to answer their question, 'Why did you do that?' It was not just a question—they wanted to beat me up, actually.

But there were also youngsters in the village, educated youngsters. They read the book and they went and fought with my parents. And my father was very angry with me and told me not to come to the house. So I was roaming around here and there.

One of the boys from the village had written a very good critique of the book. He also wrote to me, 'Don't come now, wait for some time. We will read aloud from the book and tell the people what it is about.'

And that is what they did. The youngsters collected the village people at night, after their working day was done, under the streetlights. They told the people they had misunderstood and misinterpreted the book. They read it out and explained to the people why and how I had written the book. The villagers came to know that their stories were being read by many people. They were happy about the fact that their history was becoming known to many people outside the village. Then this same boy asked me to come to the village and they organised a very big function. They celebrated me like I was a princess.

GH: So it was actually a process of their becoming confident enough to say, 'This is how our lives really are. And this is how the women's lives are.' That leads me to ask if part of the problem was not just that you were talking about dalit life, but also about dalit women's lives? Because, of course, women are doubly exploited or discriminated against, as dalits and as women. Was that part of the problem, do you think?

Bama: Not just doubly, but women are thrice exploited, actually: caste, class and gender. Religion also. So those in the community realised that there are these triple monsters in their lives. But my writing also helped them experience their strength. In my second book, *Sangati*,[59] I have recorded acts of bravery of women, how they resisted this oppressive system, which again reinforced the idea. They knew that they could protest against the system and live.

And basically that is what dalit culture is: it's loving to live. We want to live, but the system doesn't allow us to live. So the

[59]*Sangati*, meaning Events, is a collection of anecdotes and stories about the lives of dalit women. It was published in 1994, and the English translation by Lakshmi Holmström was published in 2001.

culture is very vibrant and the women too realised this. I mean, in spite of all the struggles and hardships and violence we face, we know that we are capable women. We have the strength to break through the systems that are breaking us down, and that gives us hope. So they began to celebrate their womanhood and their militancy and their life, and there was a tremendous change after that.

GH: Yes, *Sangati* is a wonderful collection of stories of the kind of brave individuals you are talking of, and also of the gestures which allow people to say, 'Look, I too can resist in this small way.' I especially like the story of that old woman who gets a free ride in a jeep to go vote. When she comes back, she's so gleeful, saying, 'I got to ride in that fancy jeep, but nobody knows who I voted for.'

So in addition to those stories of feisty women, suppose we look at what you brought up, the fact that class, caste and gender are the three axes on which discrimination plays out. Since *Karukku*, in what ways would you say you have wanted to build alliances with other movements, whether in your writing or your life? Or do you foreground the dalit identity?

Bama: I have gained and still gain strength from dalit women. Whenever I face problems in my life as a woman, especially as a dalit woman, I learn from my sisters who are in the villages. I see that I am comparatively privileged. When they are able to face all these hardships and live life with so much joy and enthusiasm, why can't I? That is a source of energy for me. With that, I move forward. And when I mingle and meet with other women, I always share this with them. I see that for nothing at all women take their lives. They lose hope in life. But I show them how life is beautiful, and beauty is simple. You can live life without having all kinds of consumeristic attitudes and values, because life is not that, real happiness is not there. Dalit women experience joy in hard labour, they live life amid their hardships. They see that life is made enjoyable by human relationships, human values—a humanistic approach gives you meaning and depth in life. That is the essential thing for our survival, not anything else.

GH: Bama, you have spoken of dalit women who lose heart to such an extent that many have taken their lives. Which actually brings us to what is happening in India right now: dalit students [such as Rohith Vemula] unable to bear the burden of day-to-day discrimination they face.[60] You've been a schoolteacher for so many years. You gave up your job in a higher secondary school, choosing to teach in a village primary school, where most of the students were dalits and first-generation school-going children. What message would you send to dalit youth today? In fact, to *all* Indian youth about our idea of [an equal] India, and this age-old caste division which is simply not going away?

Bama: This is really a very saddening thing to look at, youth losing hope. To see them driven to the point of harming themselves or taking their own lives. I feel really concerned about it. What can such people do about it? I think we need to root ourselves in our own soil and culture, first of all. Then, though thousands of obstacles may come in our way, still there

[60] This particular conversation in January 2016 took place in Delhi. Bama was in the city to take part in a panel discussion on 'Caste, Religion and Lived Experiences', organised by the Indian Writers Forum in collaboration with Ambedkar University on 20 January 2016, three days after Rohith Vemula, a dalit student in Hyderabad, died by suicide—one of the many cases of what can, arguably, be described as 'institutional murder'. (For the panel discussion, see https://www.youtube.com/watch?v=WUhd33jp-8I).

is hope, hope beyond hope. Instead of the system breaking us, or pushing us to take our own lives, we need to break through this system.

GH: Once again, we go back to the idea of the karukku, the serrated edges of a palm leaf …

Bama: Yes. One sharp side is how society cuts us in the name of caste. We bleed, we die. But the other sharp side is knowledge; that is essential. We can use knowledge. We can use our capacity to work through the system instead of cutting our own selves. The youth now, they are forgetting their roots.

It's not just the universities, Githa. Discrimination begins in the schools. Teachers in the village schools discriminate between young children. They treat them differently and the education authorities show partiality. It starts there, children having to face this discrimination and psychological harm. They don't get that positive affirmation they need, and these children really struggle. They see their equals, other children in the school, enjoy life while they are treated in a different way. They experience that. So it is a very, very painful thing. It begins there and it carries on, it accumulates through high school, in the higher grades, and then during their studies in universities—it may show up there in a more subtle way. So we need to be aware of all these things and respond collectively. I mean 'groupism' helps in the sense that you find strength in one another, like that togetherness you find in the villages.

GH: You have shared this powerful image of cutting through a system which discriminates. In practical terms, in terms of political strategy, what do you think would work? Because the anti-caste movement has had many splinters and, as you put it, the young have, in a way, 'forgotten the soil they come from'. Should there be an ongoing reassertion of dalit identity? Or should it move beyond identity politics to a mass movement? What would you suggest as a strategy?

Bama: See, as long as we live a passive life, everybody's okay, everything is okay. But not when you begin to question, when you begin to argue, when you claim your right to be human.

GH: And your constitutional rights.

BFS: Yes, constitutional right to say that I am a human person, then everybody gets agitated. They want to suppress this, that is the thing. What I think is that we need to retain this dalit identity. And you mingle with other like-minded people who respect you as a person. Because we can't really go and request or beg the people who don't accept you as a human person. So if there are people who really respect you and think, 'You are a person like me', then we can get together. Like-minded people, like-minded organisations, like-minded movements, can join together.

GH: Yes, an alliance of equals.

BFS: And another thing is that we need to equip ourselves. We need, as Ambedkar says, to educate, organise and agitate.[61] First we need to equip ourselves to fight against caste. And standing firmly on the idea [that we are equal], we can extend our solidarity to other groups, other movements, and fight for everybody's equality, fraternity and freedom.

Ultimately, we all want to be free. We want to live freely, be free persons with equal respect. And dignity. We want that recognised. We expect the other to respect us as human

[61] B.R. Ambedkar's clarion call at the All India Depressed Classes Conference in 1942 in Nagpur was 'Educate, Agitate, Organise!'

persons, equal in respect and dignity, *human* dignity. And then we too can respect that deep human dignity in others.

—∞—

Postscript: Bama's *Sangati* was part of the fifth semester syllabus in the undergraduate English Honours course in Delhi University. This was an excellent choice of text for a course called 'Women's Writings'. Indeed, it should be compulsory reading for all Indian students, regardless of the course, because *Sangati* probes the resilience of dalit women, and their courage in the face of hard work, poverty, as well as caste and gender oppression.

In August 2021, the Oversight Committee of the Delhi University removed the texts by Bama and another dalit writer, Sukirtharani, from the English syllabus. (The Committee also decided to drop Mahasweta Devi's story, 'Draupadi'.) This decision was made despite the objections of the elected members of the University's Academic Council.

Writers, academics and students issued a statement calling for Delhi University to reinstate the texts:

> Bama and Sukirtharani articulate the lived experience of being Dalit women in contemporary India. They illumine how caste oppression colludes with modes of patriarchy to produce gendered oppression and exploitation. The two writers would have constituted a very significant component of a core/compulsory paper of the final year English Hons. Syllabus, titled *Women's Writings* that aims to explore past and contemporary female lives in India (and the world)—the promises kept (or not) and the work in progress. Is this not something that the young men and women of independent India need to know and engage with?[62]

[62] 'Over 1,150 Academics, Writers Ask DU to Reinstate Texts by Bama, Sukirtharani, Mahasweta Devi', *The Wire*, 7 September 2021 (https://

The 'official' explanation came courtesy the university's registrar:

> The university subscribes to the idea that the literary content forming part of the text in a language course of study should contain materials which do not hurt the sentiments of any individual and is inclusive in nature to portray a true picture of our society … (this) is important for young minds who imbibe the content …[63]

And Bama's response? 'I am more angry than upset. I feel they are trying to strangulate our voices. But we will shout and continue to shout!'[64]

---

thewire.in/education/over-1150-academics-writers-ask-du-to-reinstate-texts-by-bama-sukirtharani-mahasweta-devi).

[63] Lekha Rattanani, 'Draupadi, DU and inconvenient truths', *Deccan Herald*, 21 September 2021 (https://www.deccanherald.com/opinion/main-article/draupadi-du-and-inconvenient-truths-1032897.html).

[64] 'Bama: Fearless, insightful writer of dalit and women's lives', *Indian Cultural Forum*, 27 August 2021 (https://indianculturalforum.in/2021/08/27/bama_fearless_insightful_writer_of_dalit_lives/).

CHINNAIAH JANGAM

How Gurram Jashuva Turned the Literary Canon Upside Down

Gurram Jashuva (1895–1971) wrote poetry that invigorated classical Telugu with the language of the people. He also took on significant real-life themes—imagining the nation, and making a plea for equality. His commitment to giving a voice to the poor and the marginalised in general, and to the dalit in particular, grew out of his own experience of discrimination.

Jashuva's mother, Lingamamba, was an 'untouchable' madiga—traditionally associated with tannery and leatherwork and, today, with agricultural labour. Lingamamba went to a school established by the American Baptist Mission, and met Veeraiah of the 'touchable' golla caste. They fell in love. Madiga and shudra shed their caste and got married as converted Christians. Their son, Jashuva, was born out of what should have been a wonderful disruption of caste and religious barriers. But it is not easy to break through the walls of a rigid society.

'There were two gurus in my life,' Jashuva said: poverty first, then caste and religious discrimination. Poverty taught him patience; and the rest, the day-to-day prejudice and cruelty, taught him to revolt. Victimhood was never his theme: 'My knife is a pen.'[65] His work was very much a part of a life of anti-caste and anti-colonial resistance.

Jashuva met the daily humiliations of discrimination upright and fighting. When he was referred to as an 'untouchable,' he retorted:

> The crows who are not equal to a seashell
> Out of jealousy, try to humiliate me
> But the talent I have will never leave me
> I will sing poems like a bell
> Present them to the people of Andhra like flowers.[66]

Jashuva lived in times when wars were being fought in the larger world; when new ideas such as Marxism were enriching the Telugu literary imagination; and when the country was fighting its way to becoming a free nation. The ideas and events of the times fed Jashuva's view of people whose shoulders bore a great deal of oppressive weight—of work, poverty and injustice. Yet they fought, whether it was for a country free of colonial rule, or for a home of their dreams, a genuinely free country. And so did Jashuva.

That was then, we wish we could say. But Jashuva's 'agenda' is startlingly (and sadly) relevant in our own times with the persistence of exclusionary fault lines:

---

[65] Hemalatha Lavanam, *Maa Nannagaru*, p. 10, quoted in the Introduction by the translator Chinnaiah Jangam, *Gabbilam*, Yoda Press, 2022, p. xxvi.

[66] Gurram Jashuva, *Kandakavyam*, Jashuva Foundation, Vijaywada, 1994, p. 64, quoted in ibid., p. xxvi.

I will not be bound by caste and religious lines
And will not let them cage
World can judge
It will not reduce me
I am a universal human being.[67]

What resonance these brave lines have for us today—for citizens and movements who are witness to old and new manifestations of caste in twenty-first century India, along with discrimination on the basis of class, community, gender and sexuality.

It is in such a context, in our times of rampant exclusionary politics, that I discovered Gurram Jashuva through the English translation of his long poem, *Gabbilam*. If it was painful for me to have my ignorance about both Jashuva and *Gabbilam* hit me like a punishing slap in the face, it was, perhaps, even worse to read of the translator's experience. Chinnaiah Jangam, a historian whose areas of research cover dalit studies, caste, and social and intellectual history, describes his encounter with Gurram Jashuva's work. His description is an indictment of the prejudices and erasures of our education system:

> Gurram Jashuva was the only Dalit poet I read in school as [a] few stanzas from his writings were included in Telugu textbooks. While teaching, teachers always reminded us that Jashuva was a Madiga untouchable and still wrote excellent poetry … Given the Brahmanical nature of [the] Telugu curriculum, references to Jashuva faded away from the syllabus as I moved up in my studies …[68]

---

[67] Gurram Jashuva, *Kandakavyam*, Jashuva Sarvalabhya Sankalanamu, MaNaSu Foundation, p. 652, quoted in ibid., p. xxvii.

[68] Chinnaiah Jangam, Acknowledgements, ibid., p. vii.

But, says Chinnaiah, Jashuva's poems were sung by dalit performers; his words were heard in the fields. Jashuva had become, just as he described himself, 'a people's poet'.

Luckily for us, Chinnaiah was encouraged by friends and teachers to engage with Jashuva's work in depth, and translate the extraordinary poem, *Gabbilam* (1941). Over the years, he discovered afresh how unique Jashuva the poet and intellectual was, 'especially in the context of anti-colonial nationalism and the growing political assertion among Dalits.'[69]

Gabbilam is a long poem divided into two parts; each part begins with a preface by Jashuva. In Part I, titled 'An Untouchable Odyssey', a bat enters the dark and miserable house of a dalit. The dalit protagonist asks the bat to carry the story of his suffering to Shiva in Kailasa. He also describes the route to Kailasa in the Himalayas, so that two narratives unfold simultaneously as if reality must be viewed on a split screen. One narrative describes the country's history, and its physical and cultural beauties. The parallel narrative gives voice to the suffering of those who have toiled for the country:

Without his labour
Even the crops hesitate to grow
By sweating day and night, he feeds the world
But has nothing to eat (p. 3)

At the end of Part 1, the bat sets off for Kailasa, and 'The untouchable labourer tied his loincloth/ And readied himself for work in the field.' (p. 28)

---

[69] *The Yodakin Podcast, Episode 18*, Yoda Press publisher Arpita Das in conversation with Chinnaiah Jangam, 21 April 2023 (https://rb.gy/0narew).

Part II, 'Meditation on Freedom', takes us to 1946. The country stands at the threshold of freedom. But will the dalit find his rightful place in this free country? 'What share does each community get in independent India?' (p. 39)

On the one hand there is heady hope:
Brother Harijan! Do not be afraid
The chariot of independence is here
You will have a place in it
Come along to pull it forward
Mother India welcomes you to join in her songs. (p. 32)

On the other hand, the monstrous reality of caste still looms everywhere, every day:

A god on the mountain respects me based on caste
Will he try to wipe away my tears?
A society addicted to mental slavery
Will it ever forge a friendship with me?

Jashuva asks in the tragic voice of his hero, 'Which holy man let me be born into this unkind world?' But can such a life, whether that of the hero of *Gabbilam*, or Jashuva's, or the reader with a conscience, continue without resistance? The poet's preface to the second part of *Gabbilam* ends with a call to keep up the good fight: 'His efforts will be realised, if not today, tomorrow.' (p. 29)

Indeed, *Gabbilam* sets out to convince the reader—in multiple ways—that poetry and protest live in exactly the same place. First, Jashuva used the Sanskrit meter in classical Telugu to prove himself equal to brahmin pandits. But the tradition of classical verse is turned on its head so it lives and breathes the dalit experience. Thus he challenges the literary canon, the cultural canon, by choosing the bat to travel across the country, as the peripatetic messenger of dalits to speak of their status as 'untouchables'. The bat, 'gabbilam' in Telugu, is believed to be neither bird nor animal, hence a bad omen. Jashuva subverts Kalidasa's classic, *Meghaduta*: Rather than the elegant messengers used by the 'upper castes' or savarnas—swans, parrots, peacocks or clouds—he uses the stigmatised bat that hangs upside down in temple towers, to send his message of suffering to the god Shiva.

> When you hang upside down inside the temple
> You will be closer to the ear of the God Shiva
> Make sure the priest is not around
> When you recount the story of my life.

Such a message is usually beyond the pale of officially sanctioned poetry, history and religion. But in *Gabbilam*, the message—the reality of caste—seizes the stage of the 'classical literary form' for its unfolding of dalit life. Not surprisingly, Chinnaiah Jangam chooses *A Dalit Epic* as the subtitle for his translation of *Gabbilam*.

In more than one way, Chinnaiah Jangam seems the perfect translator—and conveyor—of Jashuva's message, and in linking the then and now. Chinnaiah has said he was born in a poor family of labourers; his mother was a jogini (devadasi).[70] Despite all odds, he went to school, then several institutions of higher learning. He now teaches at Carleton University, Canada, and works on the social and intellectual history of dalits in modern South Asia.

---

[70] See Nirupa Vatyam, 'Child Labour to Professor in Canada', *The Times of India*, 31 October 2021 (https://timesofindia.indiatimes.com/city/hyderabad/jangam-child-labour-to-prof-in-canada/articleshow/87410448.cms).

I first came across Chinnaiah when I read his *Dalits and the Making of Modern India* (2017). The book presents dalit perspectives on nationalism, and argues that dalits were equal participants in the imagination and the politics of the formation of independent India. We exchanged an email conversation about the book in 2018, a few months after the bicentenary celebrations of the Bhima Koregaon battle in January 2018, leading to the infamous 'Bhima Koregoan case'. One of the questions I asked him: 'The Bhima Koregaon anniversary complicates the 'nationalist' narrative—in this instance, it's the battle against the Peshwas that holds meaning, not the mainstream narrative of the battle against the British. Your comments?' In response, Chinnaiah said his book

> ... challenges and complicates the singular narrative of nationalism in India—we have to see nationalism as a plural narrative. The danger with the singular narrative is that it plays into the hands of right-wing conservative caste Hindu elites. That is why the recent rise of the Hindu right in India is able to capture the imagination of ordinary people by using the rhetoric of nationalism, even though it has made the least contribution—by way of either ideas or participation—to actual anti-colonial nationalism.[71]

Four years later, in 2022, Chinnaiah published his translation of Gurram Jashuva's *Gabbilam*, and we spoke of the notion of a dalit epic, and of the long road that remains to be travelled if we are to annihilate caste.

[71] *Indian Cultural Forum*, 'Conversation: Chinnaiah Jangam on Dalit Memory, Imagination and the Nationalist Narrative', *Battling for India: A Citizen's Reader*, ed. Githa Hariharan and Salim Yusufji, Speaking Tiger, 2019, p. 109.

26 November 2022

Githa Hariharan (GH): From the title invoking a bat rather than the stereotype of a 'classical' swan or peacock, *Gabbilam* writes back, powerfully, to Kalidasa's *Meghaduta*.[72] How does this literary strategy become a process of countering caste (and class) domination?

Chinnaiah Jangam (CJ): It is fascinating that you have begun with the idea of writing back. The primary purpose of the title *Gabbilam* is to turn the literary and cultural canons upside down. Jashuva uses a subversive strategy to counter status-quoist writings by exposing their hypocrisy. The title begins this project of subversion, as a counter-narrative to dominant brahminical narratives. It questions the legitimacy of caste, and it protests the inhuman treatment of untouchables and their dehumanisation.

GH: I found Gurram Jashuva's own story extremely moving. His struggle to survive poverty and casteist discrimination, and his resistance to the scorn and neglect of fellow poets encapsulates, in one life story, the story of resistance to all orthodoxy. What do you think?

CJ: Jashuva's life is incredibly inspiring, not just as a poet, but also as a human being. His parents had an inter-caste marriage and he experienced poverty and discrimination all his life. As an untouchable, Jashuva was prohibited from learning

[72] *Meghaduta*, literally Cloud Messenger, is a lyric poem by Kalidasa (c. fourth to fifth century CE) that is considered a masterpiece of Sanskrit literature. A yaksha, an attendant of the god of wealth, Kubera, has been punished with exile for a year. The yaksha, longing for his wife, sends a message of love to her via a passing cloud, which will describe all the beautiful sights it sees on its way. *Meghaduta* inspired a range of 'messenger poems' and has been a source of inspiration for writers and artists.

Sanskrit, a classical language considered holy—the language of the gods. Jashuva taught himself Sanskrit and he wrote in classical Telugu, in a poetic form closer to the Sanskrit meter, to prove himself equal to brahmin pundits. He also worked as a scriptwriter in a theatre company. But because he read Sanskrit classical literature, he lost his job in a Christian missionary school. He struggled a great deal to support his family. He had just one set of clothes that he washed in the Godavari at night and dried on the riverbank. A friend would bring him food from a restaurant since Jashuva was not allowed inside. Despite all this humiliation, there was no hatred in him. He said poverty and caste discrimination taught him patience, even as they made him rebel against the caste system.

GH: You call *Gabbilam* a dalit epic. Its canvas is extraordinarily wide; it travels through the history of different times in India, its different religions, cultural practices and achievements, the changing physical landscape from South to North, and the diverse people, from rulers to the oppressed. Are there other qualities that make you describe *Gabbilam* as an 'epic'? Or are we seeing—as with his choice of the stigmatised bat—a subversion of the form itself, since it is a *dalit* epic?

CJ: Thank you for this question. You summed it up nicely. It is a dalit epic precisely because of everything you have listed as part of the work's canvas. *Gabbilam* is the first dalit text that is not inward-looking, limited to defining the dalit self through a narrative of oppression. Instead, it is forward-looking—in terms of the future and in terms of possibilities. At the same time, it is firmly based on the country's historical and cultural roots. Its claim to this heritage makes it unique as a true dalit epic. Moreover, the text empowers the most stigmatised creatures, including the bat, by relating them to the existential condition of dalits. It humanises all aspects of natural creation and inaugurates dalit universalism. That is why I call it a dalit epic.

GH: *Gabbilam* has an important subtext about language and power. You write that Jashuva learnt to use the Sanskrit meter to prove himself equal to brahmin pandits. But he also makes his work accessible (to be read and heard) by using the 'people's language'. In *Gabbilam*, Jashuva makes a case for the mother tongue as the best medium for poets, as opposed to any foreign language. Today we may point out that our languages are caste-ridden. How do we reconcile these apparently conflicting choices?

CJ: Yes, the subtext of *Gabbilam* involves challenging the hold of brahminical supremacy on the Telugu language. That is why Jashuva made the choice to write in the classical tradition—to dismantle brahminical power. Also, he liberated the language from a brahminical hold by using the people's everyday language, and making it accessible to the illiterate. The text is written in the context of anticolonial nationalism, and it expresses love for the mother tongue and the nation. In that context, there was no conflict regarding national liberation and the assertion of affinity to the mother tongue, Telugu. But in post-independent India, the savarna obsession with English language-centric education devalued education in the mother tongue. The dalit-bahujan were left out. They felt marginalised as they saw no future in pursuing education in regional languages. The irony lies in the attitude of savarna elites towards the local languages. Even now, vibrant literature in most of the regional languages is produced by dalit-bahujan and minorities; the brahminical elites left this sphere a long time back.

GH: We often talk about the politics of translation in the sense of what is chosen to be translated and disseminated to a broader audience. And that definitely applies here, because poets such as Jashuva and Yogi Vemana[73] are not known to too many people, especially outside the Telugu readership. But what you have written about the politics of translation takes this exclusion to another level. Would you describe how a translation of, say, *Gabbilam*, could focus on the 'poetic' or the 'literary' to 'cleanse' the poem of its political intent and articulation—its rage against casteism, its passionate narrative of resistance?

CJ: To answer this question, we have to look at colonial history—in which colonial and brahminical elites collaborated to eulogise brahminical texts and define them as everything 'Hindu/Indian'. The history of translation in colonial India revolved around reviving the brahminical texts. Even in regional languages like Telugu, brahminical and colonial elites reproduced brahmanical texts. The Madras School of Orientalism and its translation projects of classical Telugu centred on the revival of brahmanical classics to valorise and present brahminism as the dominant cultural aesthetic.

Poets like Jashuva faced an uphill task—writing poetry to meet the standards of classical brahminism while offering a distinct dalit voice. Till recent times, hardly any dalit text was translated by an established scholar. The time has come to produce socially and intellectually engaged and meaningful

---

[73] Kumaragiri Vema Reddy or Vemana, (b. 1652?) popularly known as Yogi Vemana, was a philosopher and Telugu poet. Written in a simple style, his poems addressed social themes; many lines from his poems are now colloquial phrases in Telugu.

translations that pay attention to the voices of the oppressed, instead of the privileged few.

GH: In the poem, Jashuva says, 'Condemn old and ignorant traditions, and spread education/ like alms.' Other than education, what would you say are his prescriptions for a more egalitarian India?

CJ: Across India, the dalit tradition of emancipation believed in education as a tool of liberation, and Jashuva reasserts this belief powerfully. Along with education, Jashuva demanded an equal share of the nation's resources and freedom from exploitation and dignity. He considered himself a 'vishwanarudu', a universal human being.

GH: *Gabbilam* is replete with allusions, historical and literary. But perhaps the most significant strand of allusions would be to anti-caste traditions. Would you describe a few of these traditions and histories which have, all too often, been rendered less visible?

CJ: If you read the text carefully, Jashuva consciously revives the anti-caste traditions erased by the brahminical texts. For example, he writes eloquently about the hero, Palanati Brahmanaidu, who tried to open temples for all castes, including dalits.[74] Jashuva also talks about the egalitarian ethic of Buddhism and writes fondly about the Buddha. Within the Telugu historical context, Jashuva writes about the anti-

---

[74] Palanati Brahmanaidu (*fl.* twelfth century) was a minister of the Haihaya kingdom of Palanadu (in today's Guntur district), and is remembered particularly for his egalitarian initiatives, such as the Chapa Kudu programme of common dining, where all sections of society would share a meal together, and for opening temples to all caste groups.

caste visionaries, such as Pothuluri Veerabrahmam[75] and Yogi Vemana. Interestingly, C.P. Brown[76] collected Vemana's poetry, and the brahmins tried to prevent the dissemination of this poetry.

GH: Would you say Jashuva writes something of a primer for poets in *Gabbilam*, covering the use of language, folklore and themes?

CJ: Yes, he does. But it is difficult to follow his path as his poetry is written in the classical meter. No other dalit poet could write like him.

GH: *Gabbilam* raises a poetic voice against the erasure of people, lives, and histories because of their caste. The poem was written in 1941. Today, in 2022, we find NCERT textbooks diluting accounts of caste discrimination,[77] anti-caste figures and movements, and dalit lives. For instance, an account of the life of a manual scavenger, invariably dalit, has been dropped; and this at a time when there is a campaign called 'Stop Killing Us' to protest manual scavenging.[78] What does this disconnect tell us about our journey toward equality?

---

[75] Pothuluri Veerabrahmam (b.1608–? *fl.* seventeenth century) was an astrologer and spiritual leader, considered the author of *Kalagnanam*, a book of predictions about the future.

[76] Charles Philip Brown (1798–1884) was an official of the English East India Company. Working in several places in the Andhra region from 1820 to 1834, he collected manuscripts and studied Telugu prosody, going on to produce a range of books, from dictionaries and grammars to translations of prose and poetry.

[77] See, for example, *The Wire*, 18 June 2022 (https://thewire.in/education/ncert-deletes-mentions-of-caste-discrimination-anti-caste-movement-from-class-12-sociology-book).

[78] Despite being banned multiple times, manual scavenging continues to take lives across the country. The Safai Karamchari Andolan, founded in 1994 by Bezwada Wilson, Paul Divakar and S.R. Sankaran, issued

CJ: India is walking backwards in terms of social justice and the equity agenda. The aggressive push of Hindutva is undoing all the progress made in the last seventy-five years. Moreover, the Indian state under the BJP is in denial of every form of oppression. Instead it pretends to sleepwalk its way to superpower status. But in a few decades, India will witness significant upheavals by the dalit-bahujan as they are being left behind, crushed under the weight of both brahminism and the crony capitalism which flourishes in this nefarious tie-up between the state and global capital.

GH: Anti-colonial nationalism is very much part of the context of the poem. (It brought to mind your earlier book on the dalit role in the freedom movement.[79]) Jashuva talks about 'the chariot of independence', but also asks if he will 'get a place in the mansion of independence'. He asks, 'What share does each community get in independent India?' Would you comment on the tragic resonance of Jashuva's questions for us in India today?

CJ: The future looks bleak for the oppressed in India, as the state is withdrawing from its primary responsibilities and acting as a facilitator to the rich and powerful. In the last eight years, dalits, Muslims, adivasis and human rights defenders have been subjected to hatred and violence. More than ever, people have been excluded and demonised for asserting their right to equality and freedom. In this context, a dalit text like

---

the slogan 'Stop Killing Us' in 2015, at the launch of the Andolan's first march across 500 districts to protest this continuing and abusive form of employment. In 2022, the now annual march lasted 150 days, and ended in Gumla, Jharkhand (https://www.newsclick.in/Safai-Karmachari-Andolan-150-Days-Stop-Killing-Us-Campaign).

[79] *Dalits and the Making of Modern India*, OUP, 2017.

Gabbilam reminds us of the threat to the foundations of our nation, built on the principles of justice, liberty, equality and fraternity.

—∾—

Postscript: In a conversation with the publisher of *Gabbilam* in English translation,[80] Chinnaiah responds to the controversy over the right-wing attempts to erase and/or rewrite chunks of history. The Hindu right, he says, is trying to rewrite the history of the nation through the lens of communalism. But they face an important problem with caste: '… the caste question is a very important embarrassment for the Hindu right.' He goes on to locate *Gabbilam* in this context. Such a text, he says, 'poses a very important challenge to the very idea of Hindu nation and Hindu histories …' Anti-caste discourse, dalit discourse—including texts such as *Gabbilam*—present a fundamental challenge to the Hindu nationalist agenda. How will they respond to dalit activism without 'engaging with the question of caste'?

---

[80] *The Yodakin Podcast, Episode 18*. Yoda Press publisher Arpita Das in conversation with Chinnaiah Jangam, 21 April 2023 (https://rb.gy/0narew).

MILIND AWAD

Striking a Blow to Change the World with Eknath Awad

In 2018, I came across a book with a powerful title: *Strike a Blow to Change the World.*[81] This was the first English translation of an autobiography in Marathi, *Jag Badal Ghaaluni Ghaav,*[82] by an important leader of the anti-caste movement in Maharashtra, Eknath Awad (1956–2015). The fine translation by poet and novelist Jerry Pinto opened up many worlds for me.

First, there was Awad's life in caste-ridden rural Marathwada. This is what Eknath's early life was like. He was born in the mang caste, a dalit community now listed as a Scheduled Caste. His father was a potraj.[83] This meant he would go from house to house in the village, beating his drum, begging for alms and, in exchange, taking others' sins on himself. He would

[81] Eknath Awad, *Strike a Blow to Change the World*, translated by Jerry Pinto, Speaking Tiger, 2018.

[82] Samakaleen Prakashan, 2012.

[83] A religious mendicant dedicated to Laxmi or Mari-Aai, the potraj was identified by a ceremonial length of hair often worn in a bun at the top of his scalp.

use a whip on himself to atone for these second-hand sins. This function exempted him from mangki, the compulsory unpaid labour other members of his family, like all mangs, had to perform.

In the ordinary course of things, Eknath was expected to become a potraj when he grew up. Luckily, his mother was insistent that he get an education. Eknath's 'education' was an obstacle course, an endurance test—travelling long distances, coping with penury and hunger, and always, always, kept outside the classroom, isolated from those who should have been his 'classmates' and his 'teachers'. And always there was poverty or illness or grim responsibility waiting for him at home.

No matter how many stories and images you have in your mind about what caste does to the individual, the family, the community—what it does to *people*—there is the shock and anger that pierce you when you witness, even from the outside, and merely through the written word, such suffering.

We can only imagine the brave determination required to persist when the whole world was holding him down. And persist Eknath did, going to college, learning from the ideas of change of Ambedkar, Jotiba Phule, Annabhau Sathe and Marx, finding a place for himself in movements. There was the Namantar Andolan, the movement to rename the Marathwada University as Dr Babasaheb Ambedkar University. There was the radical group of the Dalit Panthers, fighting to overthrow the caste system.[84] Eknath learnt the politics of resistance in

[84] Inspired by the Black Panthers movement in the United States, the Dalit Panthers was founded in the 1970s by young dalits, largely mahars, from what was then Bombay. In the course of its fight against the caste system, the Dalit Panthers produced a considerable body of literature that attacked brahmin cultural dominance.

these organisations and movements. Like other dalit radicals, he too saw how violent the price of protest can be, how horrific the backlash from caste Hindus—murders, rapes, houses burnt. Lives destroyed.

Later Eknath studied law. That would help, but he also knew that was not enough: 'The law had made the practice of untouchability illegal, but did the law have any say in the village?'[85] What he learnt to do, and did all his life, was work on the ground so the day-to-day struggle translated to a better life for the oppressed. A better life could mean, among other things, access to well water, or grazing land, or livelihood, or education. It could mean getting rid of bonded labour; or superstition; or the sharp divisions imposed by the caste system between people, not only between 'upper' and 'lower' castes, but also between two 'lower' castes such as the mangs and the mahars.

It is such a life that Eknath Awad speaks of in his autobiography. He gets to the point almost immediately:

> Over the last twenty-five to thirty years, I have crossed paths with about fifty thousand Dalit families. We came together to struggle and the sutra for our struggle was:
>
> *Jag badal ghaluni ghaav*
> *saangun gele mala Bhimrao.*
>
> Over me, Bhimrao left a banner unfurled,
> Strike such a blow as will change the world. (p. 3)

This is the man I saw in the autobiography: someone who refused to accept the status quo, give in, concede defeat. A doer, a man on the move. (Not surprisingly, his autobiography

[85] Awad, 2018, p. 7.

was 'written' by transcribing a series of recordings made by Prashant Kunte, who travelled with Awad for many months.)

I saw a fighter, but a pragmatic fighter, who wanted to create small changes, win small battles while fighting the bigger war against caste. So if you couldn't be 'the master of your landlord', you could at least 'stop being their slaves.' The long-term struggle for social and political change, *emancipation*, needed to be accompanied by shorter term support to survive—through development projects that would generate sorely needed income.

I saw a man brutally honest about people, their everyday conflicts, as well as their resilience and courage. In his translator's introduction, Jerry Pinto sums it up:

> He is honest about his own tendencies to use violence to settle disputes, he is honest about the methods his activists use, he is honest about the casteism he sees among his own people and he never suggests that his monumental courage and his awakening to the consciousness of the injustices of the caste system was his alone. (p. xi)

I saw in Awad someone who struggled to take the fight—all the aspects of his activism, whether 'reformist' or 'revolutionary'—beyond individual suffering to 'his people'. And for Awad, 'his people' went beyond the collective closest to him, the mang caste, so that

> … his definition of 'his people' was an inclusive one. He worked hard to erase the age-old war between the Mang and the Mahar. He did not see the Muslim or the Dalit Christian as the Other. 'His people' were defined simply as those who had been turned out of the fold for whatever reason …[86]

[86] 'My Father, Our Jija', Introduction by Milind Awad, ibid., 2018, pp. viii–ix.

Above all, I saw in Awad's life a variety of movements, sometimes complementing each other, sometimes coming together in alliances which may seem natural, but are, in reality, difficult to achieve on the ground. Eknath Awad sums up his life—the deprivation, the attacks, the campaign against bonded labour, the fight for a better life for dalits and adivasis, for bahujan:

> ... I have experienced every facet of the Dalit's life.
>
> A seed of the thoughts of Phule and Ambedkar was planted in me. A vine grew in my head. From that seedling, a peepal tree began to grow. Around that tree many activists twined themselves as creepers do. Those vines I had planted at the huts of the Backward Classes and Nomadic Tribes have begun to climb their trellises. (p. 282)

What words of hope for the future, words that give us heart to live in the present! The book made me want to talk to someone who knew Awad. So I was delighted to find that Awad's son, Milind, teaches in the School of Language Literature and Culture Studies in JNU, New Delhi.

The book served as the springboard for our conversation about Eknath Awad, the man and the activist—his rejection of the life he was assigned by caste; his resilience over personal and collective travails; the sources of his inspiration; his view of a united fight against caste as well as religious division; and his legacy for campaigns and movements.

31 October 2018

Githa Hariharan (GH): I want to begin with the personal. What was it like growing up with an activist, a fiery activist, for a father? That also meant being part of a family that had rejected its caste identity—what was that like?

Milind Awad (MA): This book is about a person who has worked at the grassroots level throughout his life, and my father was like any of the others who have done that. A lot of people have been engaged with the community, the people's movement, and he's one of them. While this book is about Eknath Awad, my father, it is equally about a process, the simultaneous activism he talks about—through dalit NGOs, the dalit movement, and various locally articulated struggles such as the campaign for human rights that he formed, the Manavi Haq ka Abhiyan. This book is, of course, about the person, but more than that it is about the parallel movements happening at the same time. The Gandhian movement, the Marxist movement, the Dalit Panthers—all this was contemporary—along with various fusions of the Dalit Panthers, and the socialist and communist movements. How they worked collectively at the grassroots level, how they articulated the issue of the land rights movement, anti-dalit atrocities, the claim on common civic amenities: these are issues people have been raising in Maharashtra and throughout the country. So the book is about various stories of struggle, particularly in Marathwada and some parts of Vidarbha. And it is a very interesting compilation of stories of the contemporary struggle in Maharashtra.

GH: And that, of course, is what really speaks to the reader and to the fellow citizen, because these are human stories, not theory. You spoke of a grassroots movement, and perhaps the sharpest aspect of that grassroots activism is within the mang community itself, and the struggle of the movement to get people out of occupations and practices traditionally associated with a subordinate status. So, for example, your grandfather being a potraj. Would you speak a little about that and how important that was?

MA: Potraj is basically a caste profession, and it is one of the characteristic features of caste that your profession becomes your identity. And your identity becomes stigmatised because of a certain kind of profession. The association with your caste identity makes the stigma a part of your everyday life. My father has written about being a mang, a social activist, a progressive Ambedkarite social activist, and he's talking about the interiorities of caste. Within the Scheduled Castes, he's talking about the mang struggle …

GH: There is mention of how difficult it is for the potraj to say, 'All right, we'll cut this long hair that we have.' And your father uses a combination of coaxing and bullying to actually get them to do it.

MA: Yes, there were some rituals assigned as caste rituals, and their practice would make the people 'polluted'. These were barter-based villages, and the programme of the anti-caste movement was to remove whatever caused people to be stigmatised in the village's barter economy. So attempts were made to cut off the potraj's hair, or prevent mangki,[87] or remove whatever made the mangs in rural Marathwada of that time 'untouchable', stigmatising them in the village's barter economy. Leaving behind certain caste professions and rituals associated with untouchability was a strong Ambedkarite message. Ambedkar had said that villages are garbage bins full of pride, so just leave them …[88] So the ex-untouchables,

[87] The obligations and work traditionally imposed on mangs as their caste duty.

[88] Speaking in the Constituent Assembly Debates, on 4 November 1948, Ambedkar said: 'What is the village but a sink of localism, a den of ignorance, narrow-mindedness and communalism.'

particularly the mahars in Maharashtra at the time, left behind practices considered untouchable or polluted.

My father was working in a time of mangki—it was still prevalent in Marathwada till the eighties and nineties. He was highly influenced by Ambedkarite thought and the Ambedkarite vision. Hence his activism, and the incident which is narrated in the autobiography, about how he opposed practices that caused his people to be excluded, making them stigmatised or 'polluted'.

My father's book is about the many stories of people overcoming stigma, and claiming social amenities such as the handpump, temple entry and so on. Each story is about a certain kind of struggle.

GH: One of the powerful aspects of the book is that it is so grounded in reality and doesn't speak merely in generalities about overcoming all these instances of discrimination. You get a very clear sense of what it is like to be a mang. You don't see the Scheduled Castes as a homogenised group. There is much talk of how the mangs feel vis-à-vis the mahars, for example. You spoke of your father being an Ambedkarite, that there was a feeling among the mangs that the mahars were lucky because Ambedkar, in a way, belongs to them. I got the impression that one of your father's tasks, and one of the tasks of the movement, was to say, 'Let us find our own leaders, but let us also follow Ambedkar and follow the path.' Was there a sense that the mangs had to catch up?

MA: I think this graded inequality is very typical of Indian society. Each caste is ritualistically and culturally composed against the others—its neighbouring castes. So there is antagonism, right? This antagonism exists at the village level, in the traditional social system.

GH: So there's a structure of power and everybody remains engaged.

MA: Power, yes. It's very interesting to see how castes are brought into culturally antagonistic positions. Within the Scheduled Castes, you will see that certain castes who have secure professions are considered unpolluted in the ritualistic structure. But those whose position is not secure in the barter system are considered the polluted and polluting castes. So this competition over purity-pollution extends even up to them.

GH: It permeates the whole system.

MA: Yes. But when we talk about the anti-class and anti-caste movement in modern times, it is important to note that while new caste struggles are emerging locally, they follow the grand narratives of the anti-caste, anti-class movement. Ambedkarism is a grand narrative of the anti-caste movement, Marxism is another grand narrative.

Nationally, you see that dalits are politicised as Ambedkarites, but under this umbrella, there are various splits among them. There is a certain traditional antagonism, which continues in modern India through processes, both political and social, which may further the antagonism.

So, in Maharashtra, since Dr Ambedkar was from there, his message was picked up in the early days by today's Buddhists. The mahars left behind the constraints of the barter economy and those imposed on them through gawki—their obligatory functions according to custom. Non-mahar Scheduled Castes in Maharashtra and throughout the country have been picking up Ambedkar's anti-caste message through their own activism. This is a simultaneous process taking place among, and emerging from, different sections of society.

GH: It's also very much a narrative of resistance. Throughout the book, you get a very strong sense of what strategies should be employed for specific campaigns as well as the objectives of the larger movement. And there's a question I wanted to pose here, one not unique to dalit movements but which figures very much in dalit movements, about the NGO as a means or an ally to conduct a campaign with.

The book brings out very sharply what the advantages are in terms of resources and access, but also the limitations. And I bring this up because you've just mentioned the alliance, the natural alliance, almost the vexed alliance between dalit movements and the left. So, what of the NGO?

MA: I think one can have a critique of the NGO, and I think that's very important—the prevailing critique of NGOs from a larger left perspective. But it is also very important to see that communities who are historically excluded are trying to come out of their exclusion through various avenues. They have limited means to assert themselves, limited resources. The kind of struggle they are initiating comes about through certain kinds of processes.

This book talks about a very important historical fact, that the dalit NGO, or civil society activism, has initiated larger processes such as asserting a claim on natural resources like land. Land issues are raised through local strategies. There is no national standardisation here, no single grand strategy; situations vary and so do the possible solutions. Activists respond to a given situation, and a strategy emerges. These responses form their strategy. Because of the absence of structure, of a grand strategy, we see these responses turning, effectively, into a strategy. The strategy is different each time, different from previous responses and other strategies in use.

Communities are beginning to respond. Their campaigns against exclusion, humiliation, against atrocities, are possible because they gain a certain kind of strength through the resources that arrive with outside intervention, such as the NGOs. So, of course, one can have a critique of NGOs in the larger context, but it's very important to see the specific intervention of NGOs in making local communities capable, empowering them to campaign on their own issues.

GH: It seems to me that there are two challenges the book implies at the end. One is the splintered nature of various dalit campaigns and movements. There is also the challenge of making alliances with other progressive movements. Would you respond to this from the viewpoint of the immediate present?

MA: This is a very important time when we can see various peripheral groups and politics emerging and coming together, right? This book is part of the context. But it's important to see how, nationally, various groups, grassroots NGOs, various local mobilisations, local political parties, can innovate an activism from their local situation, from the ground up, to create a larger solidarity. And then, a certain sense of collaboration of ideas follows nationally.

GH: But this is also a time when the right-wing is anxious to create a myth about a Hindu monolith and use caste in ways that are self-contradictory, because, of course, we know Hindutva is casteist. This is why there's a special challenge in the here and now.

MA: That's true. And perhaps we need to think about Ambedkar's response to Hinduism or Ambedkar's response to brahminism. It is very important to see how Ambedkar is criticising Hinduism/brahminism by and large, and talking about the possibilities of egalitarian movements in various avenues. There are a lot of instances of this, if you see the corpus of dalit writing, adivasi writing, women's writing or various peripheral literary movements and social mobilisations. There is forward movement; these ideas keep growing in mutual correspondence.

They are growing in correspondence and they aspire to form a certain kind of collective. It is important to see all these egalitarian ideas, emerging from their structurally composed periphery, a location where they are emerging as collective ideas—and this book is perhaps one of the important articulations we have. It talks about activism, it talks about the aspiration to get out of a caste-ridden society, it's trying to talk about collaborative movements, the various simultaneous movements, and looking to collaborate with them. The land rights movement and the movement against anti-dalit atrocities: these are in collaboration in Marathwada. The temple entry movement and movements pressing for the claim on basic public, civic amenities are proceeding together.

We need to see the multiple as essential. With local struggles, it's important to observe how people are emancipating themselves through activism as well as through their writing. There are various avenues, various ways to articulate the way forward—I always see that. I think of how my father joined and led struggles throughout his life, in his own limited way, with morchas asserting rights on certain issues. But when he writes, I think he also emancipates his readers on a broader front.

ARAVIND MALAGATTI

Ambedkar's Spectacles and Gandhi's Walking Stick

On 11 October 2015, Aravind Malagatti resigned from the Sahitya Akademi General Council, saying, 'I have resigned condemning the killing of Kalburgi and [the] silence of [the] Akademi over the issue. It should have spoken out and expressed its condemnation against such acts.'[89] His letter to the President of the Akademi was forthright: 'Dr M. M. Kalburgi's assassination is a clear attack on freedom of expression ... Defending freedom of expression must be [the] Akademi's priority.'[90]

This was my introduction to Malagatti. The moment, it now occurs to me, was apposite. Since then I have read his work in English translation, and I understand the unsaid behind that statement he made in 2015. His work is rooted in protest—literary, social and political protest—all born of the

[89] 'Keeping Count of Dissenting Voices,' *Indian Cultural Forum*, 12 October 2015 (https://indianculturalforum.in/2015/10/12/keeping-count-of-dissenting-voices/).

[90] See http://aravindmalagatti.blogspot.com/

actual experience of deprivation and discrimination. But by no means is this lived tale aimed at evoking pity or even sympathy. The work serves as a mirror to the conscience—that of the writer, spurring him to tell the truth about the persistence of caste, whether in obvious or less visible forms. It mirrors, in equal if not greater measure, the conscience of the reader, the citizen who lives in a country put together with a constitution that promises equality to all its people.

I got further confirmation of the inextricable link between the man and the writer, the man and the activist, when we met in Dharwad, at the May festival in 2017. This is a literary festival quite unlike the usual noisy and celebrity-driven sort. Some five minutes before I went onstage, I was asked if I would speak in Kannada. Since my Kannada is definitely below 101 standard, I was too nervous about holding forth on 'creeping fascism' to listen carefully to the other speakers. Besides, most of them spoke in Kannada that flowed like a rushing river, too swift for my glacial mental translation. But this much I understood: there was general consensus that Ambedkar's ideas needed to be revisited and put into practice.

Presiding over the session, Malagatti made a sharp comment or two about the violence wreaked by right-wing 'activists', and the questionable association between state and religion. Did human life matter less than that of cattle? Should 'sanyasis' become politicians and rule the state? Should religious institutions control democracy? And Malagatti quoted a poem of his to describe the India he wants: an India he can see through 'Ambedkar's spectacles', an India with Gandhi's walking stick at the border, gentle guard of the country.

Malagatti's autobiography, *Government Brahmana* (1994), is a series of simply told vignettes about a life, but also a community: 'It is not the life story of a person, rather it is a story of a community.'[91] 'Simply told' requires careful explanation. There is nothing naïve about these memories, whether of the child or the man, or their literary account. But clearly there is no need to embroider them or indulge in verbal gymnastics. The stories of the man, the community and communities are tightly held in the closed fist of caste. If these stories jump off the page and scream at you, it is the kind of scream that is even more awful because it has been quietened for so long, and still quietened so often, and so easily.

There are two comments Malagatti makes about the autobiography that are painfully eloquent about how deep-rooted casteism is in our lives, past and present. Speaking of the 'differences' among castes that become part of received wisdom, tradition and social norms, Malagatti remarks that 'Even our mythological stories and folklore justify these differences.' As illustration, he relates the folk story he had in mind when writing the incident of sacrificing the buffalo before goddess Maramma. The story is about an inter-caste marriage. A dalit boy marries a brahmin girl. He has convinced her that he is brahmin; once they are married, she finds out he is not. She kills him and he becomes a buffalo. 'The practice of sacrificing the buffalo to goddess Maramma remains,' says Malagatti. '... What we face in our life is reflected in folk stories as well as our mythological stories ... Our [dalit] life stories talk about the present status of our lives, and it is our history, the history of India, that is passed on through our life stories.'[92]

---

[91] Surya Simon, 'A call for mutual change and progress: An interview with Aravind Malagatti and Dharani Devi Malagatti', Sage, 2019 (https://journals.sagepub.com/doi/full/10.1177/00219894211049091).

[92] Ibid.

Again, speaking of the title, 'Government Brahmana', Malagatti describes how he would be teased for being a beneficiary of reservations: 'They used to tease us and say, "In the government's view, we are not brahmins, you are brahmins."' But Malagatti subverts this mockery and, in the time-tested tradition of dignity politics, uses 'the same word as a symbol of self-respect'.[93]

Malagatti's novel *Karya* (1988) takes on the milestone of death, and the ceremonies associated with death, to critique religious beliefs and rituals that erode a rational life. *Karya* does more; it also probes the power politics that play out within a caste and among castes.

The use of death rites brings to mind another powerful novel in Kannada, U.R. Ananthamurthy's *Samskara* (1965). Both *Samskara* and *Karya* reveal what ossified rituals and practices can do to the individual and the community. The tragedy of caste plays out in both and, arguably, in complementary settings. If *Samskara* holds a magnifying glass to the dehumanising conservatism of a traditional brahmin community, Malagatti's *Karya* takes on the question of justice in the context of the divisions among castes and communities. In Malagatti's words, it 'highlights the tragedy of Dalit lives and the politics and power play involved.'[94]

Aravind Malagatti and I spoke about *Karya* to uncover some aspects of the historical and ongoing exploitation of dalit communities.

---

[93] Ibid.

[94] Latha Srinivasan, 'Dalit movement has reached threshold, almost ready to explode: Malagatti', *The Sunday Guardian*, 17 April 2021 (https://sundayguardianlive.com/culture/dalit-movement-reached-threshold-almost-ready-explode-malagatti).

12 April 2021

Githa Hariharan (GH): The exploitation of dalit groups by 'ascetics' is a very sharp section in *Karya*. How does such exploitation get 'institutionalised' by the custom of revering 'ascetics' as the vessels of wisdom, and so of authority?

Aravind Malagatti (AM): In the novel, [the old woman] Bangaravva's death is just an excuse; it is a narrative strategy. Through this strategy, the novel tries to portray the tragic lives of the dalit community. The landowners exploit the community financially, and the ascetics exploit them mentally. The ascetics sow seeds of ignorance in the minds of dalits, making independent thought difficult, even impossible. The landowners use the same ignorance to drain the dalits financially. Both landowners and ascetics have long made a living out of exploiting dalits—deprived as they are of education, and even a sense of self-worth.

GH: *Karya* brings out, subtly, the division not only between 'upper caste' and 'lower caste' but also the numerous hierarchies among those who are not upper caste. Is there a difference in these hierarchies between rural and urban settings? Has this changed at all with the building of movements against caste?

AM: Similar to the divisions among the 'upper castes', there are numerous divisions among the 'lower castes' as depicted in the novel.

There may appear to be no differences in these divisions between rural and urban settings, but that's only if we look at it superficially. If we look more carefully, the contrast is visible. I could say rural life is one of imitation, while urban life is more pretentious. But life in both circumstances is dependent on caste. This dependence seeps through economic, social and spiritual dimensions.

The movement against caste has definitely weakened the roots of casteism, but its impact is mostly concentrated on the literate and socially aware pockets of the population. The penetration has not been as effective in rural areas. Human relations have been strengthened with organising and agitation. But inter-caste marriages are more frequent among the upper strata than in the lower ones.

GH: *Karya* is filled with detail about 'custom'—much of which could be described by a rationalist as superstition that oppresses or exploits people. What is apparent in *Karya* is also the fluidity of this custom—no one really seems to know what the requirements are or how people are supposed to fulfil them. Is such a reading intended?

AM: Your reading of the novel gets the perspective right. The rituals are described in the novel in emphatic detail to reach the reader's consciousness. There isn't a declaration of protest in the novel. The main intention is to make the reader feel dissatisfied. I believe that such dissatisfaction acts as a driver for change in society. The usual pattern of protest in literary work satisfies the readers without giving them the impetus to think through the situation in reality. Of course there are instances of conflict in the novel. For instance, Dasharatha regrows his moustache despite upper-caste objection, and Malappa elopes with the Gowda's wife, Padmavati.

GH: While the novel never loses sight of the condition of dalit lives, it is also very natural in its description of rural lives and people, including in its use of humour and irony. Some of the humour seems to be entangled with the tragedy of their lives—the repeated bouts with toddy and alms, for example. Also, does this tragedy lie in the self-image the dalit group in the novel has of itself?

AM: Even though social life in the novel is tragic, individual lives are filled with humour, sarcasm and irony. The novel indicates that there is life beyond rituals and traditions. In the midst of the community's journey with death rituals, the woman called Akkamma finds her lost buffalo swimming in the pond. She hands over the ritual pitcher to someone and rushes across to catch her buffalo. Her act symbolises the fact that life is much more important than any ritual.

GH: The ending is open and unexpected, as if to say there is no resolution to this situation in real life. Would you comment on the ending—the body buried with such difficulty turning up above the ground?

AM: So many complications arise in the novel because of a lapse in the ritual of carrying the 'kullaggi'—the wind blows and the man carrying the sacred ritual fire drops it on the ground. But at the end, what do they do when the corpse is dug out of its resting place? This basic question confronting them shows the meaninglessness of the rituals they struggled to follow in burying the body. The complicated rituals for burying lead to the pointless deaths of many more—that is the irony. This story is a never-ending one. Why has the corpse been dug up? Was it done under the influence of the ascetic? Was it done because people are superstitious? Because they are incapable of independent thought? Or because they lack education? Is it a conspiracy by Shanta Gowda? Or is all without purpose? These questions themselves make up the answer.

In a country like India, where multiple languages, dialects and 'registers' flow into each other; in a country like India where caste is also deeply embedded in language, how does a translator take on a text like Karya *and render it in English? I spoke to award-winning translator Susheela Punitha*[95] *about the challenges she faced in the process of translating Malagatti's novel.*

GH: One of the points you mention in the translator's note is how several languages leak into the novel and mingle in the text. The reader notices this clearly with 'kala numbri'. Is this confluence of Kannada, Marathi and Urdu a phenomenon close to state borders? How did you address this as a translator into English?

Susheela Punitha (SP): This confluence of Kannada, Marathi and Urdu is peculiar to the regional variety of Kannada spoken in North Karnataka. In 'Vasudeva's Family' and 'Worlds Within Worlds', Vaidehi[96] uses a local variety of Mangaluru Kannada, which is a mix of Kannada and Tulu. In 'Ibadat', Bolwar Mahammad Kunhi[97] uses a blend of Malayalam and Urdu expressions, typical of the Kannada spoken in the Kasargod region along the Kerala border.

---

[95] Susheela Punitha's translations from Kannada to English include writer-activist Lakshman's autobiography, *Samboli!*, Vaidehi's *Asprushyaru*, S. Diwakar's *Hundreds of Streets to the Palace of Lights*, and U.R. Ananthamurthy's *Bharathipura*.

[96] Janaki Srinivasa Murthy (b. 1945), better known to readers as Vaidehi, is a poet, playwright, novelist, biographer and translator, best known for her short stories.

[97] Bolwar Mahammad Kunhi (b. 1951), one of the most highly regarded writers from Karnataka in terms of state awards and recognition, is celebrated for his pioneering contributions to Kannada poetry for children, and for introducing a Muslim ethos into Kannada fiction—including a historical novel set in the life of Muhammad—as also for his shorter fictional works, such as the extended short story 'Onu Thando Gode', or 'A Bit of Wall'.

Yes, I do remember being flummoxed by 'kala numbri' in *Karya.* It is a compound word that blends Urdu and English to make an expression used in the regional variety of Kannada spoken in North Karnataka. 'Kala numbri', Malagatti explained to me, refers to Section 144 of the Indian Penal Code. It is a kala or black number because it prohibits people from gathering on the streets during a curfew. But even more confusing was 'dus numbri' in his story, 'Ayyappa of the Ahimsa Slippers'. 'Dus numbri,' of course, means 'number ten'. But this bit of lexical information does not help us to grasp the contextual significance. It has to be subtly worked into the translation. 'Dus numbri' in the story refers to the supplier of beef; dus, meaning ten, is the highest number used to grade meats like fish, chicken, mutton, beef … And so I retained dus numbri for its local flavour, and added a sentence to bring out its meaning: 'Only one lives on, Hussain saab, the dus numbri. Only that beef-seller knows the whole story.' Such an interpolation is not an intrusion since it is more organic than structural, drawing the reader's attention to the subtle connection between Hussain saab the butcher, and Ayyappa the cobbler.

And it is not only the regional varieties of Kannada that pose a problem. Characters in some stories become bilingual, just as it happens to us as we speak. In Bolwar's 'Ibadat' and Banu Mushtaq's[98] 'Not a Woman', they switch from Urdu to Kannada with ease. In Na D'Souza's[99] stories with Christian

---

[98] Banu Mushtaq (b. 1948) is a lawyer and social activist who writes poems, short stories and novels.

[99] Norbert (Na) D'Souza (b. 1937) is a prolific writer of novels, short stories and children's literature, who has published over ninety titles. In October 2022, he revealed that he had received threatening letters from someone who signed off as Sahishnu (Tolerant) Hindu, directing D'Souza to stop opposing the changes the BJP government was making to school textbooks (https://www.thehindu.com/news/national/karnataka/

themes, such as 'God's Labourer' or 'The Day the Crucifix Came Home', the characters shift between Konkani and Kannada. And then, there are cultural nuances of Sanskrit in U.R. Ananthamurthy's[100] novel *Bharathipura*, and of the Alwar saints in S. Diwakar's[101] 'Kraurya' that I have retitled 'Epiphany' in the English translation. In fact, transferring the ambience of Tamil culture in the setting of 'Kraurya' earned me a compliment when a professor at a conference said, 'I thought you translated only from Kannada. I didn't know you could translate so well from Tamil too.' I had to tell him that Diwakar's 'Kraurya' was a story in Kannada! The compliment was as much to the writer as to the translator ...

GH: There are points in Malagatti's *Karya* when an apparently casual comment holds an entire history. One example: 'No one asked them why the tea was black; they lived dark lives anyway.' This is powerful in translation and makes me curious about the original, and other such sharp thrusts we may miss in the translation. Would you comment on the language and craft of the novel?

SP: There is a similar sharp thrust in the reference to 'mangagala upavasa' in the last paragraph of the chapter, 'Broken Pot and Leaking Issues'. It is a description of the mourners 'fasting like monkeys'. It seems a casual comment on a way of life. But a literal translation of the expression would miss the point. I had to rewrite and make it, '... some people fasted like monkeys

---

novelist-na-dsouza-reveals-death-threat-at-kannada-sahitya-parishat-meet/article66052427.ece).

[100] U.R. Ananthamurthy (1932–2014) was, as both writer and critic, one of the most influential figures of twentieth-century Kannada literature. *Bharathipura*, the novel mentioned here, was published in 1973.

[101] S. Diwakar (b. 1944) is best known as a writer of short stories and a translator from world literature into Kannada.

who fast when they have nothing to eat, anyway.' Note the undercurrent of irony: just as monkeys fast only when they get nothing to eat, these people fasted because they had no food anyway. This is an example of the gut-wrenching humour typical of Malagatti's style, not only here, but in his short stories as well.

While Malagatti's enigmatic style makes the implications all the more forceful, I had to use interpolations as scaffolding to interpret culture-specific rituals that point towards their deeper significance in the context. For instance, in the last chapter, I had to elaborate Channappa's musings on the rites connected with the fifth day after death to highlight the magnitude of the desecration that follows. Malagatti's narration is cryptic: '"Tomorrow makes five days since Bangaravva died," Channappa grumbled to himself.' Readers familiar with the rituals following death in the machegara [cobbler] community will understand the implications of Channappa's grumbling. But I had to use a lengthy interpolation describing the fifth-day ritual in detail—here we have a community eager that 'Bangaravva's face should be embossed on silver as a hiriyamukha; she's now a forebearer.' Of course, I could not have done this if Malagatti had not given me a detailed description of the ritual.

After editing the text, Mini Krishnan[102] wondered about juxtaposing *Karya* with U.R. Ananthamurthy's *Samṣkara* since the themes are similar, of death rites going awry. And I recalled an insight I had gained when I interviewed U.R. Ananthamurthy in 2012 for the Oxford Perennials edition of *Samskara*. He had

---

[102] Mini Krishnan has had a long career in editing and publishing translations. She is, at present, the coordinating editor of the Tamil Nadu Textbook and Educational Services Corporation.

explained the significance of the rituals on the days following the cremation, and said that the brahmin community refused to cremate Naranappa because they did not want to accept him as a pithru or progenitor.

The contrast in the treatment of the situation in the two novels is obvious. But there's an incipient irony in the similarity: both writers have made the caste identity in the men so overwhelming that they cannot think beyond the stringent demands of the death rites leading to the acceptance of the dead person as a progenitor. Only the women, Chandri in *Samskara*, and Akkavva and Padmavathi in *Karya*, have been given a sense of agency to act as individuals who are capable of looking beyond the dead-end situation to find a breakthrough for themselves.

Postscript: In May 2022, a textbook revision committee in Karnataka decided to remove the work of several writers from 'the progressive stream' from school books. Writers such as S.L. Bhyrappa, a supporter of Hindutva ideology, would, however, be included in the revision process. Aravind Malagatti's poem, 'Marali Manege', was replaced with S.V. Parameshwara Bhatta's 'Hemantha'. In response, Malagatti said, 'Academics should not be guided by a particular ideology or agenda. [The] school curriculum should be like ever flowing water. The committee is free to revise any text, but doing so based on an ideology or agenda is dangerous to society and our education system.'[103]

---

[103] Jayanth R., 'Texts of many progressive writers dropped in Karnataka school books,' *The Hindu*, 18 May 2022 (https://www.thehindu.com/news/national/karnataka/texts-of-many-progressive-writers-dropped/article65427144.ece).

In June 2023, the BJP government in Karnataka lost to the Congress in the Assembly elections. The newly elected state government followed up on its pre-poll promise to look into the 'saffronising' of textbooks. To begin with, the government declared its intention to form a committee to undertake the 'full revision' of school textbooks in 2024.[104] And in March 2024, the Congress government approved the suggestions of the Karnataka Textbook Revision Committee to restore, in the academic year 2024-25, the work of 'noted progressive writers' in Kannada school textbooks.[105]

---

[104] Express News Service, 'Committee to be formed for full textbook revision next year: Karnataka CM Siddaramaiah', 17 June 2023 (https://indianexpress.com/article/education/committee-full-textbook-revision-next-year-karnataka-cm-siddaramiah-8661242/).

[105] Sanath Prasad, 'Karnataka: Works of progressive writers back in school textbooks', *The Indian Express*, 7 March 2024 (https://indianexpress.com/article/cities/bangalore/karnataka-works-of-progressive-writers-back-in-school-textbooks-9200043/).

MARTIN MACWAN

'You Cannot Kill Caste by Living Within the Caste System'

How does caste show its ugly face every single day?

Its cruel features are quite visible. Less or no choice of livelihood. Men having to go down sewers to clean them in a country and time that boasts of high technology. Men and women condemned to work as manual scavengers. Women vulnerable to harassment or rape. People not allowed to use the village well or the water pump. People left out of social and cultural activities. Children forced to sit separately from others in school. Students isolated, mocked, harassed in colleges and hostels. Barbers refusing a haircut. A lifetime of hearing casteist slurs. Not finding a place to rent or buy. Not allowed to ride a horse. Not allowed to grow a moustache …

This list barely touches the surface of what caste can do to people; these instances make up just bits and pieces of everyday truth. To count all the ways caste rears its head, or its full monstrous face, requires much travel—from now to then, and from way back in the past to the present day. From north to south, from mountain to sea, across region and, arguably, religious community; from village to city; and from infancy to old age.

Caste can even live after death, it seems: it is not always easy to find a place to bury or cremate the dead. And it is not always easy to escape discrimination or violence in the course of the funeral or funeral rites. Just three examples will suffice.

Parbhani District, Maharashtra, 2017: a dalit family cremates a body outside the tehsildar's office since caste Hindus have prevented them from holding the funeral in the village.[106]

Vaniyambadi Taluk, Tamil Nadu, 2019: the body of a dalit man is lowered from a bridge to the burial ground because the upper caste locals do not allow it to be carried across their lands, nor do they allow dalit processions to take the road.[107]

Lucknow, 2020: A dalit woman's body is taken off the funeral pyre by upper-caste men who object to her being cremated on communal land. The men remove firewood from the pyre as the body lies on the ground. The police, called in by the woman's family, do nothing.[108]

It is such a cycle of discrimination, from life to death, that many activists, organisations and movements have fought against, and continue to struggle against. One such organisation is the

---

[106] Saumya Kalia, 'No Dignity in Death', *The Swaddle*, 8 December 2021 (https://theswaddle.com/set-up-common-burial-grounds-without-caste-segregation-madras-hc-to-govt/).

[107] M.K. Ananth, 'Humanity dies in these villages where caste has no cremation', *The Times of India*, 13 December 2021 (https://timesofindia.indiatimes.com/city/chennai/humanity-dies-in-these-villages-where-caste-has-no-cremation/articleshow/88248393.cms).

[108] Saurabh Sharma, 'Anger in India after lower-caste woman's body taken off funeral pyre', Reuters, 28 July 2020 (https://www.reuters.com/article/us-india-landrights-caste-trfn-idUSKCN24T23O).

Gujarat-based Navsarjan Trust,[109] that activist Martin Macwan set up in 1988. Over the years, Navsarjan has been involved in a range of activities and projects to highlight discrimination and atrocities against dalits and adivasis, to fight for their rights, and to improve their day-to-day lives. The activities include campaigns against manual scavenging and for the basic rights of sanitation workers; field visits to track cases of discrimination and violence; and running private residential schools for dalit and adivasi children.

In 2010, Navsarjan conducted a study called 'Understanding Untouchability', covering 98,000 people in 1,569 villages in Gujarat. The study found as many as ninety-eight forms of discrimination practised against dalits. In response, the Gujarat government commissioned a study by CEPT University in Ahmedabad, 'to counter our findings', said Macwan. 'Their study only covered five villages and there was no mention of untouchability. Their only recommendation was to extend the mid-day meal scheme to higher secondary levels ...'[110]

In July 2016, four dalit men were attacked in Una, Gujarat, on the pretext of cow protection. The men were flogged in public by vigilantes for skinning a dead cow. Protests broke out. Using information from reports by the National Commission for Scheduled Castes and the National Crime Records Bureau,

---

[109] Founded in the aftermath of a brutal caste massacre in 1986 at Golana, in Anand district, the Navsarjan Trust began work in 1988 by fighting a thirteen-year-long legal battle that saw ten of the murderers sentenced for life. The Trust has since extended legal assistance to various communities of the disadvantaged and discriminated-against (https://navsarjantrust.org/navsarjans-history/).

[110] Vidya Venkat, 'Atrocities, discrimination led to Dalit wave of anger in Gujarat', *The Hindu*, 22 July 2016 (https://www.thehindu.com/news/national/Una-incident-Martin-Macwan-on-Dalit-wave-of-anger-in-Gujarat/article60527712.ece).

Macwan pointed out that 'Gujarat has a mere 2.33 per cent of India's Dalit population, but when it comes to atrocities, it ranks in the top half of the country.'[111]

The challenge was, and is, huge.

In December 2016, the central government described Navsarjan's activities as 'undesirable' and cancelled the licence it held under the Foreign Contribution Regulation Act (FCRA) to receive funds from foreign sources. The Union Home Ministry's order, in 'public interest', stated that the Trust was involved in 'undesirable activities aimed to affect prejudicially harmony between religious, racial, social, linguistic, regional groups, castes or communities.'[112]Navsarjan was going to find it even more of a challenge to continue its work in more than 3,000 villages in Gujarat.

'We were also the first organisation in the state trying to end the casteism that higher Dalit castes practice on the lowest Dalit castes,' said Natubhai Parmar, a long-time member of Navsarjan. 'Our work at Navsarjan has always been about non-cooperation with casteism ... How can the government consider this anti-national or even undesirable?'[113] These words come from a man whose life is inspiring. He gave up the traditional caste occupation of leather tanning and exhorted other tanners to do the same. Parmar also led a protest against the Una assault, dumping cattle carcasses on streets and highways.[114]

---

[111] Ibid.

[112] Aarefa Johari, 'With its foreign funding cancelled, can Gujarat's oldest Dalit NGO survive?' *Scroll.in*, 12 January 2017 (https://scroll.in/article/826311/with-foreign-funding-cancelled-and-employees-laid-off-can-gujarats-oldest-dalit-ngo-survive).

[113] Ibid.

[114] Ibid.

If one part of the story is a series of challenges, the other part is resistance in all its forms, in every form imaginable.

In 2019, I came across a publication called *Bhed-Bharat*, brought out by the Dalit Shakti Prakashan. The book was first published in Gujarati but was now available in Hindi and English. *Bhed-Bharat* brings together incidents of discrimination and violence—atrocities against dalits and adivasis—between the years 2014 and 2018. The list is based on news stories in the regional and national media. And the incidents are not represented as 'data'; they are real life experiences of real people. Just five years in the long life of the place called India, and how crowded, how overpopulated the list of indignities and cruelties heaped on its own people!

My conversation with the editor of *Bhed-Bharat*, Martin Macwan, was about this awful chronicle of injustice dalits and adivasis have continued to face in recent years. The exchange makes it clear that changes within the system are simply not enough. In Macwan's words: '... You cannot kill caste by living within the caste system.'[115]

28 April 2019

Githa Hariharan (GH): The first thing I see from the regional and state-wise organisation of data in the book is that dalits and adivasis have been at the receiving end of injustice across the country. And this picture emerges from registered cases alone, and those reported in the media—in other words, incomplete data.

---

[115] Ajaz Ashraf, 'Dalit includes all who oppose inequality, regardless of caste', Newsclick, 11 May 2022 (https://www.newsclick.in/dalit-includes-all-who-oppose-inequality-regardless-caste-activist-martin-macwan).

Martin Macwan (MM): Yes, because of the regionalisation of the media, a comprehensive picture of atrocities and injustice against dalits and adivasis has not emerged. Besides, only the sensational cases get reported. Given the fact that there are so many kinds of abuse, often they are perceived as something 'routine'—they do not disturb the conscience of society at large.

Also, the understanding of 'atrocities' has, unfortunately, been confined to physical violence. What about the non-implementation of policies and measures? This marginalises such communities even more. I have noticed that English language newspapers do sometimes report on policy issues, but not regional papers in local languages.

GH: So, on the whole, the media tends to limit itself to reporting the more violent, obvious, physical cases—the ones you describe as sensational. What about the government?

MM: We really do not see an attempt to present a comprehensive picture in the state assemblies and Parliament. So it is difficult, even for enlightened dalits and adivasis, to strategise articulation or action. Besides, what gets presented in government reports is pure figures—they do not convey the human picture as the narratives in this book do. This is the context: most dalits and adivasis struggle for basic survival. Their condition makes it hard for them to know and understand the plight of fellow community members across the country. So, for instance, a dalit from Gujarat may not even know that there are dalits in Assam or Mizoram.

Then there is the critical question of the veracity of atrocity figures. West Bengal, with a dalit population of as much as 23 per cent, does not report beyond 80–85 cases[116] under the

[116] West Bengal's dalit population (of 2.1 crore) is second only to Uttar Pradesh (with over 4 crore), but compared to Uttar Pradesh's rate of caste-

Atrocity Act.[117] It is clear that facts are being suppressed. How do you explain the fact that the number of cases the National Commission on Scheduled Castes and Scheduled Tribes reports is 20 per cent higher than the cases reported by the National Crime Records Bureau? A related question is whether the police in local stations are sensitive enough to help dalits and adivasis register cases.

Besides, there are discriminatory practices in government institutions such as schools and anganwadis, which are mandated to inculcate the value of equality. There have been cases of rape, pregnancy and childbirth involving minor adivasi girls in ashram shalas [boarding schools] that are specially financed and run for them. There have been deaths of adivasi children in these ashram shalas.

GH: What about the response from civil society, or from students and teachers? Do you find the same situation of the blunted conscience as you do in the media and in the government?

MM: Unfortunately, caste discrimination—mostly manifested through atrocities—has generally been perceived as the problem of dalits rather than the problem of the nation, though it is the biggest challenge to the Constitution of India and its core value of equality. Even in interaction with students and faculties of colleges and universities, I find they admit to ignorance about such happenings. Most of their questions at

---

crimes in 2021, which stood at 31.8—or nearly 32 crimes against every one lakh dalit residents—West Bengal recorded an incredibly paltry 0.5 (https://theprint.in/india/madhya-pradesh-rajasthan-have-highest-crime-rate-against-dalits-heres-why/1110399/).

[117] The Scheduled Castes and Scheduled Tribes (Prevention of Atrocities) Act, 1989.

the end of my talks are on reservation for dalits and adivasis, reservation being an irritant to them.

GH: Atrocities against dalits and adivasis make up a terrible old story in India. But this compilation from between 2014 and 2018—is this a continuation of the old story, or does it indicate new forms of injustice? Of atrocities?

MM: While atrocities against dalits and adivasis are not new, there are some features which are certainly 'new'.

The BJP-led National Democratic Alliance (NDA) coalition made promises to both these communities during the 2014 Lok Sabha elections, but atrocities have continued. The government, over the last five years, claims enormous development in the country, but again, the facts on the ground do not show a reduction in atrocities against dalits and adivasis.[118]

One would think that with increase in education, urbanisation and modernisation, there would be less caste prejudice, and so a lower number of atrocities. But what we find is that caste discrimination co-exists with development in all its manifestations. The new generation of the so-called educated have protected their caste status.

There has been a systematic growth in caste-based organisations as social, political and religious platforms. Applying sections of the Atrocity Act against a religious body is especially difficult. That would mean organised protests from the dominant caste groups.

In the absence of research-based study and evidence, the Supreme Court strengthened prejudice in dominant castes

[118] The three years from 2019 to 2021, during the BJP government's second term in office, saw a nationwide rise of 11 per cent in caste crimes against dalits (https://www.newsclick.in/India-Enters-Amrit-Kaal-Growing-Atrocities-Against-Dalits).

through its order that the Act has been misused by dalits and adivasis.[119] In a way, this was also used to justify the low conviction rate in the offences under the Atrocity Act.

A strikingly unique feature emerges from Gujarat, the 'model' state. Compared to a mere 7.01 per cent dalit population (some sources say 6.7 per cent), 32.9 per cent of the total convicts in Gujarat are dalit, and 23.4 per cent of undertrials in Gujarat's jails. What does this mean? That the community, by and large, are the most criminal community and not the victims of criminal abuse?

A new feature is that minor girls are increasingly the targets of caste-based sexual abuse. From my experience, I have seen that the atrocities committed earlier were the result of blatant caste prejudice and the structure of social power in rural areas. Nowadays, we also see that many atrocities against dalits are committed because of jealousy. A dalit man is attacked for riding a motorcycle. A young man is murdered, crushed under motorcycles for playing an Ambedkar song as a ringtone. Or dalit college-going youth are assaulted for tucking their shirts in or for sporting a moustache.

GH: You point out that in spite of the National Democratic Alliance government giving dalits and adivasis more seats, there has been an increase in atrocity cases since 2014. Is this linked with the consolidation of power of the right-wing across the board?

---

[119] In March 2018, a Supreme Court bench of Justices U.U. Lalit and A.K. Goel stated that the Atrocities Act was being misused to blackmail innocent citizens and public servants, and 'perpetuate casteism'. Their judgement removed a provision for the automatic arrest of anyone accused under the Atrocities Act, instead allowing the police seven days to pursue preliminary inquiries on a complaint (https://scroll.in/article/873072/supreme-court-says-sc-st-atrocities-act-is-misused-so-what-explains-the-low-conviction-rates).

MM: On a larger note, we need to stress that the root causes of the atrocities are poverty, subjugation and social-economic powerlessness. Most atrocities are around the issues of land, wages and entitlements. While the state has confined its response merely to providing compensation, social and economic inequalities have become pervasive and systemic. In 2010, Navsarjan conducted a study to map the prevalence of untouchability practices.[120] This study, often quoted in assembly and parliamentary debates, found that in 90.2 per cent of the 1,589 surveyed villages in Gujarat, dalits who practise Hinduism are not allowed to enter temples. Hindutva organisations such as the RSS have never dared to undertake any agitation to ensure temple entry for dalits even when they want them to remain Hindu. Religion has become a platform for political power in present times. Since untouchability is perceived as a creation of Hinduism, given the systemic nexus between political and religious (Hindu) power, there is no political will to address the question of untouchability.

This also speaks of the complete ineffectiveness of the dalit and adivasi parliamentarians. Dr Ambedkar had foreseen this when he pursued the demand for a separate electorate for dalits, which he considered the best constitutional remedy to ensure effective political representation to dalits. Those elected on reserved seats are more preoccupied with being advocates of their party, and less with the urgent concerns of the community they are to represent. At the village level, often those dalits and adivasis who are elected as sarpanch are labourers in the farm of the deputy sarpanch.

---

[120] See https://navsarjantrust.org/2010/01/28/navsarjan-trust-releases-study-on-untouchability-in-gujarat/.

GH: One concrete manifestation of this current nexus between 'religious' and political power you speak of has been the rush of attacks by 'cow vigilantes'. Could you comment on the repercussions of these attacks, on livelihood, food and nutrition, in addition to the physical danger?

MM: The profitable business of the dead cow has been captured by the so-called dominant castes which make money out of the skin, bones, horns and the tail hair. The waste is transformed into chicken feed—here too the dominant castes have captured a large share of the business. The fat often finds its way to the bakeries. But all these businesses and factories have never been the targets of the cow vigilantes.

Nor have the panjrapoles [animal-shelter homes] been on the radar of the so-called cow protectors. These panjrapoles flourished in Gujarat after Independence, especially because the agricultural lands held by them were declared exempt from coverage under the Gujarat Agricultural Lands Ceiling Act of 1960. It was a good programme for many landlords to turn their agricultural land into a 'gaushala' to save it from being given away to landless dalits and adivasis under the terms of the Act. Besides, there is no audit of the number of cow deaths in these panjrapoles or the reasons for death or the money earned by selling the dead cows.

While Kerala, West Bengal and Tripura had the most successful land reforms, Gujarat has had the most disastrous implementation of land reforms which were supposed to benefit dalits and adivasis.[121] True, the most successful land

[121] As Jignesh Mevani writes: 'Successive governments in Gujarat have shied away from doing the bare minimum [...] Most of their policies were even aimed at achieving, to borrow from the preamble of the Gujarat Agricultural Land Ceiling (Amendment) Bill 2015, "rapid industrialisation and urbanisation".' *The Print*, 26 December 2019 (https://theprint.in/

reforms post-Independence took place in Kathiawar State.[122] Here, in a short span of four years, 3.75 million acres of land were transferred from the feudal castes to the present-day patidars or Patels who were then considered shudra.

Dalits and adivasis have mostly been reduced to landless agricultural labourers. To survive in the rural areas, they are forced to stick to caste-based occupations such as manual scavenging and disposal of carcasses. In present times, with the soaring of land prices, the lands given to dalits for skinning the carcass have become a bone of contention. Remember what happened in Una—in the name of cow protection, dalits were attacked to remove them from those pieces of land.

There is another angle to the phenomenon of cow vigilantes. Under the influence of the Ambedkar-Phule ideology, dalits have invested a lot in education. Despite a poorly implemented reservation policy, they have been able to secure benefits in jobs. But OBC youth have little education, and so, meagre employment opportunities. There is little ideological work done among them. Hence, their only 'capital' is their caste—they can use it to get power when politicians encourage them to act in the name of cow protection. More cows die eating plastic but no one is concerned about that, neither these people nor the state.

GH: And the economic consequences of this nexus between caste and religion?

MM: True, this nexus has economic consequences for dalits and adivasis. There are several incidents recounted in *Bhed-Bharat*

---

opinion/gujarats-dalits-tribals-are-getting-back-land-they-have-so-far-owned-only-on-paper/340870/).

[122] The United States of Kathiawar (or Saurashtra) carried out these land reforms under U.N. Dhebar, its chief minister till 1956.

which show how social and economic boycott follows from incidents of atrocity. Dalits and adivasis are then deprived of work, of the type of tenant farming usually referred to as sharecropping.[123] They are denied places for defecation. They are denied credit, common village services and much more.

GH: Again, demonetisation and growing unemployment are among the problems we have faced in the last five years. In particular, what has this done to dalit and adivasi lives?

MM: I asked an adivasi man in a village about the impact of demonetisation on his family. He said there was no impact simply because he did not have a currency note. As for dalit women, they lost all the hard-earned savings they had made for social occasions without the knowledge of their husbands, as the savings became public during demonetisation.

Unemployment has been the major problem. With increased wages, farmers prefer wheat and paddy cutting machines in rural areas. The factories prefer migrant labour from other states to ensure they do not organise around labour rights. So labourers from each state are forced to migrate. Factory wages seem higher but they are not—as the working hours are often twelve instead of eight. Besides, employment is often insecure as it is based on the volume of work.

There have been more cases of caste confrontation in the factories as opportunities have reduced. Also, unemployment among the educated has been sharper among dalits and adivasis, with no implementation or weak implementation of reservation. Too often, the burden of running the family

---

[123] Only 17.1 per cent of Scheduled Castes own land, as against 39.4 per cent of rural socially advanced classes (SACs). However, 58.9 per cent of rural dalit households are employed in agriculture, compared to 26.2 per cent rural SACs. (See Jignesh Mevani, *The Print*, 2019.)

has fallen on women. You can see them every day, carrying fodder on their heads to feed their animals and earn some supplementary income.

Postscript: The new Parliament building in Delhi was inaugurated with great fanfare in May 2023, accompanied by spectacle and ritual. There was a sceptre that was made much of. Supposedly a symbol of justice, it was handed over to the Prime Minister by 'men of religion' who installed it next to the Speaker's chair.

Less than a year before, in August 2022, a group of 375 dalits from Ahmedabad was nearing the capital with a precious load on a truck: a huge coin engraved with the image of Ambedkar and the words 'Bhim *Rudan*' ('The agony of Bhim'). An engraved line encircling the image of Ambedkar asked the question, 'Will the 1947 dream of an untouchability-free India become a reality in 2047?'[124] The coin was to serve as a reminder to the rest of India, specifically its ruling class as well as its political parties, that untouchability still lives in India.

The coin was to be presented to the Indian Parliament on 14 August 2022; other programmes were planned around this event. But the guardians of the coin—and their call for an equal India—were stopped at the border in Haryana by a large number of policemen. The state police had placed boulders on the road, summoned water cannons to stand by. The group decided to go back to Ahmedabad, their coin not accepted, their message unheard.

---

[124] Syeda Hameed, 'Dalit Villagers Wanted to Present a Coin to the President. The State Stopped Them.', *The Wire*, 9 August 2022 (https://thewire.in/caste/dalit-villagers-wanted-to-present-a-coin-to-the-president-the-state-stopped-them).

Holding Up Many Skies

SHASHI DESHPANDE

Listening to the Woman's Voice

I always assume Shashi and I have known each other from the days of our childhood. But obviously this is not possible since she is older, as she likes to remind me, especially when we squabble ghoulishly about which of us should be drafting an obit for the other. Perhaps my imaginary childhood memory says something about the quality of our friendship as women and as writers.

Actually I first met Shashi when I was in my late twenties, a closet writer, and for all official purposes, an editor in a publishing house. I well recall an editorial meeting when we were dividing genres among the editors, and I waved my arm excitedly for fiction, social science, and, to the scorn of my male colleagues, women's studies, which had just about then entered our dark basement office in Delhi's Asaf Ali Road. (The new entrant was often called 'women studies', as if unwilling to give women a word to own.) I must have taken my assignments seriously; when I read that Shashi's novel, *Roots and Shadows*, had won a prize, I sought her out in Bangalore with a bunch of flowers. We quickly forgot about prizes and publishers and began a conversation of our own. All these years later, that conversation continues.

We spoke, we speak, interminably, of what feminism means to us in our individual lives and circumstances. It would be impossible to understand Shashi's voice as a writer, or her passion as a writer, if she were not viewed as a woman writing about the world; and, in much of her fiction, as a woman probing every crevice of the power equation within the family unit, an eloquent microcosm of Indian society.

My first impression of Shashi's voice—as woman and writer—was of its honesty; she actually said and wrote what she thought. To this day, whatever the subject, whatever our individual views on the matter, that sense I had, of reading or hearing transparent honesty in her words, has never faded.

We also spoke of ourselves as writers rooted in India but writing in English. This may no longer be the case, but a decade or two back, those of us living in India and writing in English often had to deliver a well-prepared explanation for why we wrote in English. I loved Shashi's true story: when it was time for her to go to school, her father, the well-known Kannada playwright Adya Rangacharya, naturally opted for Kannada medium. Her mother (whom I would much later meet, and who was made of stern stuff), insisted on Marathi. Living in Dharwad, close to the border between Karnataka and Maharashtra, they settled the border dispute with a compromise language: English.

It is only in more recent years—especially since Kalburgi was assassinated in Dharwad in 2015—that I have questioned Shashi about what the Dharwad she grew up in was like. Her memories are truly of another era. She remembers a place with treasures such as the Karnatak Granthalaya, 'a proper library' where she began her passionate relationship with books. She recalls friendships that began there with, for instance, Maria Aurora Couto, who would go on to become a teacher and a writer in her own right. Most important, this was a Dharwad and an India where Hindu supremacists did not terrorise scholars like Kalburgi. In her obituary for Maria Aurora, Shashi described the India the two of them grew up in:

> Both of us had come to the age of understanding during the Nehru years. We had imbibed that wonderful vision of India he, and Gandhiji before him, had held out to us. An India with many differences, but living together with tolerance and understanding. 'Unity in Diversity' was not just an empty slogan, it meant a way of living in this country. Was this vision to be sacrificed now to a different ideology?[125]

It must have been this vision that led Shashi to react as she did when M.M. Kalburgi was assassinated. On 9 October 2015, she wrote to the President of the Sahitya Akademi, resigning from its General Council:

> … I have always respected the Sahitya Akademi's role as the single institution in India that brings together all the Indian languages under one umbrella, at the same time giving each language its rightful place and dignity.
>
> Today, I am deeply distressed by the silence of the Akademi on the murder of Professor M.M. Kalburgi. Professor Kalburgi was a noted scholar … he was also a Sahitya Akademi awardee and a member of its General Council until recently.
>
> If the Akademi, the premier literary organisation in the country, cannot stand up against such an act of violence

[125] Shashi Deshpande, 'My Friend Aurora', *Indian Cultural Forum*, 18 January 2022 (https://indianculturalforum.in/2022/01/18/my-friend-aurora-by-shashi-deshpande/).

> against a writer, if the Akademi remains silent about this attack on one of its own, what hope do we have of fighting the growing intolerance in our country? …
>
> Sadly, it has become increasingly important to reaffirm that difference of opinion cannot be ended with a bullet; that discussion and debate are the only way a civilised society resolves issues. It has also become clear that writers, who are supposed to be the conscience-keepers of society, are no longer considered intellectual leaders; their voices no longer matter. Perhaps this is the right time for writers to reclaim their voices. But we need a community of voices, and this is where the Akademi could serve its purpose and play an important role. It could initiate and provide space for discussion and debate in public life. It could stand up for the rights of writers to speak and write without fear; this is a truth all political parties in a democracy are supposed to believe in. Silence is a form of abetment, and the Sahitya Akademi, which should speak for the large community of Indian writers, must stand up and protest the murder of Professor Kalburgi and all such acts of violent intolerance …

Our conversation, since 2015, has grown wider and deeper. We have struggled to understand, all over again, the many meanings of words like 'secular' or 'democracy' or 'dissent'. We have tried to imagine how these meanings can be reflected in our work. No word, no meaning, has been exempt from being tested in the practice of our daily lives. That old catch phrase 'the personal is the political' stays with us in one new avatar after another, helping us view, critically, our lives and work.

This is what we did when Shashi's literary memoir, *Listen to Me,* was published in 2018. Using the memoir as a starting point, we spoke of the personal circumstances of her life, the places she has lived in, and the languages she has heard and spoken. All these matters fed into the central question of a writer's sensibility—a writer who is a woman, and a writer who has known many Indias, past and present.

December 2018

Githa Hariharan (GH): Your memoir, *Listen to Me*, is preoccupied with location in many senses of the word. And so is your other writing. In the memoir, you take us from the Dharwad of your childhood, to a changing Parel in Bombay-Mumbai, to both old and new Bangalore, and to the houses you have lived in. Would you comment on this continuous process of defining your home?

Shashi Deshpande (SD): I have always had a very strong attachment to place. I lived in Dharwad for only the first fifteen years of my life, but it has stayed with me through the years. So has the ancestral 'wada' of my mother's family in Pune, which we visited every year in my childhood days. Some years after my marriage, the 'wada' was demolished, but it still lives with me, inside me. As do the hospital quarters in Parel, Bombay, where my children were born and grew up, and the quarters in NIMHANS,[126] Bangalore, where they moved into adulthood and left home in pursuit of their own careers. But above all, each place contributed to my growth as a writer. From Dharwad, where I became an ardent reader, thus laying the foundation of my writing, to Bombay, where, first as a student, and then as a married woman, my experiences and observation of life around me shaped my thinking, to Bangalore where I recognised that writing was my life's work and settled down seriously to it—each place has played a role in my writing life.

[126] National Institute of Mental Health and Neuro-Sciences.

But I consider Bombay the place that shaped me as a writer. It was this phenomenally active and bustling city which never sleeps that set my imagination alight. It was the women who came to work for me who gave body to this imagination. Many had drunkard husbands and were almost always victims of domestic abuse. I saw how hard they worked, how unflinching they were in their determination to see that their children had an education, their determination that 'My daughter should not become like me, she should not live the kind of life I do.' Their hard lives, the way they coped with cruelty, made me understand—as a girl who had lived a sheltered life—the injustices in life. It was this understanding that pushed me into writing, or so I like to think now.

GH: But beyond place, you also address the rich but slippery business of living a life with many languages.

SD: Yes, when I came to Bangalore, I relocated myself in the language of our lives in Dharwad. In Bombay, I was familiar with Marathi, but it was only the language spoken in the family. Here, in Bangalore, Kannada was spoken all around me, we saw Kannada films, Kannada plays, heard Kannada songs. Through my father, I came upon the world of Kannada writers, of Kannada drama, and the world of Purandaradasa[127] and Basavanna,[128] whose songs my father chanted tunelessly all the time. It gave me a rootedness which I, as an English writer, had lacked till then. If my writing language was English, the world of my two languages—Kannada and Marathi—was where my writing was located. My connections to the cultures of these

[127] Or, Purandara Dasa, a sixteenth-century Haridasa philosopher in the bhakti tradition, revered as a founder of Karnatik music.

[128] Or, Basava, the twelfth-century philosopher, poet, social reformer and founder of the Lingayat movement.

two languages were very strong and my writing reflected this. Yes, Bangalore dispelled that sense of not belonging, or of not belonging entirely, to any place. In *A Matter of Time* (1996), *Small Remedies* (2000), *Moving On* (2004) and *In the Country of Deceit* (2008), I returned to the world into which I had been born, easy and comfortable now in that world, the language in which I wrote becoming naturally a part of it.

GH: You raise the question of politics in the novel, and indicate that this refers to any sort of probing of power structures, including the family. This enlarges our understanding of the political, and brings into play the principle of the personal being political. Would you say gender, rather than caste or class, is the main prism through which you view power politics?

SD: The family is a microcosm of society, and the same power politics that exists in society is in play in the family as well. Power politics begins in the family and it is gender that separates the powerful from the powerless. I remember reading a report which came out after the World Conference on Women that women workers are the most poorly paid everywhere in the world. That however poor a man is, a woman is always poorer. She is at the bottom of the pile. It substantiated my idea that all women, whatever class, religion or even caste they belong to, have been deliberately, from times immemorial, deprived of power, even power over their own bodies and lives.

As a writer, I often felt at the receiving end of this idea that since women are less important, their lives are not important either. That women who write about women confine themselves to the family and home. I remember in my early days as a writer, an interviewer asked me that since I wrote only about 'in here' and not about 'out there', did I not feel circumscribed, limited? And I had to think what 'in here' and 'out there' meant. I then understood that I could not think of them as two rigidly exclusive categories, one more important than the other. Think of Tolstoy's *War and Peace* without the peace, its 'in here'. Of Tagore's *Home and the World* without the home. Like the world, home was a battleground in which injustice was rampant. Home was the first place where the inequalities, the injustice, began. Home was where girls and boys learnt the truth and the reality of patriarchy. Reading cases of divorce, separation and custody of children for my novel *Shadow Play* (2013) I came across a sentence, 'The categories of cruelty can never be closed.' These chilling words gave me a glimpse of the cruelty that can exist within the home and the family. This is cruelty which is always concealed within the walls of a home, and not spoken of, so, more dangerous and harder to fight.

It was some time after writing *That Long Silence* (1988) that I realised this book was about the politics of gender. About the belief held, perhaps since human life began, that in the family, the man is the master and the women (and children) are his subordinates. By chance I came across Engels' *The Origin of the Family, Private Property and the State* (1884) and found in it this statement: In a family he (the man) is the bourgeois, the woman represents the proletariat. And this one: The first class oppression is that of the female sex by the male.[129]

That Long Silence was not written to substantiate these statements. I wrote the novel before I read these words and it seemed to validate these statements—to my mind, at

[129] 'The first class opposition that appears in history coincides with the development of the antagonism between man and woman in monogamous marriage, and the first class oppression coincides with that of the female sex by the male.' (II. The Family 4. 'The Monogamous Family')

least. And yet, to the literary world, *That Long Silence* and all my subsequent novels were just 'women's novels'—which immediately put them in a small frame. Not even a miniature, which has a beauty of its own, but just a novel about women set in the family. The personal, not the political. Trivial and insignificant as compared to novels which were 'out there', set in the large frame of the nation, of the world. Novels which could aspire to the descriptor 'epic'.

I do not want to dramatise myself and say that my entire writing life has been a struggle against this idea. But I have to say that to go on writing despite the way my novels were received, labelled, categorised and put in their place, was never easy. Yet it was possible, because of my own belief in what I was writing, my certainty that my novels were about women's struggle to understand what they were, beyond the stereotypes they had been made to believe in. A class struggle has some validity, it is taken seriously. A woman's struggle against whatever is stacked against her is never a serious struggle. Even today this has not changed. Not completely.

In November 2021, a collection of essays by Shashi, selected and compiled by Nancy E. Batty and Dieter Riemenschneider, was published. Entitled Subversions: Essays on Life and Literature, *the volume includes essays that address a range of subjects, from the role of the writer and the power structure within which women writers function, to assorted texts and writers.*

Our conversation was in two parts. Part 1 went back to her 'writer's country.' Shashi spoke of the complexities of belonging, especially in the Indian context. The complexities include the claims of several places and languages, the multiple legacies of myths and tales, and the communities within the larger community of writers, whether it is that of women writers, or Indian writers in English, or Indian writers …

8 November 2021

GH: In your book of essays, *Subversions*, you write of Bengaluru and Dharwad with layered memories, in loving detail. You also write of your complex relationship with languages—English, Kannada, Marathi. Where do you as a writer feel the greatest sense of belonging? Or is it a quest to belong that drives you?

SD: A.K. Ramanujan has this rather interesting take on the multiple languages spoken in his home in Mysore. On the ground floor, which was the women's domain, Tamil ruled. Upstairs, which was the realm of the men, there was English. And outside the house and on the streets, the language was Kannada. In our family too we had an arrangement in which all the languages had their place. I spoke to my father and brother in Kannada, to my mother and sister in Marathi (my mother was from Pune), and in school it was English. As we grew up, English became, increasingly, the language in which we siblings communicated. We did not see this as remarkable, but certainly I know that some of our schoolmates regarded it as unusual, especially the fact that we, sisters and brother, spoke in English among ourselves. Today this has become commonplace. But at a time when there was not much movement of people, it was a rarity. I must say I did not have the feeling of belonging to any language. All the languages were mine; I would move from one to the other when necessary.

The question of where I belong came to me only after I began writing. Initially, I was not even conscious of the fact that I was writing in English. Since my reading was entirely in

English, it became the only language in which I could frame my thoughts and ideas. But that there was a problem was brought home to me when I was questioned about my writing in English. My father was a Kannada writer, so why was I writing in English? I steadily deflected this question; for a writer it is not which language, but how you use it that matters. Yet within me a question grew: I did not belong with the writers in the various [Indian] languages. We were separated by the different languages we wrote in. But it was not just that; after all, the Kannada poet Bendre[130] grew up in a Marathi family, while Masti,[131] another eminent Kannada writer, was a Tamilian but wrote in Kannada. No, it was the fact that I wrote in a 'foreign' language that made me an outsider. In fact, not only did I feel that I did not belong to the literatures in the various Indian languages, I also rejected the idea of belonging to the group of Indian writers who wrote in English. Theirs seemed a strange kind of writing to me. I was very confident that I would never write that way, where the discrepancy between the language and culture was bridged very consciously and the effort showed. Ultimately, I found my own way of bridging the gap between the culture my writing came out of and the language I was writing in. To get to this point, I had to carve my own path. And after writing *The Dark Holds No Terrors* and *That Long Silence* (1989), I knew that if I had to belong anywhere, it was here, in the great complex of Indian literature in many languages, English being one of them.

As for belonging to a territory, although Bangalore is home, I also lay claim to the territory I inhabit in each of my novels.

---

[130] Dattatreya Ramachandra Bendre (1896–1981) is considered one of the finest lyric poets of Kannada literature.

[131] Masti Venkatesha Iyengar (1891–1986) played a central role in the development of the short story form in Kannada.

As long as I am writing, I am part of the territory I create in my writing. Belonging is no longer a problem. If I am driven by anything, it is by a great desire to tell women's stories, to show women as they are, not as they have been painted through the centuries: frivolous, vain, irrational, hysterical, childish and so on ... As a writer with a pen in my hand, I could write the truth and the reality of a woman as no man could. This was what drove me, made me persist despite condescension or being ignored or dismissed.

GH: So many of us women have made use of myths to comment on societal norms but also, as your book is titled, on subversions—the dramatic and visible sort, as well as the quiet, private gestures of assertion. What is your take on our living legacy of myth?

SD: I wonder how many countries there are in the world in which myths have had such a long and continuous existence among the people and which continue to have great power. In India our epics are still alive, they still mean much to us. Writers continue to be fascinated by them, and the language [bhasha] literatures have always brought myths into their writing. In recent times, writers in English have also taken to retelling the myths.

That myths mean something more to women came to me after I began writing. They give women an idea of their roles, role models so to say. For centuries, Sita, Draupadi and Savitri have been held up as role models for women. I started looking at these stories differently when I came across a story which served as a wake-up call for me. This is the story of a woman, a pativrata (a very unsatisfactory translation for this word is an ideal wife). The woman's husband was sleeping with his head on her lap. Then she saw her child going close to the fire. She was faced with a dilemma. As a pativrata, she could not disturb her husband's sleep. But what if the child fell into the fire? And so she prayed to the god Agni to help her. Agni, knowing she was a pativrata and doing the right thing by not disturbing her husband's sleep, moved the child away from the fire. The child was saved, the woman had triumphantly proved herself a pativrata, and the man slept undisturbed. An all-round success. But I thought it was an incredibly stupid story. Any normal mother would have just shoved the man's head off her lap and rushed to her child. And I realised that the story was addressed to women. It told them: your duty to your husband is paramount, above even your duty towards your child. Clearly, the story had been written or told by a man to give women this message.

I discovered that if I were to ask some questions about mythical stories, they would yield quite a different meaning. For instance, was it really Draupadi who started the Mahabharata war? Would her kshatriya husbands have refrained from war if she had not egged them on? And Sita—was she so meek and docile that she took Rama's sentence of sending her back into the forests without anger? Without questions? Punished a second time—and for what? Why did Rama not have the courage to tell the world that he believed in his wife's innocence and chastity? And Karna, the child who was born to Kunti when she was only a girl. She was in the ashram then, where her father had placed her. Had she been impregnated by someone in the ashram? Or had she been pregnant earlier which is why he sent her there?

The first story I wrote about a woman from our myths was about Sita. Then I wrote about Amba after reading Iravati Karve's *Yuganta*.[132] (That book gave me a new vision.) In

[132] Written in Marathi and a winner of the Sahitya Akademi Award in 1968, the full title of the book, as translated into English by Norman

the Mahabharata, Amba's story is important only because it leads to her becoming an instrument of Bhishma's death. But what drove her to her death does not do great credit either to Bhishma, or to his brother who was to marry Amba. If this story left me angry, I found one of the more interesting, though less-known stories in P. Lal's[133] retelling of the Mahabharata. In this story, Subhadra, Arjuna's newly-wed wife, asks Draupadi, Arjuna's senior wife, 'How do you manage to keep all your husbands happy?' (Indeed, a question to which many of us would like to know the answer.) And Draupadi says, 'I don't let them know what I think.' I don't know whether the story really exists in the Mahabharata, but it reconciles me to much that I objected to in stories about women.

Recently I wrote a story about Madhavi, Yayati's daughter. King Yayati sends his daughter to several kings, one after another, to sleep with each and produce a son. Once a son is born, she has to leave the baby behind and move on to the next king. Even the great rishi Vishwamitra wants to have her for a year. A father doing such a thing to his daughter? How could they even narrate this story without any comment, as if it was a commonplace story? The only unspoken comment comes when Madhavi walks away from everything. A ghastly story. I wrote it, guided by the fact that Madhavi left everything behind and went away.

I had great pleasure though in writing a story about Indra and Nahusha. It is a story about Indra being toppled from

---

Brown, is *Yuganta: The End of an Epoch*. A pioneering sociologist, Iravati Karve (1905–1970) studied the main protagonists of the Mahabharata and attempted to locate the story in an identifiable historical period, using socio-political details as clues.

[133] Purushottama Lal (1929–2010) was an essayist, poet, translator, and the founder, in 1958, of the Calcutta-based publishing firm, Writers Workshop.

his throne and Nahusha being installed as King of the Gods. The story has only one woman in it, Sachi Devi, Indra's wife. And she is there only as the subject of Nahusha's desire and lust. I brought in Nahusha's wife as well and made the two women active participants in the story. Why should it not have happened that way?

An example of how a creative writer can tell a story differently comes from Kalidasa's play *Shakuntala*. According to Iravati Karve, the original story which came from the Mahabharata is 'concise, hard and unpolished'. In this story, both the King and Shakuntala are shrewd and cunning. The king trifles with her; then, though he remembers her, he says he has forgotten her. He finally accepts her because of her son, since he has no heir. Love is nowhere in the picture. But Kalidasa converted the story into a lyrical play in which Shakuntala is an innocent girl (look at the setting—an ashram set amid nature), and Dushyanta forgets her only because of a curse.

One cannot rewrite myths. They are there, they have been there for centuries. One cannot ignore them either. But they can be retold and given a twist that makes you look at them quite differently.

Part two of the conversation took us to even more ambitious territory. Shashi spoke about dissent, feminism, and the role of a writer amid the growing polarisation in the country. Over the years, Shashi has expressed, in her writing and in public space, her straightforward stand on any assault on constitutional rights. 'The Constitution gives us all equal rights,' she has said. 'Any government in power must respect that.'[134] *She links these*

[134] Shoba Warrier, 'Some of the middle class cling to Hindutva', Rediff.com, 18 May 2023 (https://www.rediff.com/news/interview/shashi-deshpande-some-of-the-middle-class-cling-to-hindutva/20230518.htm).

rights with democracy, with the people's power to decide who will represent their interests and serve their needs: 'Democracy gives us the right to change governments which are not working well.' Dissent is important, Shashi underlines, whether as a woman, a writer, or a citizen.

GH: Your collection of essays, *Subversions*, has a powerful epigraph that seems perfect for the times. It quotes the indomitable Ruth Bader Ginsburg: 'Some of my favourite opinions are dissenting opinions.'[135] This choice of epigraph says a great deal about your aspirations as writer, woman and citizen in search of democracy and freedom of speech. Shall we begin with the question most relevant for our times? What, for you, is dissent?

SD: Among the numerous judgements by Ruth Bader Ginsburg (RBG), many of which were on contentious matters, there is one in which RBG and two other judges dissented. While the other two judges wrote the usual 'I respectfully dissent', RBG simply said, 'I dissent.' Or so the story goes. Perhaps she meant that there is no need to apologise for dissent, or qualify it.

Dissent comes out of questions. The idea of dissent began, for me, with the personal, which is so often the case. My questions began when I moved from a free, unrestricted childhood to an adult world ruled by the idea that women have to live restricted lives. And so, the questions: Why was marriage so important for a girl that she and her parents had to subject themselves to humiliation from the family of the future groom? Why was a girl 'given' in marriage? Why did they speak of a girl being 'allowed' or 'not allowed' to do something after

[135] Joan Ruth Bader Ginsburg (1933–2020) was an Associate Justice in the US Supreme Court from 1993 till her death.

marriage? Things have changed since then, though perhaps only for the privileged few. What has not changed is that a wife remains subordinate to her husband, and her life and personality are subsumed into her husband's. I was pretty sure that mine would be a marriage of equality, that I would never be 'the woman behind the man'.

When I began writing, things became clearer; writing always clarifies one's ideas and thoughts. And the questions within me moved to the outside world. In fact, one of my early novels [*Roots and Shadows*, 1983] came out of Indira Gandhi's policy of taking total control of her party and of the country. Soon, any dissent against her policies or views became almost lèse-majesté. Sycophancy, almost a hallmark of politics in our country, followed. But our brush with the idea of a Great Leader taught us this: if dissent is stifled, democracy is threatened.

We seem to have come once again to the same place. Intolerance of dissent has reached the stage when dissenters are called Naxalites, terrorists, unpatriotic and anti-national. I can remember a sick Girish Karnad sitting with a board round his neck which said, 'Me Too Urban Naxal'.[136] A powerful image, and a new word coined[137] for those who disagree with

---

[136] This was at a public protest in Bengaluru, on 5 September 2018, marking one year since the assassination of Gauri Lankesh. On the same day, the Hindu Janajagruthi Manch and the Sri Ram Sene held demonstrations in support of those accused of the killing (https://scroll.in/latest/893572/karnataka-lawyer-files-complaint-against-girish-karnad-for-wearing-sign-saying-me-too-urban-naxal).

[137] The term 'urban Naxal', thrown at activists, union members, scholars and protesters, implies that they are Maoist operatives working covertly to overthrow the state. In *Modi's India: Hindu Nationalism and the Rise of Ethnic Democracy* (2021), Christophe Jaffrelot traces its origins to the BJP leader Arun Jaitley, who first used 'urban Naxals' in 2014 to smear activists of the Aam Aadmi Party. In a May 2017 article for the right-wing magazine *Swarajya*, the filmmaker Vivek Agnihotri repurposed Jaitley's term to target

the powers that be. To consider dissent unpatriotic and anti-national is the beginning of the end of democracy. Democracy means dialogue, debate, discussion. To stifle dissent is to take away the voice of the people. What despots want is a chorus of sycophants, not a healthy exchange of views and opinions.

We talk a great deal about the right to freedom of speech and expression. To me, the right to dissent is the other face of the freedom of speech and expression. I also consider dissent the agent of progress and change. If democracy means that the views of the majority prevail, there is still always a dissenting minority. And this can, at times, be more powerful than a dumb, unthinking and accepting majority, ruled by slogans. A servile and subservient population guarantees a weakened democracy. After all, democracy does not mean that there is universal agreement. It only means that the majority view will prevail, and this after there have been debates and discussion about the issues.

In a recent case, Supreme Court judge D.Y. Chandrachud spoke of dissent as the safety valve of democracy.[138] Dissent which is suppressed can result in a violent explosion, while dissent expressed can lead to healthy debate and discussion. I also consider dissent not just a negative. It means positively standing by your beliefs. One of the most alarming things in our times is the punishment given to dissenters. It not only punishes the dissenter, it instils fear into would-be dissenters.

'urban intellectuals, influencers or activists of importance' as 'the "invisible enemies" of India'. Without any basis in social science or recognition in law, 'urban Naxal' has nevertheless transitioned from right-wing opinion pieces and demagoguery to police charge sheets.

[138] Now Chief Justice of India. The reference is to 15th P.D. Desai Memorial Lecture in Ahmedabad on 15 February 2020 (https://www.hindustantimes.com/india-news/dissent-is-the-safety-valve-of-a-democracy-justice-chandrachud/story-1vOft3QfRvszjGuBBWSuLI.html).

It may make them think, 'I better keep my mouth shut. I don't want to get into trouble, or get my family and friends into trouble.'

GH: For those of us who have seen the women's movement in different phases in India and elsewhere, what does it mean to write texts informed by feminism? And what does it mean to live feminism day to day?

SD: It has been a very long journey for me, as I am sure it has been for many women, moving from a vague sense of dissatisfaction and inchoate thoughts to confused ideas of something being wrong. And then, connecting it to the way women are regarded and treated, before finally stumbling on feminism.

I first saw the word feminism in an American journal, *The American Review* (issue of 1973, it is still with me). There was a longish article in it, written by Isa Kapp about 'the new feminism'. It began by saying, '... After more than a century of legal, social and cultural advances ... the American woman is today in the throes of a new feminism more articulate, widely supported and militant than any in history.' I read this article not just with interest, but with a sense of release. Finally, I was hearing something that chimed with my own thoughts. Yet my own ideas of feminism did not come out of this 'widely supported movement', but out of what I saw around me: gross inequalities in every sphere of life between men and women, a subordinate status given to women in almost every field of life.

It was the Mathura rape case [1972] that showed me the extent of the injustice. It was a case in which a young adivasi girl was held overnight in the police station and raped by two policemen. While the lower court and the High Court held it to be rape, the Supreme Court reversed their judgements. They concluded that since the girl showed no signs of struggle, and had no bruises, she must have consented, and so it could not be rape. What I remember most vividly is the letter written by four law teachers to the Supreme Court (published in newspapers) arguing that the Supreme Court was mixing up submission and consent. They held that submission was natural when a young girl was in a police station in the middle of night, confronted by policemen who were figures of authority for her; she had no choice but to submit. That did not mean she consented. It was rape.

This case woke me up to the injustice which women had to face, even from a judge. It also showed me, through the protests that followed, that this injustice could be questioned. Moving to Bangalore, I found myself very peripherally involved with the work of an NGO working for women. One of their volunteers, who dealt with the victims of dowry deaths, told me that the suffering of the dying women was so terrible she could not sleep for months. By this time, I was seriously involved in my writing. But I knew even then, with just four novels written, that creative writing cannot bear the burden of an ideology, that no writer can write a story, a novel, or a poem to directly convey a message. To do so would mar the aesthetic of the work. And for writers, the aesthetic of creative writing is as important as the content. At best, the work can only be 'informed', as you rightly put it, by your ideas ...

To live feminism day by day is just as hard as reconciling your feminist views with your writing. To live with feminism means a moral struggle within yourself. All of us live in a complex web of relationships which we nurture and depend on. To bring feminism into personal life could mean hurting a relationship. What do we do? Compromise on one's ideology and save a relationship? Or forget one's ideology? When it comes to children, especially very young children, there can never be any compromise with children's needs. No ideology can stand against a child's needs.

What makes it hard to bring feminism into your day-to-day life is the way feminism is looked at. I consider it one of the important movements of our times. Obviously, for it is a fight for equality by one half of the human race. But to the world, to the male world, and even to many women, it was and is a joke. Never has any movement been so derided and ridiculed as the feminist movement. Never has a movement been as misunderstood as the feminist movement. Feminists are aggressive, they are man-haters, they don't want children, they are troublemakers—these are the perceptions, the prejudices. I know that I was the constant butt of jokes in the early days because of my views. Strength and affirmation came through books. And through the tireless and selfless work of activists, who are now, thankfully, getting some appreciation for the work they are doing. There is also some hope now, with the judiciary, especially the higher courts, taking serious note of any injustice against women, and with young people coming back into the fight. And more men (though still a pitifully small number) becoming sympathisers.

GH: What can we, as writers, do about making the powerful cliché 'unity in diversity' live through our work? And what can we do, through what we write, or what we say in the public space, about the growing polarisation in the country?

SD: The idea of India being a country where there was unity in diversity, which had seemed so magical and meaningful after Independence (and which had proved true during the freedom fight), today sounds both meaningless and irrelevant. Is it because we know it is unachievable? Have we given up on it, knowing it is something impossible to achieve? Whatever the reason, it lies in our past, covered with dust and totally forgotten. The truth is that we have moved so far in our intolerance that we cannot bring back the idea of the underlying unity of this country. Religion has become a tool to divide people. People are encouraged to be intolerant of 'the other', they have been manipulated into mistrusting one another, the differences between them deliberately exaggerated. One would have to be extraordinarily optimistic to imagine that we can reverse the movement of the chariot which set off for Ayodhya thirty years back.[139] That we can turn it back and make it go on a pilgrimage uniting the entire country.

But change will come, changes have to come. The wheel of fortune never rests, it keeps turning.

As far as writers are concerned, I am afraid I am not sanguine. Writers can do very little. People have been brainwashed into accepting a divisive ideology. The times when writers could influence people are way behind us. Religion has got such a grip over the country that rational thinking and understanding have no place in a person's thinking. Besides, writers no longer have that larger-than-life image which made people look up

---

[139] L.K. Advani had planned on riding a customised Toyota minibus, calling it a 'rath', from Somnath to Ayodhya, between 25 September and 30 October 1990, taking a roundabout route that crossed ten states. Following outbreaks of communal violence in North India, Advani was arrested in Bihar on 22 October by Lalu Prasad Yadav's government, and was unable to go any further. Tens of thousands of his followers reached Ayodhya and attempted to scale the Babri Masjid, but the Janata Dal government of Uttar Pradesh, headed by Mulayam Singh Yadav, had ordered a substantial deployment of police who defeated the karsevaks' attempt by firing and conducting mass arrests (https://frontline.thehindu.com/politics/india-at-75-epochal-moments-1990-lal-krishna-advani-embarks-on-rath-yatra/article65725588.ece).

to them. There are too many influences working on people now, too many voices speaking. The writer's voice is lost in this cacophony. Politicians and the entertainment industry, both replete with money, have poisoned the wells of culture. We who write in English are even more impotent. English writing reaches a small minority and despite the fears of English threatening our languages, these languages are what reach most of the people. They have a kind of power and influence which English lacks. I do believe that a number of factors have to come together to make a real impact on the thinking of a people. A small, maybe very small, part of this will be the contribution of those who write in English. One has to comfort oneself with that thought.

MANGAI

Conscience-Keepers, from Avvai to Inquilab

Mangai's journeys have helped her to be many people. She is Mangai, but also A. Mangai, or Mangai Arasu. She is, (perhaps officially), Padma Venkataraman or V. Padma.

Mangai is a professor of English; a researcher; a translator from English to Tamil. She is an actor, a theatre director and a founder of theatre groups. Her journey with political theatre began somewhere around the 1980s, as part of her involvement with the women's movement. The theatre groups she is associated with are not shy of experimenting, or of asking searching, uncomfortable questions, or of taking a political stand. Her life in theatre gives deeper meaning to her activism by bringing together the politics of gender and sexuality with theatre practice:

> We live in a society where the woman's body is consistently subjected to shame or treated as an object of gaze. In theatre, the socially constructed images around the body are broken. When it is a trans body or a queer body, it becomes an even

bigger statement. Theatre lets you be free with your body, to own it.[140]

Theatre is also, Mangai discovered, 'democratic in the process, collective in aesthetics and absolutely participatory as a product.' It has enabled dialogue and negotiation between her artistic and activist personas: 'I have forever been a "devil's advocate",' she says. 'At an activists' meet, I would argue for artistic efforts; at an artists' meet, I would voice the concerns of the activist and the academic.'[141]

There is yet another dimension to Mangai's engagement with theatre, deepened by her research, her negotiations with classical texts, and her engagement with Tamil on multiple levels. 'It is indeed a pity,' she writes, 'that the Tamil tradition which is as ancient and classical as Sanskrit did not find a place in the construction of post-independent modern theatre …'[142] She goes on to describe her own rewarding experience when she took 'a gendered lens' to this rich material in the Tamil tradition—when, for instance, she directed the play *Avvai* by the Tamil poet and playwright Inquilab.[143] The play, a modern retelling of Avvai's story, reimagines Avvaiyar, the conventional wise old woman figure. And this Avvai, who celebrates love, life, song and drink, was brought to life on the stage as 'an

---

[140] Kavitha Muralidharan, 'Mangai and her theatre of liberation', *The Hindu*, 3 September 2020 (https://www.thehindu.com/entertainment/theatre/mangai-and-her-theatre-of-liberation/article32514603.ece).

[141] 'I have forever been a devil's advocate"', Interview with A. Mangai, LeftWord Blog (https://mayday.leftword.com/blog/post/i-have-forever-been-a-devil-s-advocate).

[142] A. Mangai, *Acting Up, Gender and Theatre in India, 1979 Onwards*, LeftWord, 2015, pp. 178–179.

[143] Tamil speakers know Makkal Palavar as 'Inkulab' or 'Ingulab'. The spelling has been Persianised for broader recognition.

exceptional female bard' by playwright Inquilab and theatre director Mangai.

For a long time, Mangai and I knew each other, reader to reader. The *Indian Cultural Forum* brought us together more directly. I recall badgering her to write for the Forum's site; she signed many of the statements the Forum released, a series of unhappy (though brave) signs of the times. But it was the camaraderie of reading and writing that finally led us to friendship. She read my novel *I Have Become the Tide* (2019) and wrote to me, describing it as 'an agit-prop novel'. I read the final draft of her English translation of Inquilab's *Avvai*.

I knew Mangai had taken up popular female figures from mythology and history and interpreted them as women with strong voices of their own. So Mangai's interest in Avvai did not surprise me. Nor did the fact that she expressed this connection with Avvai, Inquilab's *Avvai*, on the stage, as well as through a translation of the text. What struck me was the creative trio that came together as something of a 'team' in the text I read, and the play I was then moved to watch: Avvai, Inquilab, Mangai.

Avvai or Avvaiyar is a generic term in Tamil for a well-respected woman; the title refers to more than one poet. Apparently, there have been at least three Avvaiyars—poets in the female canon—at various points in Tamil history, from the Sangam period through medieval times. But there is only one figure that lives in the popular imagination: a bent old woman, stick in hand, always on the move, ready with advice for kings and commoners, old and young.

Inquilab's Avvai is somewhat different. In Mangai's words, 'Inquilab emphasises the values Avvai stood for—chieftains who protected their fold; nature in its highest bloom; people sharing resources; and women making choices and speaking their minds.'[144] Inquilab's Avvai is a strong woman, young, sensuous, creative, free; she is, quite naturally, going to take on the patriarchy.

Inquilab's work was fed by his rational outlook and his political commitment. In addition to being a poet and a professor of Tamil, Inquilab was an activist on several fronts. He was a communist; he was passionately anti-caste; he was a thoroughgoing rationalist. Even after his death in 2016, his worldview sent a reminder, like a precious legacy. In 2017, he was conferred, posthumously, the Sahitya Akademi Award. His family refused to accept the award; they were quite clear that Inquilab would have turned down any award from a government that 'does not act against communal and casteist elements'. The family's letter of refusal went on to say, 'Today, there is a major spurt of violence, classism, communalism and oppression. The persons who criticise and question the powers are executed in broad daylight … It [accepting the award] will be a betrayal to Inquilab's writings and the life led by him …'[145]

Avvai, Inquilab, Mangai. What brought them together as artists? And what are artists really meant to do? Mangai has a succinct answer: 'Artists are the conscience-keepers of

[144] 'Inquilab led a secular life until the end', *Indian Cultural Forum*, 8 April 2022 (https://indianculturalforum.in/2022/04/08/inquilab-led-a-secular-life-until-the-end/).

[145] 'Family of Tamil Poet Inquilab Refuses to Accept Sahitya Academy Award from a Govt That "Doesn't Act Against Communal & Casteist Elements",' *Outlook India*, 22 December 2017 (https://www.outlookindia.com/website/story/family-of-tamil-poet-inquilab-refuses-to-accept-sahitya-academy-award-from-a-gov/305843).

society.'[146]This was the gift I received through the play *Avvai*: I read, saw and heard an extraordinary collective of conscience-keepers. Avvai, a woman and artist reimagined for our times; Inquilab, a poetic communist and dramatist; and as translating curator of the printed page and the play onstage, Mangai.

8 April 2022

Githa Hariharan [GH]: This project—the play as well as the translation—is, as you say, on the 'cusp of the classical and the contemporary'. This is true on several levels—for the Avvai figure[147] from Sangam times to the statue on the Marina beach; for the play by Inquilab; and for your translation that negotiates both classical Tamil and the living language. Would you comment on how these strands come together?

A. Mangai [AM]: For Inquilab and myself, I think the flicker of this thought—of working with the Sangam classics—began from the contemporary; the demolition of the Babri Masjid, to be exact. The south of India, especially Tamil Nadu, did not experience the Partition and its aftermath. Also, mosques and dargahs have always remained part of our culture, irrespective of the religion you practise. I still remember how my grandmother, clad in her nine-yard saree in the brahminical style, would take us, her grandchildren, to Nagore Dargah. We lived in Nagappattinam. Velankanni and Nagore were very much part of my psyche.

---

[146] Ibid.

[147] Avvai is a legendary figure to whom several poems from the Sangam corpus are attributed. Her biography, entirely the work of popular tradition, maintains that the young poet sought, and received as a boon, direct transfer to a venerable age to avoid the demanding and subservient life of a young woman.

I am not sure what triggered Inquilab. He was born in a lower-caste Muslim family that practised medicine. His native place, Keezhakkarai, had the most glaring class differences among Muslims, who formed the majority in the area. Early in his life, he was influenced by the Dravidian movement, by Periyar and by Marxism. He led a secular life until the end. His decision that his body should be handed over to the hospital was only one of many such moves. And he was a professor in Tamil, steeped in classical literature; he was emboldened to use this great resource as a springboard. The passion with which he spoke of Avvai, traversing the land of the Tamil region with her bardic community, toddy-pot in hand, struck a chord in me. So, apart from making the figure of Avvai contemporary to us, the thrust was to also find alternative resources to Hindu mythological sources like the Ramayana and the Mahabharata.

Within the Tamil milieu, the play *Avvai* broke the image commonly held of Avvai as the old, grey-haired, hunch-backed, pious, didactic and celibate woman. The Avvaiyar statue on the Marina beach is essentially constructed from the 1953 film *Avvaiyar* by Gemini Studios and Vasan.[148] That film was produced primarily to counter *Parasakthi* [1952], which stood for the Dravidian ideology. Questioning the acceptable image of Avvai within patriarchy created, in turn, an Avvai who challenges the norms. She is young, sensuous, intelligent, nomadic, outspoken and unattached, except on her own terms.

Also, the text bridged the classical usage of Tamil with a language prevalent in the twentieth century. Inquilab is

---

[148] Subramaniam Srinivasan (1904–1969), more widely known as S.S. Vasan, was already a businessman and the publisher of *Ananda Vikatan* when, in 1940, he set up the Gemini Studios. He went on to direct films in Tamil, Hindi and Telugu, and in 1964 became the first person from the film world to be nominated to the Rajya Sabha.

essentially a poet. He walked into dramatic literature because of my prodding. His skills in poetry helped him create that bridge between the classical past and contemporary usage. I am not sure if the translation has fully captured that distinction.

GH: The use of the past for the present is a central preoccupation for creative work. Keeping the Avvai figure in mind, would you speak about the importance—and the challenges—of using the past in general, or figures from the past in particular, to make sense of the present?

AM: The use of the past for the present is like walking on thin ice. And there is also the prospect of a selective choice of the past, or a lack of criticality. India is paying a heavy price with the ghosts of the past vying with each other. I have also been sceptical of glorifying the most ancient as the most significant. That goes against the dialectics involved. But, despite all these apprehensions, we need to know our past; engage with it critically; learn and unlearn from it to build a meaningful, egalitarian, just society in the present. Basically, images from the past have been pressed into serving the interests of those in power.

Tamil is no exception. We can speak of the Tamil language as 'forever young'—which is partially true, since 'she' has survived till date and has not gone out of use in the way of other classical and semi-classical tongues like Sanskrit or Pali. Within the Tamil culture too, Kannagi reigns supreme as the chaste wife of a merchant husband who falls in love with a dancing girl, Madhavi. In most cases, the past has served to consolidate caste and religious differences, gender discrimination, and to validate untouchability, all in the name of gods and destiny! The alternative values within the culture are not highlighted. In fact, they are denied or covered up.

Avvai brings to the fore the life of Tamils when it was closest to nature, perhaps just when it was giving way to empires being formed. Inquilab emphasises the values Avvai stood for—chieftains who protected their fold, nature in its highest bloom, people sharing resources, and women making choices and speaking their minds. Avvai also witnessed the new hierarchies in play. Her poetry stands testimony to these. And the play leads us to engage with the past critically.

GH: From the craft point of view, did you have to work hard to balance an awareness of time past and present, while also compressing or collapsing time? I ask this especially because the text is meant to be staged, not just read.

AM: Structurally, the play works on this challenge in a linear fashion. The exploration of the Sangam Avvai texts is flanked by two scenes—the first one and the last. The former brings in the audience in relatively present times—schoolchildren learning by rote the texts ascribed to Avvaiyar, an eighteenth-century author who wrote didactic poetry—before it moves back into the Sangam age. It is the popular grandma Avvaiyar who leads us to the Sangam Avvai. The latter is set as a scene where the two Avvai-s meet and discuss their respective trajectories and end up meeting a new Avvai, a poet from Sri Lanka. These two scenes seem to be the prefix and suffix to the depiction of Sangam Avvai.

I think Inquilab's intention was to raise questions about the historiography of Tamil literature, and not stop with resurrecting the classical bard Avvai. Performatively, those two scenes helped me 'make and unmake' the mimetic ideal of art in the classical period. In fact, the contemporary ensemble of actors found that the ancient bardic community struck a chord with them—through all the clashes of ideas, the distribution of work, rehearsing their art before they present it, meeting people of varied classes and being 'roadies', documenting the rough-and-ready feel of their lives.

GH: That poems and songs live pretty much in the same place is something we are in danger of forgetting. Does theatre help reveal the intimate relationship between the two? Does work like Inquilab's, and theatre practice that uses forms like therukoothu,[149] remind us of this relationship?

AM: Theatre in India is total theatre—opera, ballet and drama combined. Till the mid-twentieth century, we had plays written with songs—implying they should be sung and danced, with the dialogue in prose. Of course, those of us who grew up on the staple of Western education forget this. Even in English literature, we know that Shakespeare needed to be sung, narrated, spoken and enacted. In post-Independence India, we have tried to provide an impetus to work with pre-colonial, ritualistic forms. 'Back to the roots' has been on the agenda of Indian theatre practices during the independence struggle and after. This is especially true of Indian regional language theatres, where it flows organically. In Tamil, when we decided to go back to the idiom of therukoothu, it added to the classical milieu we wanted to create—music, costumes, stylisation, balancing the classical and contemporary language. It heightened the energy and transported us to a new experience.

[149] A theatrical form of storytelling that combines spoken lines with music, song and dance. Traditionally, therukoothu performances took place on the move, as part of processions, and were distinct from kattaikoothu, overnight performances that unfolded in a fixed setting. Koothu performances originated in Tamil Nadu and eventually spread across much of South India.

With the English text at hand, more experiments are in order. I am excited to see how *Avvai* will inhabit English and other Indian languages like Hindi, Malayalam, or Kannada. Some languages will find resonances of Avvai with other poets in their own languages (perhaps not as ancient as hers), enriching the complex multi-layered cultures of India.

VAASANTHI

'I Continue to Write Because I Dare to Hope'

Consider this body of work written over forty years: as many as thirty novels, six short-story collections, three biographies, four volumes of journalistic articles and four travelogues in Tamil. That makes the count nearly fifty books. The numbers are astonishing enough, but there is also the variety of genres, and the wide range of subjects, from women's lives to political leaders to the Eelam war in Sri Lanka.

Surely this is the work of several women? Apparently not. How does this one woman, Vaasanthi, do it? She must have a racing pen; or two of them, because she writes in both Tamil and English. Maybe she needs two more, four in all; say a more 'balanced' pen to be a journalist, and a more 'wayward' pen to guide her imagination as she writes novels and stories.

Like many writers, she began by using her pen to describe something that disturbed her—the treatment of a widow in the extended family. She simply had to write about it; but she didn't want to hurt her family, so she assumed a pseudonym.

Pankajam became Vaasanthi the writer—the kind of writer who feels deeply about her subject.

Over the years, her stories and novels have dealt with the wider world, asking searching questions about places and lives new to her. Often, the fiction is built on a substantial foundation of research that has taken her not just to libraries, but to the field, to hear directly the stories of the people concerned. Her novel on the complex past and present of devadasis, *Vittu Viduthalaiyagi* (2012), translated into English by N. Kalyanraman as *Breaking Free* (2022), is an example. Vaasanthi's interviews and long conversations with these artists of another era brought home to her 'the wounds, agonies and humiliations suffered by those women—some of whom were great artists—over many generations …' This had 'a profound impact on their descendants … who have sought aggressively to reject the markers of their past.' As for the writer Vaasanthi, 'The shock of that discovery and the effect it has had on me over the years, along with my research as a journalist into the devadasis' art practice, gave me the impetus to write this novel.'[150]

By this time, as a mature writer dealing with complex subjects, Vaasanthi's other life—as a journalist—gave her the opportunity to research, and also to see the world, many worlds, up close. She learnt to be persistent: she sent Jayalalithaa a fax every day for ten years—in which time her subject had become Jayalalithaa—asking her repeatedly for an interview.[151] She became adept at understanding political players in Tamil Nadu—enabling her to write popular (and sometimes

[150] Vaasanthi, 'Afterword', *Breaking Free*, HarperCollins, 2022, p. 326.

[151] It didn't help. Vaasanthi went ahead and wrote her book on Jayalalithaa, and described it as a portrait rather than a biography.

controversial) biographies of Jayalalithaa, Karunanidhi and Rajnikanth. There is an empathy, a sensitivity in her approach to these figures, that ensures that she is never dogmatic or simplistic in her portrayals. In the Acknowledgements section of *Amma: Jayalalithaa's Journey from Movie Star to Political Queen,* she makes it clear that she has 'only tried to decipher Jayalalithaa's many-layered personality. She is too complex and reserved to reveal herself fully.'[152]

Her 'definitive' biography of Karunanidhi is notable for its meticulous research. And the research is used to make the story of a life comprehensive, complete with multiple contexts. There is the boy, the son of isai vellalar parents, drawn with memorable clarity; and the man with painful memories of caste discrimination: 'Why did his father, so talented and learned, have to stand at a respectful distance with his head bent and shoulders bare before much lesser men who sat on their teak wood swings chewing paan, just because of his caste?'[153] There is the man shaped by the secular principles of the Dravidian movement, but also the party leader and chief minister entangled in the compulsions of realpolitik.

In short, Vaasanthi the journalist is evident in her fiction as well as non-fiction. The journalist brings together individual stories, secrets hidden away in human nature, community histories, astute observation of the political terrain, and sharp commentary on social and cultural landscapes. She

---

[152] Ramakrishnan M., 'The enigma that is Amma: telling the Jayalalithaa story', *The Hindu*, 23 May 2016 (https://www.thehindu.com/books/books-reviews/The-enigma-that-is-Amma-telling-the-Jayalalithaa-story/article14335267.ece).

[153] Vaasanthi, *Karunanidhi: The Definitive Biography,* Juggernaut Books, 2020. Quoted in the extract published from the chapter 'Autumn of the Patriarch' in the *Indian Cultural Forum*, 20 May 2020 (https://indianculturalforum.in/2020/05/20/on-the-kalaignar/).

acknowledges the value of her experience as the editor of the Tamil edition of *India Today*:

> The best period of my writing/ journalistic career was during my ten years at *India Today*, which were both challenging and rewarding in the long run. Till my posting there, I just had a superficial knowledge of Tamil Nadu politics and the State, though I had been writing in Tamil and had become quite a well-known writer among the Tamil reading public. But I had one advantage—I was a familiar name that enabled me to easily access politicians, artists and common people. I did a number of pathbreaking stories that made *India Today* Tamil edition a highly respected weekly. My weekly columns received critical acclaim from readers as well as leaders of political parties. Karunanidhi would never miss my columns. He would call me the very next morning and express his views ...[154]

Years later, when Vaasanthi and I spoke, she was clear that she viewed all her writing, 'journalistic' or 'creative' as 'political acts'. I chose to use her short stories as the take-off point for our conversation. *Ganga's Choice and Other Stories* (2021), a collection of stories translated from Tamil into English,[155] begins with an intriguing question-and-answer dedication to her grandson. The five-year-old child 'asked a profound question, "Are we real?" I told him, "We are. Because we feel."'

---

[154] 'Meet the Author: Vaasanthi', *All About Book Publishing*, 7 October 2020 (http://www.allaboutbookpublishing.com/7329/meet-the-author-vaasanthi/).

[155] Translated by the author, Sukanya Venkataraman and Gomathi Narayan.

18 May 2022

Githa Hariharan (GH): The stories in the collection *Ganga's Choice and Other Stories* look closely at women's acts of resistance, but never without probing the human costs of choice—how difficult it can be to cut loose, even impossible sometimes. Indeed, the stories portray women who are defeated by fear as well as women who manage to overcome their fear, even if only for one triumphant moment. Would you say your stories make a painfully realistic assessment of the choices available to women?

Vaasanthi (V): I write about what I see happening around me, what I have observed in the course of my life's journey as a member of a large conservative family in my childhood, and as a daughter, a mother, a wife and a journalist. Also as a citizen of this country, a citizen with dreams and expectations and hopes for a better future. Fiction writers draw from lived or heard experiences or something they have witnessed and been moved by. My fiction writing began during my college days. It centred on the family and on gender discrimination within the four walls of home. The sorrow of the childless woman, the miserable life that widows live but silently accept as their fate—I wrote about these and other unspeakable wounds women have endured.

As a journalist, I had the opportunity to travel the length and breadth of Tamil Nadu. During the nineties I was the editor of the Tamil edition of *India Today* and that was when I lived in Tamil Nadu at a stretch for the first time. (I grew up in Karnataka and was never in Tamil Nadu, although I became a writer in Tamil.) My travels as a journalist served as an eye opener. I saw, from up close, a world I did not know—different cultural hues of course, but most sharply, the condition of women in a range of rural settings, the patriarchal pressures on them, and the mythological beliefs that are always directed at suppressing their freedom. The women I saw, the most vulnerable rural women, illiterate and dependent, were caught in this web. I could sense their anger and frustration at not being able to break free. All these impressions that I gained as a journalist stayed with me, in my memory, you could even say at a subconscious level of awareness. They emerged later when I was writing so I could weave them into short stories. This is how stories such as 'Murder', 'Poison' and 'Dance of the Gods' were born.

The young women who had migrated from villages to cities and worked as maids told me a different story. They too suffered from patriarchal pressures; they experienced class alienation. But the economic independence they enjoyed, at least to a certain extent, made them bolder. They could make decisions defying the accepted order of things. Writing about these people revealed to me the many stories hidden in their tears and silence. There is a redeeming factor in how they deal with their pressures. This is what stories like 'Ganga's Choice', 'Voice' and 'Mouse Trap' capture.

The stories had to be realistic. Some stories write the ending themselves, as in 'The Testimony'. I thought that was the honest way to portray them. I cannot write fairy tales. Yet even in a tragic ending, there is always a stream of hope. There is an undercurrent of redemption that comes through the women's realisation of oppression, through the rebellious thoughts in their minds, and the various reactions they have to these thoughts. Even with a woman putting an end to her life, her suicide is an act of protest and fury, a gesture of defiance as in the story 'Dance of the Gods'. The protagonist Panchali thinks of the many cages in the village, one for women during their menstrual cycle, another the kitchen. The cage is a metaphor that describes the status of women in our villages. I don't know how many women truly get to rebel and be free of the cages they live in, but my Panchali does. It is in the kitchen, in the end, that Panchali finds her route to escape from public humiliation, ridicule and betrayal. Her death is an expression of her refusal to succumb to the heartless patriarchal system.

GH: Your stories seize the contemporary moment, from the vilification of Muslims as terrorists, to the human tragedies created by the COVID lockdown. Is this the news-conscious journalist in you providing stories for the present moment?

V: Perhaps you are right. I began my career as a fiction writer. As a girl, I was deeply influenced by my maternal grandfather who was a Gandhian and an English teacher. He was a liberal, always deeply disturbed by discrimination in the name of caste, class, gender and religion. I developed an academic interest in the history and sociology of various states. For instance, I happened to reside in Northeastern India when my husband, an engineer and central government employee, was posted there. I found that the rest of India, including the Centre, was ignorant of the anger and aspirations of the people there who were ethnically different. When we were posted back to Delhi, I was thirsting to write journalistic articles on subjects that the Tamil readers were not familiar with. I was already a prolific writer of fiction in Tamil, and when the Tamil magazines requested me to write about events in the capital—Indira Gandhi's assassination being one such—I began to write quite a few journalistic articles in Tamil along with my fiction writing. It was a learning process. It helped me delve deeper into the way things unfurl in the political world and how the world keeps changing. From then on, I began to feel that no writer could remain apolitical.

I have been very deeply affected by the vilification of Muslims as terrorists—it is like a stigma that seems to have been stuck into the community deliberately. The fear and sense of alienation felt by my Tamil/Kannada Muslim friends; their mental agony and shock, all so clear in their silent gaze; their feeling of insecurity increased manifold. How can a writer not write about all this, describe and analyse such a social crisis? The images I saw of migrant labourers walking to their villages during the COVID lockdown left me devastated—I was disturbed to a degree that I could not explain. I had to give vent to my feelings. Call it being news-conscious or whatever, it was the natural reaction of a writer who takes things to heart.

GH: In this collection, I found the recurring contrast of urban and rural settings striking. In fact, the theme of the dislocated 'immigrant' seems to run like a linking thread throughout the collection, intersecting, of course, with gender, community and class. Would you like to comment?

V: Ours is a country of great contrasts. There are great divides between the urban and the rural, there is the gender divide, the communal divide, the class divide—division is all-pervading in the country no matter which language you speak. In a society that is becoming more unequal in every way, we become, metaphorically, immigrants—crossing over borders, over the line of control, breaking walls constructed by the system—first the family, clan and tribe, then the state. Crossing borders is a constant endeavour manifested in many forms of defiance. Paradoxically, some of these forms may appear cowardly or defeatist. But the fact that we endeavour is what is reassuring.

GH: Your stories travel all over India and speak powerfully of contemporary India. Would you say the changes you portray are generally for the worse? From poverty to inequality to the active exclusion of people, what sort of assessment do your stories make of the country today?

V: Creative writing is not only an aesthetic or artistic craft, but also a political act. I have been lucky to have travelled in most parts of India, and I have been overwhelmed by the feeling of oneness with people of different regions speaking different tongues. I grew up in Karnataka in an amazingly secular and inclusive atmosphere and still carry the richness of that experience in my heart. I am pained when I see that the scene has changed. As a journalist and a creative writer, I am deeply conscious of my duty as a writer. I am aware of what is going on around me—economic and gender inequality, the growing fear experienced by the minorities, the draconian sedition laws that still exist from colonial times and that often get misused by the state. Writers write about what affects them deeply; they try to decipher the meaning of what they perceive. That is my effort in these stories—I am trying to understand why people behave the way they do. It is a fascinating journey, at once humbling and baffling. I believe there is always a ray of hope in the writer's mind. We are always looking for a glimmer of redemption and retribution. A reviewer said of my stories that they 'conclude on a certain tone of triumph—sometimes darkly shadowed—(but a) triumph of a sort, nevertheless'. The humane, in one form or the other, redeems not only the characters, but also the readers.

I have faith in the youth of today who are more intelligent and better informed than all of us when we were young. They are politically aware and conscious of what is wrong and what is right. I hope and believe there is light at the end of the tunnel and beyond. I continue to write because I dare to hope.

VOLGA

Building Solidarity Through Sisterhood

Popuri Lalitha Kumari, the award-winning Telugu writer, feminist and activist, uses Volga as her pen name. The name, she told me, is personal *and* political. Lalitha's sister was named Volga, after a brave Soviet soldier who fought the Nazis. When her sister died, Lalitha, just sixteen at the time, became Volga when she wrote. This way, her parents still had two daughters, and the name was apposite. It suits her politics, says Volga.

Indeed, the pen name is something of a signpost for Volga's work. It signals the invariable entanglement of the personal and the political, so central to the development of a feminist worldview. At first, there was a trio of women, two of them memories, who resided in this small space of a two-syllable name. But even a small space can aspire to become spacious, grow into a long river, let an entire sisterhood of women flow from past to present, all striving for emancipation.

This is what Volga made a commitment to: bringing together the work of politics and feminism with the work of the imagination. Her journey to this point was not exactly straightforward, nor easy. She was part of quite a range of leftist movements at one time or another, from the Students Federation of India (SFI) to the Naxalbari movement of the CPI (ML) and later, the Revolutionary Writers Association, also a Marxist-Leninist group. She moved on in the 1980s, looking for ways to create a space in which she could engage, as a woman, with both politics and literature. As she struggled to make sense of her personal, political and literary lives, she became a forerunner in constructing a feminist framework for the political discourse of Telugu literature.

Her early novels *Sahaja* (1986) and *Svechcha* (1987)[156] questioned the extent of freedom a woman can experience within marriage. *Svechcha*, in particular, sold in large numbers; it was also controversial and led to intrusive speculation on her personal life.

But Volga was nothing if not a fighter. She was well on her way to creating a 'women's space', whether it was through a resource centre for women, or her translations, or her writing of non-fiction and fiction. This women's space, Volga discovered, is necessarily diverse, with room for debate as well as unanswered questions. In the case of her fiction, this meant that 'Volga's stories are layered with collective pasts, and varying memories of the past. Equally plural are the ways to frame this raw material to understand what a life in the present is all about, and where it should move ahead to make more complete individuals, and more egalitarian societies.'[157]

---

[156] Translated into English by Ari Sitaramayya as *A Quest for Freedom*, National Book Trust, 2003.

[157] This is what I wrote about Volga when the *Indian Cultural Forum* published a piece on *The Liberation of Sita* winning the Laadli Media Award for Gender Sensitivity in Fiction for 2017. 'Liberating the Sitas of India',

Volga wrote about women's lives and their struggles to be full-fledged, free partners in the political, professional and personal spheres. But there remained a cultural context that she had to address if she was to look at women's lives in a continuum: mythology. So she built on the 'liberal tradition' of Telugu literature—of questioning the gender and caste assumptions of mainstream myths. The collection, *Vimuktha* (2011) translated as *The Liberation of Sita* (2016), imagines Sita's life after she was banished from Ayodhya. Sita's life gains new meaning as she learns from the lives that other women from the Ramayana, from Surpanakha to Ahalya, have made for themselves. What begins as survival strategy in these stories, deepens into an exploration of what freedom from man-made norms could mean.

(Such exploration comes with danger in our times. In 2016, the Telugu newspaper *Andhra Jyoti* published a story by Volga called 'Asokam', in which Ravana's wife, Mandodari, dares to argue with him and also reject the practices associated with widowhood. Volga got some threatening phone calls about writing stories that would 'cause harm to the nation' ...)

Through this continuum of women's lives and women's stories, from mythical settings to the world we live in, Volga's own understanding of the complex category of Woman has developed, and quite specifically in the Indian context. She traces this development with characteristic self-awareness:

> When I started in the 80s, reading and writing at a feverish pace, I looked at women as a homogenous category—that all women were one, a sort of 'workers of the world unite' kind of understanding. Then in the 1990s, caste emerged as

---

19 August 2017 (https://indianculturalforum.in/2017/08/19/liberating-the-sitas-of-india/).

> a major issue—maybe because of the Karamchedu incident[158] and the debates that followed. I wrote *Aakasamlo Sagam* (*Half the Sky,* 1990), with a Dalit heroine, and with the sense that all women are not the same and that caste plays a major role. Yet, when I did an anthology of feminist poetry *Neeli Meghalu (Blue Clouds)* in 1993, there weren't many Dalit women writers in it. There were, in fact, not many of them writing then with a Dalit-feminist consciousness. Yet, I felt that it was a shortcoming of the anthology. Gradually I realised the broad scope of feminism which includes not only just caste, but also several other factors—religion, race, gender (LGBT). Feminism has given me that power to accept, understand and integrate differences. The inclusiveness that I learnt from feminism—I try to express in my writings.[159]

It is this inclusiveness that fuels her hope for the future. One source of hope is writing by 'Dalit and minority women … They are straightforward and write without hesitation about their sufferings, protests or dissent … When I hear their voices, I feel a lot of hope …'[160]

I first knew of Volga as an activist in the women's movement. We became friends through the *Indian Cultural Forum* and through each other's writing. She translated my novel *I Have Become*

---

[158]On 17 July 1985, in Karamchedu village of Prakasam district in Andhra Pradesh, several dalits belonging to the madiga caste were killed by upper caste landlords belonging to the kamma caste. Ibid.

[159] T. Vijay Kumar, 'Volga: An Interview', *The Liberation of Sita*, Translated from the Telugu by T. Vijay Kumar and C. Vijayasree, HarperCollins, 2016, p. 117.

[160]'Dakshin Literary Festival 2020: How minority women's words give Volga hope', *The New Indian Express*, 23 December 2020 (https://www.newindianexpress.com/nation/2020/dec/23/how-minority-womens-words-give-volga-hope-2240211.html).

the Tide into Telugu; I read and admired her work in English translation—including *Svechcha*, *Yashobuddha* (2017)[161] and *Vimuktha*. *Vimuktha* (*The Liberation of Sita*) yields new meanings every time I go back to the stories in the book. More recently, I read the English translation of *Gamaname Gamyam* (2016). Translated by Vasanth Kannabiran, *The Sickle and the Scalpel* (2022) is based on the extraordinary life and times of Dr Komarraju Atchamamba (1906–1964)—one of the first women doctors in the country, a member of the Communist Party of India, and a pioneer for women's emancipation in Andhra. Capturing the period of social reform in pre-Independence Andhra, through the freedom struggle, the novel foregrounds the rise of the modern Indian woman and her struggle for rights and recognition, alongside the rise of communism and the left in the newly formed nation.

My conversation with Volga used this novel as the springboard for her to talk about building a nuanced sisterhood that can take us closer to a more 'inclusive solidarity'.

23 February 2023

Githa Hariharan (GH): *The Sickle and the Scalpel* is an apt title for the translation of the novel *Gamaname Gamyam*. The title signposts two powerful paths to greater freedom—the scalpel as symbolic of a woman's advancement through a career, but also as a vocation that enables her to contribute to society at large; and the sickle as symbolic of the ideology that drives both the individual and the collective towards greater equality and freedom for all. It's a powerful link between two symbols

---

[161] Translated into English as *Yashodhara* by P.S.V. Prasad, HarperCollins, 2019.

rich with possibilities. Would you comment on the ways in which you have addressed this link between the personal and political in this novel, as well as in the rest of your work?

Volga: This novel, like many of my other works, explores how women realise, through their life struggles, that the personal is political. I try to capture their journey in the path towards this realisation.

The Sickle and the Scalpel draws on the life of Dr Komarraju Acchamamba. She was, perhaps, the first woman doctor in the India of her times to speak and write about health—women's health in particular—as a political issue. She was a founding member of the Communist Party of India. Every step and stage in her life could be described as political, including her childhood. We talk of the link between the personal and the political. Sometimes, many times, it seems to me that it is not just a link; it seems both are one. Even what we like and dislike, which may appear purely personal, have a political basis. Aren't these personal preferences deeply dependent on the socioeconomic factors of our backgrounds?

Liberation from oppression is the key issue. But liberation from the position of an oppressor, whether that of a man or a member of an upper caste, is critical too. Revolutions have mainly focussed on liberating people from oppression. They have not given enough importance to understanding how oppressive one can become in the name of the revolution, or in the process of revolution or reform. It is even more difficult to understand patriarchal oppression. Oppression has many layers. I am trying to peel away at least this one layer, patriarchal oppression, in my work.

GH: In *The Sickle and the Scalpel*, there are moving references to male solidarity with, and indeed active contribution to, women's achievement. The best example is Sharada's historian father. He is not only confident that his daughter will take care of her brother's education and career, he also thinks of her as 'a great hope that guides my life.' He says to his wife, 'Our daughter should create history, not write history like me.' How much of this character is based on a real person? Or is he almost entirely an ideal?

Volga: We need male solidarity. We know that people, both men and women, suffer from inequality. We should work hand in hand because the whole struggle is to have peace among genders. Men may have limitations in understanding what women want. But even then, how can we ignore the men who struggle for women's equality?

The father character in *The Sickle and the Scalpel* is real. Komarraju Lakshmana Rao was a historian. His sister, Bhandaru Acchamamba,[162] inspired him in many ways. She was the first short story writer in Telugu; she wrote historical booklets; she organised women into Sanghas. She died looking after victims of the plague. Lakshmana Rao gave his sister's name to his daughter. He believed in her intellectual and physical capabilities and her energy. There were people like him who loved *and* believed in their daughters.

GH: One of the recurring questions in *The Sickle and the Scalpel* is about modernity—the Indian version, the woman's version. So much confusion remains about what is 'modern' and what its value continues to be in our times. What is Sharada's vision

---

[162] Bandaru Acchamamba (1874–1904) was an early feminist historian and organiser of women's associations, starting with Coastal Andhra in 1902. Her biographical account of thirty-four women was published in 1901 under the title *Abaala Saccharitra Ratnamala* (A garland of great women's life histories).

of a modern Indian woman in her time, pre-Independence and in the early years of the nation? And all these years later, yours?

Volga: Modernity—what a puzzle it is, and how colonialism and its cultural imposition have given us the runaround with this word! I think we are still trying to figure out what modernity actually means. Before Independence, people had many clear ideas about modernism. *Modern* meant rational thinking, believing in equality, believing in liberty. It meant the intent and action to change society, through education for instance. Women had many dreams around the idea of the modern. Now we have fewer dreams about it. We even use the word less frequently, though we still engage with the idea. I think that the meaning of the idea changes, depending on who is defining it. Now post-modernism has also lost its sheen.

In Telugu, the word 'modern' carries all the previous meanings, but not when used to describe contemporary women. If we use 'modern' in a Telugu sentence now, it often has a satirical connotation, especially with reference to how a woman is dressed or how she conducts herself.

My vision of a modern woman? She is a simple, honest woman who understands the power structures of contemporary society. This modern woman steps forward to fight inequalities in whatever form she chooses.

GH: *The Sickle and the Scalpel* is based on the life of Dr Komarraju Acchamamba (1906–1964), doctor, communist, and a leader of the women's movement. How did you combine history, fiction, and the progressive ideas—as well as critical questions—that you and Acchamamba share? How much of Sharada is Acchamamba and how much of her is you?

Volga: I think the critical questions you refer to are still there, unanswered from her generation to the present day. I wrote the novel as a process of searching for answers. The character Sharada is, I can say, completely Acchamamba. When I began the novel, I thought some fictional elements would be necessary, and I changed her name and the names of her family members. But when I completed the novel, I realised that Sharada is Acchamamba and I didn't use (or need to use) any of my abilities to write fiction. Maybe I should have claimed that 'All the characters in this novel are real. There are no fictional characters or events in this novel, only the dialogue is in my words. The thoughts and meanings belong to the real people in the novel. Only the words are mine.'

As for the similarity between Sharada-Acchamamba and me: I cannot reach the heights she did. There may be some similarities—I too was part of the left, then I came out of it. But Acchamamba's energy, her magnanimity, her selflessness—all these are unreachable for me. I can say though that I learnt many things from her.

GH: Both the mythical women you write about—say Sita in *The Liberation of Sita* (2016)—and the real women—say Sharada in *The Sickle and the Scalpel*—are in search of control over their lives, choices and relationships. But arguably, your Sita fares somewhat better than Sharada in her quest for freedom, and in her subversion of notions of love and sacrifice. Is it easier for a writer to visualise a mythical woman realising herself rather than a woman from history or fiction?

Volga: I think so. Actually, a writer has quite a bit of freedom when writing about mythology. Of course, she has great responsibility too, partly because our mythology is deeply rooted in religion. And partly because of the way the fundamentalists and the right-wing react to mythology as well as religion. It's not that we are afraid. But if we are not careful as writers, the whole debate or discourse we want to engage with gets sidelined. So we have to figure out ways to make freedom and responsibility work together.

When Chalam[163] was writing, he had much more freedom than we do. (He wrote from 1925 to 1975.) His way of dealing with mythology is hilarious and thought-provoking. My approach is different—it's not humorous. And I do not ignore the original text completely. I want to retain the original flavour of the characters. I don't imagine Sita as a woman of modern thought from her childhood, or Ahalya as a wise woman from her early years. Their sufferings and struggles make these women strong, wise and free. Readers also go through this process as they relate to the struggle and the hard-earned freedom of the characters and hopefully, they grow stronger.

So freedom, responsibility, strategy, purpose—so many things work together consciously or unconsciously. In Ahalya's story, it works unconsciously, as it does in Surpanakha's strategy. In Renuka's or Urmila's, it works consciously.

GH: The rewriting of myth helps you to engage with some deeply philosophical questions in the context of a better life for women. In *The Liberation of Sita*, I was struck by Surpanakha's attempt to redefine beauty and self-esteem. She says, 'Gradually I learned to love my hands. I learned how to create, work and serve with these hands.' From the passive site of beauty, the face, which can merely be looked at, she progresses to her hands, active makers of beauty. From appearance, inviting gaze, the woman develops into someone who is recognised for

---

163 Gudipati Venkatachalam (1894–1979), a writer of novels, short stories and non-fiction—including his memoir *Chalam* in 1970—was one of the most influential figures in modern Telugu. His advocacy of women's education and of relations based on love rather than the traditional family arrangement made him controversial, a role that he embraced.

her work. From an ornament, she grows into a creator. Would you comment on how you imagined Surpanakha and rewrote her story, independent of a relationship with a man?

Volga: The characters and events are already there. We have to interpret them—or subvert them—so they gain new meaning. I have seen many Surphanakhas in contemporary society. Violent incidents that may leave women survivors mutilated, women disfigured by knives and acid. I have seen many of these women recovering, surviving with dignity and beauty and great courage. Though they may not express their survival in a philosophical way, their lives teach us a philosophy of life and a love of labour. Surpanakha represents all those women.

GH: Again, whether in myth or real life, women's strength—and their journey towards self-realisation—involves the individual woman connecting with other women and learning from them. Would you comment on the importance of this sisterhood, as well as its limitations, given caste, community, class?

Volga: Sisterhood is very important for liberation. Patriarchy, which is strongly based on caste, religion and class, divides women along those lines. This division strengthens all the oppressive factors and holds patriarchy together. Patriarchy is very deceptive: it knows how to divide and rule. It operates various power structures and hierarchies in such a way that we, who are prisoners, willingly guard our chains. We protect the walls we are imprisoned in. If we want to break or try to break these walls, we are beset by doubt. We doubt each other. It is not our fault. Patriarchy actively works to make us feel insecure. To understand and join our hands together in a joint struggle is not an easy task. Nowadays it seems almost impossible. Still, there is no other way but to go forward. We have to come together, understand each other, clear our doubts openly, fight our fears without inhibition. The situation is getting worse every day. We have to build sisterhood and solidarity on an urgent basis.

GH: The book *The Sickle and the Scalpel*—and many of our actual experiences over the years—show how difficult it is to *live* an egalitarian ideology. I am referring, of course, to how deeply men (and sometimes, women) have internalised patriarchal norms despite their location at the progressive end of the political spectrum. And we women of a particular class or caste or community background are also continuously learning that not only do gender issues manifest quite differently for working class women, but also for dalit women, or adivasis, or Muslim women. You have addressed these slippery questions through your writing, but also through your activism and research. How do we work towards a broad front among women, but also among both men and women in progressive movements, without suppressing voices or risking identarian divisions?

Volga: This is not a simple question and there is no simple answer. We have to learn to discuss and debate. We should not become like our enemies while fighting them. Remember what the poet Audre Lorde said? We cannot destroy the enemy's mansion with the enemy's weapons.[164] We have to find creative ways to do that; we have to evolve new strategies.

---

[164] This was at a conference held at the New York Institute for the Humanities in 1984, where Audre Lorde (1934–1992) found that she was the sole panellist representing the black lesbian point of view. Her precise words were: 'The master's tools will never dismantle the master's house. They may allow us temporarily to beat him at his own game, but they will never enable us to bring about genuine change.' The struggle against racism was not separate from that against homophobia, and those targeted by hate

There is so much to be done. We need to make our male comrades realise they are patriarchal in their thoughts and actions. We need to help upper-caste women and men to free themselves from their oppressive behaviour, language and attitude. There are no readymade answers—struggle is the only answer. We have to keep going ahead. If there is a wall, break it. If there is a sea, swim.

GH: You have spoken of a liberal tradition of questioning our epics on the basis of caste and gender, especially in Telugu literature. Is there anything left of this, given the growing intolerance of questioning, speculation and works of imagination?

Volga: Yes. There is space still which we have to protect. We have to grapple with intolerance with daring, intelligence as well as a sense of responsibility. Maybe we cannot write like Chalam or Tripuraneni Ramaswamy[165] in our times, but we can still find ways to challenge intolerance.

GH: You have experience of collectives fighting for the right to dissent—such as the Revolutionary Writers' Association.[166]

---

should not comply with the oppressor's design of separating one group from another (https://collectiveliberation.org/wp-content/uploads/2013/01/Lorde_The_Masters_Tools.pdf).

[165] Tripuraneni Ramaswamy (1887–1943) was a poet, lawyer, playwright and rationalist. His verse attacked blind faith, while as a social reformer he devised a simple and inexpensive wedding ceremony, vivaha vidhi, used by him to officiate at many weddings.

[166] The Viplava Rachayitala Sangram, popularly known as Virasam, was set up in 1970 by a group of Telugu writers inspired by the peasant uprisings in Naxalbari and Srikakulam. In 2021 it was banned by the Telengana government as one of sixteen organisations accused of 'waging war on the state' (https://www.siasat.com/telangana-govt-bans-revolutionary-writers-association-15-other-orgs-2127992/).

How do we strengthen these organisations that back movements as well as freedom of speech?

Volga: We should set up new collectives. Build new movements. Have clarity about whether you want to *back* the movement, or you want to *be* the movement. A lack of clarity on this point has led to the loss of both the purpose and the base of many people's organisations.

GH: I know how difficult it is to balance the demands of writing fiction with the day-to-day involvement in political causes as well as academic research. How did you, and how do you, manage this?

Volga: You respond to the need of the hour—if you need to run, you do it.

GH: You have probably answered this question a thousand times, but let me ask about your pen name, Volga. And how does Lalitha change when she sits down to write and becomes Volga?

Volga: The name is personal and political. It began as a political one in my family and became personal to me. My father called my older sister Volga. She was born in 1946, after the Second World War. That day, the newspaper carried a story about a red-army soldier named Volga; the story was about her courage in fighting with the Nazis. My father was inspired by the story and named my sister Volga. My dear sister died when I was sixteen. I had begun writing poems by that time. I took her name as my pen name. Volga is alive. I am alive. So my parents still have two daughters. That name suits my politics too.

RITU MENON

Do Women Have a Country?

The sixties, a politically charged decade, offered many young people the exciting possibility of change. This was the decade in which Ritu Menon got a degree from Miranda House in Delhi, then went on to study at Vassar, a women's college in the US. American campuses were, at the time, rich grounds for movements—whether for civil rights, or against the Vietnam War. This was also the political context for an incipient women's movement. The sixties (and early seventies), Ritu has told me in our conversations over the years, will always serve as a 'marker' for her own personal trajectory. These decades led her to feminism. They led her to the world of books, a world viewed in the light of feminism. Both feminism and books, inextricably linked, served as an impetus to change. The book, she told me once, 'articulates the movement'.

Her experience in the US gave her a ringside view of the early stirrings of the women's movement in the West, and its link with the world of books. Speaking of the 1970s, Ritu points out that

> … the three movements—women's, women's studies and 'women in print'—were products of the 1970s. They provided an impetus to the realignment in perspective that considers gender as a crucial lens to look at things from. Although the history of the former two have been well documented and researched, the 'women in print' movement, which accompanied and reinforced the other two, has received less attention till date …
>
> The 'women in print' movement was made up of feminist presses, feminist book stores, reviewing periodicals, designers, librarians, binders, and even printers, and they formed an alternative to mainstream publishing.[167]

Returning to India, she worked in publishing in Delhi, on an imprint that was 'to focus on women'—it was too soon for the word 'feminist' in mainstream Indian publishing. Then came a landmark moment. In 1984 Ritu and Urvashi Butalia decided to set up a feminist press. Friends in the business, incidentally all men, reacted to the idea:

'Women's writing, not even a footnote.'

'Look, girls, take my advice. Do a bit of fact-finding.'

'Is there enough writing? What will you publish after the first year or two?'

A kind one summed it up: 'It's a risk.' And a blunter one pronounced, 'Stupid.'

I would love to know what these well-meaning gents thought when they saw the substantial publishing list built by the first feminist press in India and South Asia, Kali for Women. Surely, they must have seen that this was no ordinary

---

[167] 'Ritu Menon on feminist publishing and alternative knowledges', *Indian Cultural Forum*, 25 March 2021 (https://indianculturalforum.in/2021/03/25/ritu-menon-on-feminist-publishing-and-alternative-knowledges/).

publishing enterprise? To begin with, Kali defined itself as 'feminist', which meant it had to go beyond producing books to attempt what Ritu calls 'development activity'—consisting of links with other women's groups across South Asia, and participation in workshops as well as activism, whether on the streets or in the courts. This was, of course, in addition to developing a body of work, of feminist analysis. A close association with feminist academics and activists in Pakistan, Sri Lanka and Bangladesh led to publishing a growing number of authors from these countries, and to a recognition of the shared histories as well as ruptures across the region.

The publishing venture was small but independent. Asked about the 'joys' of independent publishing, Ritu said,

> I can develop a list the way I want to. If I had been part of a larger publishing house, I would never have been able to initiate the series I called *Arabesque*. It is not economically viable, but it is a literary, political and personal commitment.
>
> I am able to introduce readers in India to some of the most fantastic writing that is available currently from a region in the world that we know very little about and strangely enough, have very little curiosity about, even though historically India has had strong links with West Asia. We are going to publish a book of testimonies by Palestinian women prisoners in Israeli prisons. It is an act of bearing witness to the struggles of people who have been under occupation for over 50 years.[168]

There was a great deal of learning en route, with the results reaped by readers, writers and mainstream publishers. Fiction

[168] Chintan Girish Modi, 'The Ritu Menon interview | Feminist publishing is a development activity. It is not just about producing books', *Firstpost*, 13 July 2021 (https://www.firstpost.com/art-and-culture/the-ritu-menon-interview-feminist-publishing-is-a-development-activity-it-is-not-just-about-producing-books-9796791.html).

in translation, for instance, now 'discovered' as viable by big publishers, was a conscious choice for smaller presses like Kali, wanting to respond to the multilingual nature of Indian literature as well as to day-to-day life.

Overall, there was the constant learning of what feminism can be:

> Feminism has never had a singular definition. It has always been fluid, open and evolving. There is no authoritative voice, high priestess or presiding deity. There is no foundational work that everyone has to prescribe to. It has no sworn allegiances. And it has changed from place to place.[169]

Spurred by the momentum of the movement, Kali, as well as its founders Ritu and Urvashi, were also engaging with research and writing that would bring together individual and collective experiences of women in the subcontinent. One of the most significant of these projects was to do with the Partition, that great map still burdened with unheard voices and half-told stories. Urvashi put together a major volume of testimonies in *The Other Side of Silence: Voices from the Partition of India* (1998). Earlier the same year, Ritu, in collaboration with Kamla Bhasin, focused on women's narratives, in *Borders and Boundaries: Women in India's Partition,* counterpointing their voices with official accounts. Both books were important signposts in a feminist historiography of Partition, inaugurating a serious reconsideration of how that history should, and could, be written.

The years of publishing women's stories—listening to their voices, hearing their stories—must have prepared Ritu for her desire to write women's lives. She chose women whose lives

---

[169] Ibid.

encompassed nonconformist choices, creative work, and an engagement with public space to express their view of the world. Ritu says she wanted to try something new, something which may approximate 'a feminist biography'. *Out of Line* (2014), her book on Nayantara Sahgal, is subtitled 'A literary and political biography'. In 2021, Ritu published her *Zohra! A Biography in Four Acts*.

Zohra Sehgal (1912–2014) spanned an Indian century of the arts and became, within the country and abroad, the only woman to make a mark in virtually all the performing arts, with the sole exception of music. In *Zohra! A Biography in Four Acts* (2021), Ritu Menon traces her remarkable journey—from travelling to Germany to learn modern dance at the age of eighteen, to the unconventional grandmother she played on stage and screen till well past the age of eighty.

Soon after the book was published, Ritu and I spoke about the woman Zohra; her times or context, whether in India or England; and the art of biography.

2 August 2021

Githa Hariharan (GH): The most obvious word that comes to mind when talking about Zohra Sehgal is 'unconventional', whether we consider her life choices in her times, or her work. Would you sum these up, bringing out the 'breakthroughs', but also the challenges?

Ritu Menon (RM): Actually, more than unconventional, I would say she was truly courageous. It took a particular kind of courage, also confidence, to break the mould and strike out on her own at the age of eighteen. To enrol in a dance school in Germany, an unfamiliar country, without the language, without the cushion of family or friends, without instant communication—remember, this was 1931.

And rather than breakthroughs, I prefer to think of them as decisive moments that became turning points in her life. Joining Uday Shankar's Dance Company[170] and touring with him. Then, being part of Prithviraj Kapoor's Prithvi Theatres.[171] Zohra always said that it was Dada (Shankar) and Papaji (Kapoor), both creative powerhouses, who were her inspiration. She was lucky to have been at the right place at the right time. On her part, she intuited (or realised) that performing with them meant being part of something pioneering.

Her real challenges, both personal and professional, were what she encountered in mid-century England as a fifty-year-old Asian woman, a single mother, trying to make a breakthrough in a field that was notoriously cut-throat and close-knit. It was actually in England, where she had no godfathers or benefactors, that she came into her own. Long before BritAsian became fashionable.

---

[170] Without any formal training in dance, Uday Shankar (1900–1977) created a fusion of classical and folk-dance forms, which also drew on painting, sculpture and his interactions with performance artists in Europe, as a new form that he called 'Hi dance'. In 1931, he founded his dance company in Paris, initially known as 'Uday Shankar and his Hindu Ballet'. Joined by Zohra Sehgal in 1935, the company toured widely in Europe and America. It had an enormous influence on the reception of Indian dance in the West, and also on the performance and presentation of both religious and secular dance forms within India.

[171] Prithvi Theatres was the name of the travelling repertory company founded in 1942, with which Prithviraj Kapoor (1906–1972) toured the country for fourteen years, putting on plays in Hindustani at a time when he was at the height of his cinematic success. After his death, his son Shashi Kapoor formed a trust to continue his work. The trust built a theatre in Juhu, Mumbai, now famous as the Prithvi Theatre.

GH: Many of our readers will recall her as the mischievous and lovable grandmother figure. In some ways, this figure recalls the old woman from our tales who is free to say a great deal because of her age, and perhaps because she is 'liberated' from the sexual space in the eyes of the conventional community. Do you think Zohra humanised this figure in ways beyond the stereotype?

RM: More than humanise, I'd say she rejected the Dadi stereotype, remade her as a character and rescued her from becoming a cliché. And it was this irascible, wacky, unpredictable Granny whom audiences responded to spontaneously, so much so that roles started being written for her. There hasn't been a granny like her in television since.

GH: I want us to pay a little attention to her relationship, as a dancer and an actress, to the body as a medium, but also to language. Would you comment on the view that much of her power came from a trained body, her voice, and her way with words, from Urdu to English?

RM: Anyone in the performing arts, but especially those who go onstage, know that their body is their most vital asset. For Zohra, discipline, training, her riyaz, could never be compromised or neglected. It's what enabled her to perform—and perform supremely well—till her late 90s. I don't know whether her facility with English and Urdu contributed significantly to the strength of her performances, because really, it was her whole being that spoke—voice, gesture, movement, eyes, hands, stillness ... In the film *Partition* [1987] she doesn't speak more than a few words, but her performance is electrifying.

GH: In these jingoistic times, it is especially important for us to understand the value of a 'hyphenated' cultural life. How much of an interplay do you think there was between her work in India and in London?

RM: Not very much, really. The hyphenation, if we want to call it that, was more evident in England than in India, and the better part of Zohra's career as an actor was in the former. But yes, her success in England did mean she got noticed in India, especially after she came back for good in 1987.

GH: Zohra had progressive views and lived an unconventional life. She worked and lived among the politically committed in her IPTA[172] days, for instance. But her politics remain a little cloudy in the book—did she ever take an interest in using her voice, as an actress or a woman or a citizen, for political causes, whether in India or the UK?

RM: Zohra's stint with IPTA was quite short-lived and in fact when P.C. Joshi asked her to take charge of the Party's Cultural Squad, she declined, saying she was an actor, not an activist. As far as I'm aware she was fairly apolitical. I wasn't able to find much evidence of her being politically engaged when, for instance, there was a great churning in England in the 1960s, seventies and eighties. She was there, but distant from it all. Actually, of all the siblings, it was Hajrah, Zohra's older sister, who was explicitly political; she was a communist. In Zohra's case, I think the one political decision she took was to opt for India, not Pakistan, post-Independence. She and Hajrah stayed back but the others moved to Pakistan.

GH: The book resonates, as does Zohra's life, with larger-than-life women and men with ideas, talent and achievement.

---

[172] The Indian People's Theatre (IPTA) was formed in 1943. Zohra Sehgal joined IPTA two years later.

Who among these, other than Uday Shankar and Prithviraj, influenced her and gave her a sense of 'belonging'?

RM: Her formative influences were Shankar and Kapoor. She greatly admired and respected the professionalism she found in theatre, film and television in England, so, more than individuals, I think the dedication and seriousness of purpose she encountered there were important influences.

GH: You have now written two biographies, each of an outstanding woman artist. You refer eloquently, in your Preface to *Zohra!* to the difficulty of separating the dancer from the dance. Your challenge is to 'see the face behind the mask'. Would you tell us more about this challenge and your strategies to meet it? And because we tend to get quite a few hagiographies in India, how do you keep a biography from becoming one?

RM: We're new to biography as a genre here, so whatever I say is tentative, especially as I'm trying something even newer—feminist biography. What does this entail? How should I approach my subject? How much should I reveal and how much of her life should remain private? How much detail should I go into?

You speak about strategies. I ask, 'What are my responsibilities as a feminist biographer?' In Zohra's case, the two main problems I encountered were her celebrity status, and the fact that she had already written and published her memoirs. How was I to navigate both facts? Then, she was no longer alive, so I could neither verify anything nor probe more deeply.

I decided that I would 'ignore' her celebrity status for the time being, see her as a woman in her times, locate her firmly in her context, in order to highlight what for me were the important questions. What were the circumstances in which she arrived at her decisions, made her choices? For example, if Partition hadn't taken place, would she have made her career as a dance teacher, her original ambition, and her one 'regret'. And so on.

The second was to try and see her through other people's eyes—colleagues, other professionals, family, friends. Wherever possible. And then, as with Nayantara,[173] never to speculate. One must, as a biographer, be sympathetic to one's subjects, but one cannot be overawed by them. They're human, after all.

In 2023, Ritu published India on Their Minds: 8 Women, 8 Ideas of India, *a collection of writings by eight women who witnessed and participated in the events leading up to India's independence from colonial rule. These women, through their short stories, novels, essays, memoirs and autobiographies, documented the birth of the nation and its aftermath, reflecting on the impact of these events on individual lives. Commemorating the seventy-fifth anniversary of India's independence, Ritu wondered what 'country' meant to them, and how they articulated their relationship to it in their writing.*

In this conversation, Ritu and I speak of the many-layered personal and political voices of eight different women: Nayantara Sahgal (b. 1927), Captain Lakshmi Sahgal (1914–2012), Rashid Jahan (1905–52), Ismat Chughtai (1915–91), Qurratulain Hyder (1927–2007), Attia Hosain (1913–98), Kamlaben Patel (1912–92) and Saraladebi Chaudhurani (1872–1945). What brings these women together? All of them raised their voices as

[173] Ritu Menon, *Out of Line: A Personal and Political Biography of Nayantara Sahgal*, HarperCollins, 2014.

'interlocutors, participants, and commentators, in the life of the country(ies) they lived in.' And all were deeply committed to the idea of an inclusive, diverse, egalitarian and secular nation.

And of Ritu's biographical endeavour in this book, it may help to refer to her own words on past and present in tellings and retellings: 'To understand continuity in a biography is to recognise the simultaneity of the past and the present, but also to engage with the discontinuity, which is part of their telling . . .'[174]

9 July 2023

GH: You have described these eight women's ideas of India as a combination of 'the personal, the professional and the political'. Would you elaborate on this, keeping in mind the diversity of the women whom you have included in the book?

RM: It's more of a deduction, rather than a description. Only two of the women, Lakshmi Sahgal and Rashid Jahan, were 'professional' in the generally accepted definition of the term—they were practising doctors. But social work, which is what Kamlaben Patel and Saraladebi Chaudhurani engaged in for a good part of their lives, is considered a profession today. And script-writing, broadcasting and editing, which is what Ismat Chughtai, Qurratulain Hyder and Attia Hosain did on a regular basis, are certainly considered to be that, although none of them was 'qualified' for the job. Nayantara Sahgal, by virtue of her journalistic writing, would be called a columnist today, in addition to being a novelist.

---

[174] Ritu Menon: 'Biography as Continuity', Lila Foundation, Prism Lecture Series, Event Report (https://lilafoundation.in/2014/08/20/ritu-menon-biography-continuity/).

In that sense, yes, they could be thought of as professional women, but the important point is that however they defined themselves, their writing—even Kamlaben Patel's—was nothing if not political in intent. And it was through their writing that they made a strong political point, and intervened in the life of the country by commenting on what was going on. That politics sprang from deeply felt, personal choices that each woman made, that had a direct bearing on how she thought of herself as a political being.

That said, Lakshmi Sahgal and Rashid Jahan were directly involved, politically as well—Sahgal as part of the Rani Jhansi Regiment in the Indian National Army, and later in the CPI(M) and AIDWA [All India Democratic Women's Association]; Jahan as an active member of the Communist Party of India from its inception. Ismat Chughtai was part of the Progressive Writers' Movement; Saraladebi Chaudhurani was politically active through her public engagements in Calcutta and Lahore, and via the journal she edited, *Bharati.* Nayantara Sahgal was steeped in politics, given her family background, and it provided her with the context, as well as the material, for all her writing. Hyder and Hosain's novels, short stories and non-fiction drew their inspiration from an acute understanding of 'politics', notwithstanding the fact that they may have chosen to remain independent of formal political affiliation. Their personal life choices were nothing if not deeply political.

GH: In what ways would you say independence from colonial rule, Partition, and the birth of the 'nation' were defining moments for the lives of these women—and also for their ideas of India?

RM: All three interlinked events were watershed moments for the eight women and all of them were unalterably affected by them. Indeed, if it hadn't been for the fervour and energy of the freedom movement and for the fact of Independence, followed by Partition, I would venture to say that they may well have written differently. Except for Rashid Jahan (who died soon after Independence and we can't know how she would have responded), six of them grappled with what this simultaneous freedom and division meant, for them personally, as well as for India. The only writer who has not dealt with Partition in her writing is Nayantara Sahgal. India was her main character, rather than any single moment or event. And Saraladebi retreated into a life of spirituality during the mid-1930s. [She became a follower of the 'Howrah Thakur' Bijoy Krishna Chattopadhyay (1875–1945).]

Hyder, Chughtai and Hosain remained preoccupied with the idea of what this new, independent India meant to them, and of how they should relate to 'nation' and 'country'; and certainly all of Hyder's major work dealt with this conundrum in one way or another. Lakshmi Sahgal and Kamlaben Patel, post-Independence, withdrew from an active political life, and in Patel's case, permanently. Yet they wrote. And it is through their writing that we get an insight into how they responded to these epochal events. It is also through their writing that we understand the 'political' differently, because they wrote *as women*. Inevitably, it would offer another perspective on, and experience of, a politically aware life. This fact leaps out of all their writing, fiction or non-fiction.

GH: All eight women address, in some way or the other, the concept of nationalism current in their times. Their understanding of nationalism naturally informs their practice of the concept in their writing, their activism, and their choice of alliances or allegiance. How do you think they have responded, or would respond, to the different brand of 'nationalism' that is on the ascendant today?

RM: I realised, almost serendipitously, as I was writing, that of the eight women, four were Hindu, four Muslim. These may have been subliminal identities before Independence, but Partition reconstituted them radically, and each writer was confronted with the question of where, and how, she 'belonged' in this redrawn, redefined 'country'. No longer could they think of the 'nation' in uninflected, ungendered terms. Kamlaben Patel expresses this existential anxiety with anguish as she was compelled to deal with it at an urgent, human level.[175] Hyder and Hosain are possibly the most eloquent. They also had to 'choose' 'their' country, but it was a choice enjoined on, not 'chosen' by them. Chughtai chose too, and in the bargain, all of them lost.

We know how Hyder and Nayantara Sahgal responded to today's brand of nationalism, because they have written about it. Unequivocally, and with mounting despair at the betrayal of an original, aspirational idea that liberation and freedom represented, notwithstanding the tearing asunder of the country at Partition.

Do women have a country? How is it, and one's place in it, to be understood? Hyder, for one, addresses this question, sometimes frontally, at other times elliptically, and all her protagonists contend with it throughout their lives. One cannot speculate, but if I were to go by what they wrote and said, by how they lived their lives, I would say that every one

---

[175] Her account of Operation Recovery, carried out by the governments of India and Pakistan to restore the abducted women and children from the Partition riots to their families, was titled *Moolsotan Ookhadela* (1984) and was translated from the Gujarati by Uma Randeria as *Torn from the Roots: A Partition Memoir (2006).*

of these eight women would have rejected the nationalism on display today. They would have chosen whom, and what, to align with today, as they chose then, to uphold those ideas of India that are inclusive, diverse, egalitarian and secular.

Again serendipitously, the eight women in the book personify the kind of diversity that allowed me, writing about them, to foreground the very personal, very political, very gendered voices they raised as interlocutors, participants and commentators in the life of the country(ies) they lived in.

Diversity and Dissent:
The Body and Soul of Culture

SEEMA CHISHTI

Bringing Home the Big Promise of India

The Indian version of diversity can spread a family across the subcontinent's map. It can connect lives from Mysore to Uttar Pradesh to Delhi, all within the same family. It may get a little complicated explaining 'where you are from', or why your name is what it is despite where you come from. But it also means you can lay claim to a very spacious home—extending from North to South, and encompassing Hindu and Muslim, more than a couple of languages, and certainly more than a single cuisine or culinary tradition. Such are the rich gifts of diversity, all brought home to one family. Seema Chishti's family is a fascinating example because it assures us that what every heart wants to hear is true: this diversity is also born out of love.

It was 1964. In the basement office of a magazine in Delhi, two Indians, a man and a woman, began a conversation. He was Anees Chishti, a Syed Muslim from Deoria in Uttar Pradesh. She was Sumitra Bai, a Kshatriya Hindu from Arsikere in Karnataka. (Had they met in a novel, readers would have known at once that Sumitra and Anees belonged together, since their names are near synonyms—each means 'good to befriend'. In another novelistic touch, their names are also a clue to their characters.)

Many decades later, their daughter Seema describes what followed:

> The conversation sparked a lived partnership of more than four decades, where the personal choices they made spawned a mini-India in their home …
>
> Love stories like that of my parents have now acquired a different meaning. People are attacked for the homes they happen to be born in, who they are, what they eat, drink, read, think, and of course, who they befriend or choose to spend their lives with.[176]

Seema brings this lived reality, this big promise of Indian diversity, to the heart of every home, the kitchen. In *Sumitra and Anees: Tales and Recipes from a Khichdi Family* (2022), she reveals her family's kitchen and eating habits as a confluence, in which her parents' inter-faith marriage and the new life of independent India complemented each other. As Sumitra and Anees built their life together, recipes from Sumitra's kitchen reveal an interplay of North and South, of Hindu and Muslim traditions, a taste for both vegetarian and non-vegetarian cooking, brought together in a homely cosmopolitanism—unpretentious and easy in its stride as much as it is eclectic, nourishing and economical.

Today, with food culture and inter-faith marriage transformed into points of communal friction, even of outright

---

[176] Seema Chishti, D. Sumitra Bai and Anees Chishti, *India Love Project*, 9 May 2022 (https://www.facebook.com/IndiaLoveProject/posts/d-sumitra-bai-anees-chishtiby-seema-chishtiin-a-magazine-office-in-a-basement-in/479030804015787/).

conflict, Seema's quiet evocation of the family table, its unfussy nurturing of pluralism, togetherness, hospitality and shared pleasure, reads as a powerful rebuke to India's new politics.

18 June 2022

Githa Hariharan (GH): I want to begin with your book's subtitle, *Tales and Recipes from a Khichdi Family*. The phrase holds some of the critical aspects of human experience, from story and food to family and the heart of the home, the kitchen. How did this title come about?

Seema Chishti (SC): Khichdi, a mix of rice and pulses (and more) is considered a mish-mash and has always fascinated me. I always felt I was part pulse and part rice, so to speak. Then, like all good and useful things, it is also undervalued while speaking of high cuisine. We know how invaluable khichdi is when you have a patient at home. I wanted to own the word in how I saw my home—proudly—as not monochrome, but as a 'khichdi thing'. Society does not seem to be in very good health at this time, so I thought I must draw in the khichdi reference. Then there is also my mother's recipe book that she left behind ... So it worked well, to riff on the food aspect of my book and the idea of a healthy, 'mixed-up' food item. What better way to encapsulate Sumitra and Anees's coming together than with a reference to khichdi?

GH: The khichdi is a great metaphor for a diverse country and for the story of your parents' lives together, a sort of lived unity-in-diversity. (It's also useful to remember that khichdi has vegetarian as well as non-vegetarian versions.) How do you think your parents managed to throw out all purist notions to embrace this plural 'khichdi' identity, as individuals, as a couple, and as a family? And how did you cope with this sensibility as you were growing up?

SC: My parents got together in a world that was not so openly hostile. This is not to say that prejudice, or a sense of group identity, did not exist. After all, it is not an invention of the present. It has been sharpened and weaponised, and is now articulated in ways that appear much more brazen, partly due to the times, and partly, perhaps, due to new technology. In hindsight, I think it would be fair to say that the two of them benefitted greatly from each other's influence and from living a life together. It enabled them not just to be who they were as individuals, but also something else. They created something as Sumitra and Anees together—a unit—that was more than the sum of their parts. So we were culturally happy to be Hindu, Muslim and, possibly, Christian and Sikh too, but we were also happy to not fit into one single box. By virtue of the fact of their personalities and the bond that held them together, my parents were both mature and deeply connected to their cultural roots. This made them more accepting of others. In fact, it made them eager to learn more. Importantly, the Indian state was a different creature then—we are talking of the early years after Nehru's death—so the modernity his stint as prime minister had infused into how the Indian state behaved, and what it stood for, was still alive. The fact that the state was not an active enabler of societal prejudice and biases made it possible for Sumitra and Anees to not be solely preoccupied with security issues as couples belonging to different religions would be today. They could think more about thriving than just surviving.

GH: The silly stereotype of a cosmopolitan is someone privileged, flying from place to place. But your book indicates some of the deeper meanings of cosmopolitanism, even in a small town in UP. Who is a cosmopolitan for you? And why are true cosmopolitans an endangered species?

SC: A very good and important question. It is fashionable to raise cheers for regressive 'nationalisms' in Europe and elsewhere, citing 'cosmopolitan elites' as the reason for the so-called 'rage' of those voting for far-right parties. That, according to me, is clever but deceitful propaganda. It makes crossing narrow identity issues a class issue too, by misrepresenting cosmopolitanism as something elite and alien—involving the jet set as you say. This takedown of cosmopolitans is at the heart of a sophisticated sons-of-the-soil argument, which is actually a plea for narrowing the mind.

A cosmopolitan mind is an open one, not limited by boundaries imposed by one's own ascribed identity, and happy to form partnerships and associations with others not of the same kith/kin/clan. To my mind, a cosmopolitan person is not a jet-setter or someone who has travelled the globe, but an evolved person who is a sum of all the parts that constitute life on the planet—so is happy to accept 'other' languages, ways of being, thinking, living, eating, loving, which were not known to him/her or prescribed at birth. Evolution and engagement with the whole wide world in a way that is non-hostile, and capacious thinking—where the cosmos is the unit of operation. (Maybe that is the origin of the word?)

True cosmopolitans are becoming an endangered species since politics is, in several parts of the world—and especially in India—held on a tight leash by people who do not want their electorate to think for themselves, or think deeply. That would open up minds and options. The line of 'one leader', 'one tax', 'one religion', 'one man', 'one kind of food', pushed ad nauseam is intended to shrink minds and crack down on critical thinking and reasoning. So cosmopolitanism is under attack, mocked as alienated and elite and disconnected. It is important to mock and discredit—call the dog mad before you shoot it. If a significant section of the electorate thought like cosmopolitan people, that would be the end of the narrow kind of India they are trying hard to create.

GH: Would you comment on the importance of mixed marriages, whether in terms of community, caste or region? Not only to make laws such as the Special Marriages Act work, but also to resist new laws that criminalise inter-faith marriages, or which increase the number of impediments to mixed marriages? How do they bring communalism/casteism and patriarchy together?

SC: It is interesting (and sad) that inter-religious marriages, according to National Family Health Survey data, remain at about 2.5 per cent or less of the total, and inter-caste too is at around 13 per cent. (I suspect these inter-caste marriages may not necessarily be a radical choice. They could be marriage among the savarnas or within categories of dalits—not across the big dividing lines.) The young in India today are no 1968 generation. The available data (World Values Survey and Pew Reports) suggest that they are quite conformist, and behave as their 'elders' would have them do.

Yet even this small number of 'mixed' marriages matters. How the state and society respond to such marriages is a useful barometer to judge how open-minded its people are, and to what extent society accepts pluralism. It is not as if everyone must cross-marry to prove a point, but more how you look at people who have done so, and how the state reacts. Together, this makes for a very important indicator of how democratic the place is, and how enlightened and accepting its people are of new ideas.

The laws currently targeting mixed marriages are serious prohibitors and convey a clear signal about where the state stands with reference to pluralism, modernity and patriarchy.[177] In one fell swoop, by cracking down on 'our women' marrying outside the community or region, you establish control over women, reduce them to possessions, and ensure that the patriarchy continues to reign. Inter-community ties remain fraught and social mobility is also killed. These laws, like the Nuremberg laws, are not only about showing a community as inferior or different. But as family structures in feudal setups like ours are central to maintaining all manner of regressive attitudes, to keep an endogamous and conservative family going is an imperative if you want to maintain patriarchy as well as communal and caste divides. So it becomes a political project too to control the family as that keeps society regressive.

I cannot see any way for an enabling law like the Special Marriages Act of 1954 to be made to work for the purpose it was intended, without a change in politics and without fostering a larger mindset which accepts that India must

---

[177] In November 2020, Uttar Pradesh passed the Prohibition of Religious Conversion Ordinance. Whereas the Special Marriages Act, 1954, requires a couple in an inter-faith relationship to give thirty days' notice of their wedding to a district official, the new law mandates two months' notice. There are also new criminal provisions, including a jail term of up to ten years and nullification of the marriage, should forced conversion be found to have taken place. In this regard, any relative of the couple, whether by blood, marriage or adoption, can lodge a complaint with the authorities (https://theconversation.com/indias-love-jihad-anti-conversion-laws-aim-to-further-oppress-minorities-and-its-working-166746). In March 2022, Haryana became the eleventh state to follow Uttar Pradesh's lead and table an 'anti-love jihad law' (https://thewire.in/communalism/haryana-becomes-11th-state-to-table-love-jihad-law-congress-protests-in-assembly).

modernise. Currently, the spiel being put out is nostalgia, for a return to a mythic and contrived ancient Hindu past, which means 'stability'—in other words, a social order that is unequal, divided, and certainly not one that gives women and dalits agency.

There is a telling comment in S. Rukmini's book, *Whole Numbers and Half Truths: What Data Can and Cannot Tell Us About Modern India* (2021), when she is talking of the miniscule numbers of mixed marriages. One interviewee tells her that she is looking at the wrong variable—marriage. He suggests she look at how many of those in love are choosing partners across religion and caste divides.[178] But that sounds like Madhubala in *Mughal-e-Azam*: 'Pyaar kiya to darna kya?' If that was to be written today, it could well face the censor's axe—it is far too liberating.

GH: You have a lovely description of your parents' life together: 'The big promise of India they brought into their modest home.' Would you say they were actually 'living' the Constitution as good citizens should, making those words and

[178] Lately, that too has turned riskier. Uttarakhand, India's most populous hill state, gained a new chief minister in 2021: the forty-eight-year-old Pushkar Singh Dhami, who has spent thirty-three years in the RSS. Along with the usual contributions to Islamophobia—from fearmongering about 'illegal settlers', 'land jihad' and 'love jihad'; to hosting 'Dharma Sansads' that issue calls for a genocide of Muslims—Dhami's government has also introduced a law that requires couples in live-in relationships to register themselves with the administration and receive clearance first. Should they fail to do so, they could be jailed for up to three years (https://scroll.in/article/1057843/how-state-backed-hindutva-rhetoric-is-fuelling-the-ethnic-cleansing-of-uttarakhand and https://scroll.in/article/1063457/why-enter-our-bedrooms-uttarakhands-live-in-law-leaves-even-young-supporters-of-the-bjp-worried).

aspirations real? How different was their effort to bring India home from yours?

SC: Their meeting in Delhi, hailing respectively from Mysore and Deoria, was a coincidence. But on becoming partners and building a home together, they went on to become more than what they would probably have been, had they not come together as a couple. They enabled their only child—me—to acknowledge and accept all sides of her identity and be whoever she chose to be. That is a big tribute to the kind of home they built.

I don't think they set out to do a 'model citizen' number, but allowing the wind to blow into their home from all sides, sweep in with it whatever it did, and to be able to deal with this—all this was extraordinary. No one really ever 'finds' themselves, that quest is eternal—but I could be myself in their/our home, and that meant different things at different stages in my life. The same experience was shared by my friends over the years and by the family that I chose to build as an adult. I think that is a tribute to 'the big promise of India they brought into their modest home'.

Friends of my parents, family and acquaintances will bear witness to what their presence and way of thinking meant to them and enabled in them. My parents ended up being a support system for so many people over the years, people who broke barriers—whether it was the unconventional subjects they chose in college or their choice of life-partners. As I say in the book, at the risk of sounding corny, 'Taboos were the only taboo.'

In the lottery of birth, I was the apple that fell from the tree. By the fact of my DNA and upbringing—nature and nurture both—I happened to witness and inherit values that

I absorbed and lived by. When I look back, I can say with some confidence that I always made non-parochial choices. I was never guided by narrow concerns of ethnicity or identities ascribed to people at birth which they are forced to accept as immutable for the rest of their lives. So in that sense, I did and do make the promise of the Indian Constitution a lived reality in my little home too.

T.M. KRISHNA

Unravelling Tradition and Practice

Like all public intellectuals who have achieved rockstar status—Romila Thapar and Arundhati Roy are two very different examples that come to mind—Krishna elicits adoration as well as vituperative hatred. Luckily there is a significant number of rational responses in between the two ends of the spectrum.

Krishna began as a talented young musician with a mind of his own. He was not going to simply regurgitate what he had been taught was the Karnatik[179] norm or 'tradition'. He was going to experiment, even if it was a simple matter to begin with, such as the prescribed sequence of the music in the kacheri or concert. (I began listening to his music with interest when some die-hard conservatives told me he is 'kirukku'—a 'crack' or a 'crazy fellow'. Having often been called a kirukku myself, there was a friendly edge to my curiosity.)

I don't know how long it took him to move on to experiments on a more ambitious scale, but I suspect it did not take too long. Krishna is given to questions. By the time I first met him,

---

[179] Also Carnatic or Karnatak. This conversation uses 'Karnatik' in keeping with T.M. Krishna's choice.

he was already more than just another enfant terrible; he was asking himself some rather searching questions about the art he practises.

Then, like concentric circles growing larger every month and year, his world of enquiry grew, not just in width but also depth. The questions pushed him, and so his audience, out of their comfort zone into an unusual new space of 'musical activism'. This activism seems to have grown, organically, out of his need to emerge from the safe island-colony of brahmin-dominated Karnatik music practice.

The activism took the form of singing for campaigns such as 'Poramboke Paadal', the music video that called attention to the encroachment on Chennai's Ennore Creek, or singing a poem by Perumal Murugan on the dehumanising practice of manual scavenging. It meant unusual collaborations with, for example, the Jogappas, transgender folk musicians. Krishna described the performance with the Jogappas as a 'conversation of multiple sexualities and multiple cultures through multiple music.'[180]

Activism also meant exploring new settings to enlarge the context of both performance and the partaking of the arts. For instance, Krishna has been involved in organising community festivals in locations such as a fishing village, where the performances may include a wide range of forms, from Karnatik music to parai attam[181]. Activism has spurred Krishna to mine texts well beyond the acceptably Karnatik: from the edicts of Asoka to the verses of the reformer Narayana Guru to Faiz

---

[180] Nina C George, 'T.M. Krishna's duet with transgender Jogappas', *Deccan Herald*, 14 April 2019 (https://www.deccanherald.com/india/karnataka/bengaluru/t-m-krishna-s-duet-with-transgender-jogappas-728602.html).

[181] Parai is drum and Parai Attam is, simply, dancing to the drumbeat.

Ahmad Faiz's 'Hum Dekhenge' in multiple Indian languages to 'We the people', the powerful invocation to the citizenry in the Indian Constitution.

The keywords—or the central motives—are multiplicity and inclusion. Which is why such activism demands paying attention to the terrible old fault lines of caste, gender and community as manifested in the 'traditional' or the 'classical'. The point of it all is to break old walls, and strengthen the diverse but inclusive nature of artistic and cultural practice. In the process, amid polemics and controversy, Krishna's questions and experiments have served to spark debate—and new ways of seeing, locating and practising the 'traditional' and/or 'classical' arts.

In 2013, Krishna published *A Southern Music: The Karnatik Story*, acclaimed for its combination of music practice, technique, history and polemics. He has followed this up with other books—notably *Sebastian and Sons: A Brief History of Mrdangam Makers* (2020), which serves as a cultural history that bears testimony to caste-based discrimination and exclusion. The books, the articulate responses to developments in cultural and social issues, and most of all, the choice of a life in which the musician is also a politically engaged citizen, have all helped Krishna grow into a public intellectual of the cultural community.

The *Indian Cultural Forum* benefitted from his support, as have numerous ventures that wish to address cultural politics. At the personal level, Krishna and I have had several conversations over the years, partly because we share the conviction that all art is political, and partly because of love for Karnatik music; but also because we share the difficult but necessary task of unlearning caste (and class) privilege as we practise and partake of culture, and let our political choices seep into our everyday lives.

In one of these wide-ranging conversations with me in 2015, Krishna spoke about the nature of tradition and the classical, and of exclusionary musical practice.

20 October 2015

Githa Hariharan (GH): Krishna, I want to ask you about the apparent conflation of 'traditional' and 'classical'. Is the belief that current practice has a continuous link with 'antiquity' an illusion? What happened to the 'traditional' during the shift from traditional music and dance communities to a nationalistic Indian classical music?

T.M. Krishna (TMK): There is the image of Karnatik music, and there is the truth of Karnatik music. The image of Karnatik music practice traces its origins back over several centuries with a largely unchanged core character. Almost all theoretical and philosophical narratives of this musical form end at the doorstep of Bharata's *Natya Shastra* (between the second centuries BCE and CE), or push back to the Vedas themselves. Using a short ruler and a blunt pencil, we have drawn a single line from the ancient era to the twentieth [or twenty-first] century. As with the theory of Hindu religion and philosophy, unconnected ancient musical traditions, counter-movements and deviations have been fed into this linearisation, giving Karnatik music a sense of musical and philosophical 'hoariness'—an antiquity.

But if we were to look at the reality of its musical history through the treatises of the past, and what we know of its practice, it is quite clear that what we call Karnatik music today is a result of complex interactions between people of different regions and different musical lineages over the last 500 years.

In its aesthetic evolution, what directly and incontestably connects the Karnatik with the music in the *Natya Shastra*, the *Silappathikaram* (second century CE), the *Brhaddeshi* (ninth century) or the *Sangita Ratnakara* (twelfth century) is not much. Ideas embedded in the theory and practices of periods much before the sixteenth century may exist at the foundation of some of the elemental principles of this melodic form. Beyond that, there is very little that connects Karnatik music, as we know it today, with the ancient world. Karnatik music is indeed a modern idea, with its present form only about 300 years old.

To come to its 'communities', Karnatik music has been practised, presented and patronised by the elite of South Indian society. What is 'the elite'? Basically, the 'select', often self-selected, in positions of authority and influence. The communities that practised Karnatik music included the isai vellalars,[182] the devadasis[183] and brahmins. The isai vellalars and devadasis were part of the same hereditary music and dance community. The isai vellalars came in as vocalists, as instrumentalists, [the double-reed woodwind] nagasvara and the [percussion] thavil being a speciality; as tutors of dance,

---

[182] Isai (music) vellalar (cultivators) refers to the heterogenous 'minstrel' community traditionally involved in the performance of music and dance. With the abolition of the devadasi system, and the entry of brahmins into their sphere, the traditional performers took on this term to sustain a sense of community.

[183] The conventional definition of a 'devadasi' is a woman 'dedicated' to the service of a temple deity. The word, however, bears the burden of various contentious connotations of the historical and societal perceptions of the devadasi community. Such perceptions were also influenced by Victorian and orientalist dogmas. In this conversation, 'devadasi' refers to the 'hereditary singer-dancer community' and is used with an awareness of the word's problematic baggage.

and as conductors of dance performances. The devadasis were dancers (performing Sadir, which in the twentieth century was transformed into Bharatanatyam) and musicians. The brahmins were involved in singing, instrumental music, composing, and the construction of Karnatik musicology. The brahmins, along with the royalty, used their positions of influence in temples and otherwise, to patronise and become the 'blessers' of the form.

The revolving wheel of Karnatik music as we know it today was given another vigorous 'turn'—an increasingly important one—by the upper-class Hindu nationalist movements of the late nineteenth and early twentieth centuries. Their spirit transformed Karnatik music into a quasi-religious, bhakti-based presentation. Kirtana (a form of composition) became the anchor-sheet of the music, and its lyrical meaning became the basis for bhava [emotional expression] in the music. The lyrical import being religious, philosophical and ritualistic, Karnatik music became a representation of brahminical Vedic culture, with 'purity and sanctity' as a central notion.

The influence of the brahminical harikatha tradition, a musical storytelling of mythological stories that evolved in the Tanjore district during the Maratha period, cannot be underestimated in the evolution of twentieth century Karnatik music. Many Karnatik musicians were also exponents of the harikatha tradition. So there is a cross-pollination of ideas in the content, presentation and stylisation of Karnatik music. The concert structure and presentation were the result of the structuring zeal of the urban brahmin male governed by these principles, with Madras becoming the hub.

It is around the same period that the devadasis lost their hold over the dance and music world with the 'anti-nautch' legislation.[184] The last generation of influential devadasi artists emerged in the early twentieth century. Afterwards, things changed so much that some of these women even shed their own identity to become brahmin women in the eyes of the Karnatik music fraternity. Musically, an independent feminine musical aesthetic was lost with the disappearance of the devadasis from the Karnatik cosmos.

The nagasvara vidvans [players of the nagasvaram] who possessed a parallel instrumental narrative to Karnatik music were also slowly sidelined. They did try to conform to the kirtana-based musical presentation finalised by the early twentieth century brahmin practitioners. But they were unable to establish themselves like their brahmin counterparts, who were vocalists or instrumentalists playing the flute or violin. The caste discrimination faced by nagasvara vidvans, including widely acknowledged maestros such as T.N. Rajarathnam Pillai (1898–1956), is part of Karnatik lore. Today the nagasvara is only found in temples or at wedding functions. There were isai vellalars who were violinists and mrdangam (or mridangam) players, and a few were prominent vocalists. But they too faced distinct handicaps at social levels. Though the stature of their musicality had to be recognised, appreciation of their work did not mean they were accepted as 'one of us'. Here again, the last generation of isai vellalar vocalists, violinists and mrdangam players emerged in the 1940s. A lot of musical ideas were appropriated from the isai vellalars and the devadasis,

[184] The 'Purity Movement', led by Raghupathi Venkatarathnam Naidu from 1880 onwards, was initiated in Andhra but extended up to Madras. The combined forces of dominant-caste social reformers, Christian missionaries and the colonial government resulted in an anti-nautch movement targeting the devadasis and their livelihood. A series of bills to this effect were introduced between 1912 and 1930.

but they were not made intrinsic to the twentieth century 'purified' Karnatik.

With the isai vellalars and the devadasis more or less gone, the music came under the control of the brahmin community. Needless to say, this meant that brahmin men, with their particular sense of what was 'proper' and 'pure', what could go onstage and what should not, took charge, and women became the special subject of taboos. Brahmin women themselves had to struggle against 'their own men' for their right to be public performers. Only devadasis were meant 'for the stage' and 'for the pleasure of others'. This social norm brings back the idea of devadasi impurity. To receive acceptance, talented brahmin women had to strictly follow the principles and restrictions laid out by the male brahmins who designed twentieth-century musical practice.

GH: Could you give us a brief background of the variety of exclusions in music practice on the basis of caste, gender and community? How do these exclusions actually work on the ground?

TMK: Today the Karnatik music world resembles a gated brahmin enclave. This includes practitioners, connoisseurs and impresarios. Most of the minority non-brahmin audiences come from the Tamil diaspora—from Jaffna and some (non-brahmin) communities from Kerala. Non-brahmin musicians today are mostly isai vellalar who continue in the nagasvara and thavil tradition. Very few come from other caste groups. A view contrary to this would lose no time mentioning names that 'disprove' this. But those names are, essentially, the exceptions that not only prove but shout out the rule.

The reason for this is plain. The performance and the articulation of Karnatik music is deeply entrenched in the brahminical ideas of religious practice. This is an intimidating cultural roadblock for most other caste groups. This subliminal undertone has very little to do with the music. It is more of a social identity marker. But this construction is like an iron covering. It makes it very difficult for those not part of the brahminical environment to break through. The music is held captive to this brahminism. It is also true that we wear this identity on our collective sleeve. Visit any of the Thyagaraja aradhana[185] concerts, and you will see the overt manifestation of this ritualism embedded in the musical environment. It is almost as if you need to be anointed into this religiosity if you want to understand the music.

The places where the concerts take place—'sabhas'—are geographically public spaces, but culturally private conclaves. Most members of the inner circle don't seem to understand that sabhas may have an 'All are welcome' board outside, but this does not mean that it is a welcoming public space. I can only imagine what would happen if suddenly, one day at a concert, most seats were occupied by people from a poor non-brahminical neighbourhood. This would certainly make every person, including the musicians, extremely uncomfortable. Therefore this 'All are welcome' actually addresses the 'All' of a certain cultural community and we do not want 'All and sundry' to come in. Being welcoming is very different from saying we don't stop anyone!

Today there are very few instrumentalists or vocalists who are not brahmin. And even those have not really made

---

[185] Annual music festival held as a tribute to the composer Thyagaraja (1767–1847) of Thanjavur. It is held in Thiruvaiyaru, the town where he lived. In more recent times, similar festivals are held in other places, including the United States, where the diaspora holds the Cleveland Thyagaraja Festival every year.

it to the top rung of the musical ladder. Saxophone Kadri Gopalnath and the late Mandolin U. Srinivas (1969–2014) are two musicians from outside the brahmin fold who broke the 'B-barrier'. Interestingly, both of them took up Western instruments—the electric mandolin and saxophone. I wonder whether the elitism of their 'Western instruments' somehow helped them break through the casteism in the Karnatik substratum.

Without doubt, we brahmin practitioners have a different attitude towards the 'others'. This separation is seen in the way musicians bond and share beyond the stage. It is in these spaces one can clearly see groups forming with the non-brahmin musicians (usually isai vellalars) almost always in a different group from their brahmin colleagues. It is also true that the few people of other castes, whether they are practitioners or listeners, have had to internalise the brahminical texture of Hinduism which we believe gives Karnatik music depth and direction.

We can clearly see this in the way Tamil Nadu's music colleges stay apart from the general Karnatik music scene. These music colleges are where the maximum number of non-brahmin students study Karnatik music, yet few of them ever make it to the mainstream circuit. In fact, there is very little connection between us—the 'control group'—and those students. They remain in the periphery, and most of them disappear.

We, as the control group, have done little to make this music more accessible. Nor have we consciously considered accepting students from other communities. I do believe that such affirmative action is essential. Very importantly, we should look at communities beyond even the traditionally musical isai vellalars, so that this music may touch a larger cross-section of society. The traditional notion that the 'classical' (a purely sociologically created term), can only be appreciated by a certain class of people, needs to be challenged.

Digging this music deep into the Hindu belief system has also made it very difficult for people of other religions to come into the system. A few traditional Muslim musical families that have produced nagasvara vidvans have made brahminical religious practices a part of their lives. This only strengthens the religious rigidity that informs the music.

In the early twentieth century, some attempts were made by Christian scholars such as Abraham Pandithar (1859–1919) and H.A. Popley (c. 1879–1960) to create Karnatik kirtanas with Christian themes, but these compositions are not even known to the mainstream Karnatik community. K.J. Yesudas is frequently cited as an example of the openness of the Karnatik world. But the 'real' Karnatik fan does not accept Yesudas as a serious musician. In fact, if you were to attend his concerts, you would find that the members of the audience are distinctly different from the people you would find at the concerts of many accepted Karnatik musicians.

GH: You have spoken of caste and religious community. What about gender?

TMK: The gender bias in Karnatik music is blatant and obvious. Many senior musicians who accompany vocalists on the violin or mrdangam, including many leading lights, have refused and continue to refuse to 'accompany' women musicians. Accompanying women singers is acceptable up to the point when leading male vocalists induct these violinists and mr̥dangam players into the 'men's club'. In fact, many male vocalists have told accompanying male musicians that they should stop accompanying women, or not do it too often, if they want the patronage of the leading men! Organisers too play along with the wishes of the men. The common talk among the male musicians is that in general, women's music is not as tough and rigorous as 'men's music'. Accompanying musicians claim that the women do not 'challenge' them. Other arguments include complaints from accompanists that the high pitch of women's voices makes the strings of the violin and the membranes of their mrdangam taut, so that it is hard to express themselves freely. Of course, this argument flies out of the window because these very same musicians accompany male instrumentalists who tune their instruments to the very same high pitches.

The point is that there is a clear disdain for 'women's music', and such generalisations are, let us face it, purely sexist. For a woman to receive respect from the men she has to indulge in complicated mathematical or technical musical presentations, traditionally considered the man's domain, too difficult for the 'weaker sex'! Another effect of influential musicians only accompanying 'the boys' is that young women do not get the professional support of these stars, while the young men of their generation are able to reach the top tier with greater ease. Ironically, even star female lead musicians prefer to have male accompanists. Like their male counterparts, they are 'fine' with female accompanists until they become stars. Once that happens, they prefer male accompanists whom they can control, and display the same machismo their male counterparts flaunt. The officialdom of Karnatik music is also a male bastion, making the environment quite difficult for women in general.

GH: In otherwise well-intentioned attempts to critique 'commercialisation' of music performance, do these various exclusions get masked?

TMK: Interestingly, even with the commercialisation of the music, these exclusions do not get masked. The main reason is that the aesthetic being commercialised is built on the edifice of discrimination. To be saleable, the 'product' has to conform to these standards. The receivers have built their musical receptors based on what musicians have constructed as 'music'. From the format of the music to the way the content is explored, explained, discussed and shared, these sociological exclusions are built in, co-opting all of us knowingly or unknowingly in this practice of discrimination. And don't we all know how well religion and the 'spiritual' sell?

GH: You once used a telling metaphor about access to Karnatik music today, its 'exclusiveness'. You likened this music world to an island that people in the mainland are cut off from. How is this transforming the development of music practice and the alleged 'Indianness' (as in pluralistic nature) of the 'tradition'?

TMK: Though Karnatik music has been, by and large, an elitist art form, the sense of cultural exclusivity that we practise today has sharpened over the last hundred years or more. At the core of Karnatik music practice, we hold the philosophical un-questionability of the Vedic tradition. This idea envelops our complete understanding of the form. Once we describe this music in such terms, we make lyrics and their linguistic meanings central to the experience of the music. This makes us overburden musicality with artha-bhava,[186] which, to me, has very little or no space in an art form such as Karnatik music. But this has greatly influenced the way this music is practised and experienced. Consider the numerous so-called Karnatik music PhDs awarded for religious topics, religious theme-based

[186] Literally, meaning (Artha) and emotions (bhava).

concerts/presentations and esoteric lec-dems proliferating in the Karnatik sphere. From being an abstract exploration of raga, tala and text, the music has become a creative extension of bhakti sangeet! The number of purely bhajan-like pieces in the concert has increased over the last forty years, with many members of the audience only waiting for that religious or spiritual upliftment. I would argue that there is no place for religious or spiritual intentionality in this music. In fact, there is no room for any literalism.

There is another trap in this religious-spirituality. We, the practitioners of Karnatik music, believe that we are singing a sacred form of music that rises above everything tactile and temporal. We give ourselves the status of being conduits to the divine. This self-created and self-appointed position allows us to ignore the very real discriminatory nature of our musical practice, by saying that 'Music is beyond all this,' or 'Once "in music," all these separations don't matter.' We feel we shouldn't distract ourselves with such externalities. So we forget that the very idea of the internal is the result of these external manipulations.

As a consequence of religious entrapment, we have lost the purely abstract musicality—the soul of the music. We are unable to experience language as a creation of sound, and its aesthetic interactivity with raga and tala. Every one of us experiences this beauty, yet we constantly bury it inside a religious/spiritual discourse. And that discourse is almost canonical.

GH: Finally, the question, as always, of modernity. What is the space for the modern in 'traditional' music, 'classical' music, and, in sum, the present-day practice of Karnatik music?

TMK: I have a serious problem with the word 'classical' since it really does not describe the art form to which it is attached. All it tells us is that a certain upper class or caste of society practise and patronise this art form. There is a need to either rediscover its meaning, or replace this word with some other expression such as 'art music'.

And the view that the traditional is not modern needs to be corrected. This delusion is the creation of the practitioners and patrons themselves. We proclaim cultural superiority, placing ourselves as caretakers of a certain antiquity. Almost every form that we call traditional is a modern creation. The only exceptions to this statement are probably some purely religious art practices that have not moved, aesthetically, beyond the bounds of their ritualistic function. Every other form is modern, and the modern is recreated in every generation.

This discomfort with the word 'modern' that we practitioners of the traditional have, goes back, once again, to our obsession with sanctity and purity. By constantly placing—or shall I say 'reposing'—the art in an enshrined past, we imply that it is distanced from the vulgarities of modern times, conveniently forgetting that vulgarities have always existed, irrespective of the era.

SHANTA GOKHALE

Culture and Conflict

Shanta Gokhale has much to tell us about the cultural scene in India—not just what is apparent on the surface, but its layered history and the nuances of its power politics. What makes her knowledge especially valuable is that it is rooted in practice: she is a novelist, a playwright, a translator, a journalist, a columnist and, for many of us, an inspiring figure as a woman.

I first met Shanta in Bombay in the eighties through a couple of journalist friends. I would get to know her better in later years, but then I admired her from afar. In fact, many of us young women, aspiring journalists or writers, wanted to be like her—she had, as a friend put it, 'poise'. And we wanted it too. All these years later, I ask myself again what it was about Shanta that attracted those of us in search of a role model. I think it was the fact that she did so much—she taught, she wrote, she translated, she edited. She was a divorced woman and a single parent, and she took on work she may not have necessarily liked so she could be independent. And she did it all in a way that appeared to us as cool, beautiful, poised. It all seemed effortless, though we knew it couldn't have been.

Up close, the view over the years is even better.

Shanta as writer: in addition to innumerable newspaper articles and columns, she has also written plays, film scripts, short stories and two novels. All along, her writing connects with the world she is in and asks how, in these Brechtian 'dark times', the individual can work out a creative response to violence, inequality and injustice. In other words, play a role in creating a living culture of dissent. Shanta describes this process apropos her novel *Tya Varshi* (2008), translated in English as *Crowfall* (2013):

> … I had wanted to explore how art could respond to the violence that had gripped the country and the world. This novel was written two years after the 2002 Gujarat bloodbath. Two pieces of writing guided me then—an article by an Iraqi ceramicist Nuha al-Radi and Mathew Arnold's poem 'Dover Beach'. In her article al-Radi says that she had expected her well-known book, *Baghdad Diaries*, to make some difference to America's attitude towards her country and its citizens. But that did not happen. America attacked Iraq a second time. This time around, she says, she simply put her head down, did her work, hoped that she would survive the bombing while attempting to preserve some shreds of humanity in herself. 'Dover Beach' told me how this could be done. Arnold speaks of his despair at the ebbing of faith in the world. He means of course religious faith. But to me it was faith in the principles of equality, liberty and brotherhood.[187]

[187] Shanta Gokhale, 'Singing in Dark Times', the 26th Safdar Hashmi Memorial Lecture, text subsequently published in *Guftugu*, 29 January 2020 (https://guftugu.in/2020/01/29/singing-in-dark-times/).

Shanta as translator: '... it has been the preoccupation of a lifetime.'[188] In her autobiography, *One Foot on the Ground, A Life Told Through the Body* (2019), she recalls how her mother suggested the lifetime task of a translator of Marathi literature: 'When I chose to do English Literature in England, Mother had asked me how I intended putting my knowledge to use back home. I had said I would teach. "That is one way," she had said. "But there's another which you must consider. Translate the best Marathi literature into English."'

Shanta has faithfully lived out her mother's advice. From 1970 to the present, Shanta has translated any number of Marathi plays into English. (On the way, she has learnt a great deal about censorship.) Then there are the novels and autobiographies she has translated, several of them testimonies to the woman's voice insisting on being heard.

In the introduction to *Smritichitre: The Memoirs of a Spirited Wife* (2017), her award-winning translation of Lakshmibai Tilak's[189] *Smritichitre,* Shanta shares the multiple tasks of the translator, from understanding the context—the world of the writer and the text—to making the precarious leap from the feel of the original language to a 'near equivalent' register in the target language:

> With translation, there are personal and practical factors also to be considered. It is, after all, not a mechanical process of fitting word to word. One needs to get into the skin of the writer, view the world through her eyes, find words and

---

[188] Shanta Gokhale, 'Theatre Censorship in Maharashtra', Talk delivered at Mumbai University, Teachers' Refresher Course on 4 March 2017 (https://shantagokhale.com/articles/features).

[189] Lakshmibai Tilak (1868–1936) was a Marathi writer best known for her memoir, *Smritichitre*. She also completed her husband Narayan Waman Tilak's epic poem *Chirstayana* after his death.

> phrases that hypothetically she would have used had she been writing in English. The question I had to ask myself was whether I had the capacity to get into Lakshmibai's skin and translate not so much her words as her world. It was all very well to be seduced by the easy flow of her crisp and colourful sentences and her vocabulary that smelt of kitchens and cowsheds rather than books and libraries. But was I equipped to find the right register to carry those lines, those phrases into English?[190]

And from then to now, over five decades, Shanta the teacher and cultural commentator: the role model has remained a mentor to a large number of writers, translators, possibly all those who believe in the word and in meaning. Finally, as she says, 'Writers write because they must. They have no way of shedding their lifelong habit of working with words. So the question is not whether to write, but how to write, particularly when times are dark.'[191]

In a conversation with me in early 2020, Shanta spoke of her method of dissent, of the Indian education system which is still feudal and casteist, and of multilingual theatre in Mumbai.

2 January 2020

Githa Hariharan (GH): Shanta, let's begin with what we are living through today, the shrinking space for dissent, for doubt—all the essentials of life and citizenship in a democracy. You have always spoken your mind. How do you think we should handle the situation?

---

[190] Shanta Gokhale, 'Lakshmibai Tilak, My Old Friend', *Indian Cultural Forum*, 26 June 2022 (https://indianculturalforum.in/2022/06/26/lakshmibai-tilak-my-old-friend/).

[191] 'Singing in Dark Times', *Guftugu*, 2020.

Shanta Gokhale (SG): I don't think we can speak in the plural. How I will handle it is my way of doing it. Each one of us would have to find our way of doing it. I have always spoken out and spoken very clearly, frankly, about what I believe, and why I believe it to be the case. And whether it's through my feature writing, or my columns which I started writing sometime in the nineties, it has been a continuous thing. Lately, in the last six or seven years, my friends have begun to worry. Once in a while, I have got a call to say, 'Be careful.' And I've always said, 'I'm small fry for the powers who want to crush dissent. There are big people around who are leading thousands and thousands of people, who are changing their minds, changing their hearts. Those are the people who count.'

GH: I am curious about what gives us the strength of our convictions. In your case, you began with teaching. And the college space, the university space, is great for clarifying ideas, whether you are a student or a teacher. So a kind of compulsory liberal space, that is one ground; then theatre and different sorts of theatre. Suppose we look at these spaces where we discovered what it is to speak up, express doubt or dissent.

SG: You spoke of the university as a liberal space. My experience of teaching was different—it was not in a liberal space at all. My problem is that the educational system, as it operates in many parts of this country, is extremely feudal.

At school, we were not expected to question the teacher, so speaking out didn't come naturally to us. The examination system, the so-called objective questions, meant ticking boxes where something was right, something was wrong, and there was nothing in between. So we were not allowed to develop nuances in our thinking.

At the college where I first taught—this was Elphinstone College—we had tutorial groups, and a lot of students from Indian-language-medium schools came to college and were totally at sea because the medium of instruction was English. I remember writing an article about the caste system in college where the English-speaking students were the brahmins and all the others were lower caste.

When I went into my first tutorial, I noticed there were Marathi-medium students there, and I was talking to them in English. Somehow, it seemed completely unnatural to me to be doing that. So I thought, okay, let me try and teach them through their mother tongue, and slowly bring them into the English language as they become confident. The principal, who was passing by when I was taking this tutorial, called me and said, 'I heard you talking in Marathi.'

So I said, 'Yes, the students are from the Marathi medium.'

'No, but the medium of instruction in this college is English.'

So that was the caste system, it was a restrictive space.

The liberal space which I inherited came from my family. And that, of course, is what gave me confidence. My father spoke out. My mother spoke out. They allowed us to speak out, to question, to discuss. And we grew up with this kind of empowered feeling.

GH: You have brought up one aspect of the language problem, English. We also face the challenge of harnessing the riches of a multilingual culture, not just in a token way, and without slipping into linguistic chauvinism. There were so many languages in the Bombay I grew up in: There was Tamil and Marathi and Gujarati and Hindi, at least what we in Bombay thought was Hindi. You are a translator and a theatre person as well. So how do we handle this multilingual resource successfully, in theatre for example?

SG: In Bombay, in theatre, it hasn't been handled at all. You find theatre in four languages in Bombay. There's English in South Bombay, Gujarati in Central Bombay, Marathi in North Bombay, and Hindi further north. And whereas the Gujarati-Marathi constituencies do go north and south, the north and south don't come to the centre. It was only during Satyadev Dubey's[192] time, because he moved in cosmopolitan circles, that people from South Bombay came to the centre and watched Hindi and Marathi plays and, sometimes, Gujarati plays. So these are linguistically watertight compartments …

If you are doing theatre of the kind which is movement, music and colour, it may get across language barriers. People watch because their senses are aroused. But if language is the main vehicle, then that acts as a barrier. There are a whole lot of people living in Bombay who don't know Marathi. What sense would it make for them to watch a Marathi play? Because Marathi theatre is very word heavy. The same goes for Gujarati. So English and Hindi are 'accessible' to everyone, but these two languages are not.

GH: What is the relationship between language in theatre and language in film? After all, most of us learnt our Hindi from Hindi cinema.

SG: Absolutely. And it also killed other language cinemas. That's true equally because it was accessible. After all, it was

[192] Satyadev Dubey (1936–2011) was a playwright, scriptwriter for film, producer and director. He is best known for producing Girish Karnad's *Yayati* and *Hayavadana*, Badal Sarkar's *Ewam Indrajit* and *Pagla Ghoda*, Mohan Rakesh's *Aadhe Adhure*, Vijay Tendulkar's *Khamosh! Adaalat Jaari Hai*, and his scripts for the films *Junoon* and *Bhoomika*.

glamorous. And everyone went and watched, everyone sang those songs. Marathi cinema died in the process. It had its time earlier, in the forties and fifties. Then it died. And then there was a resurgence once again with television. A lot of people migrated from television to film and made some great films that got attention at the national level. But yes, for people who want to foist Hindi on the whole country, I always feel the work has been done by Bollywood. But the language has also been accepted with a lot of love and affection, so we should just let it be.

GH: Marathi theatre has contributed some phenomenal plays, many of which you have translated. Take playwrights like Vijay Tendulkar. If we were to describe them today, would they be called modernist or progressive? For example, what would Tendulkar's relationship with the right-wing have been? The RSS or the Shiv Sena, how would they have viewed somebody like him?

SG: Tendulkar was always targeted by right-wing people, the Shiv Sena, for instance. His *Ghashiram Kotwal* (1972) was targeted by the brahmins of Pune, many of whom were (and are) members of the RSS. So he had to bear the brunt of [opposition to] his opinions, which he put out there for everyone. And he never felt the need to shut up in his lifetime. It was still a time when people weren't intimidated in quite the same way they are now. So he could write what he thought and say what he thought. And sometimes what he said was not particularly acceptable even to liberals. But he spoke out.

When he did *Sakharam Binder*,[193] for instance, what used to be 'trolls' in those days would call and say horrible things about

[193] First performed in Marathi in 1972, the play was banned in India in 1974.

him. They would call the director whose wife was acting in the play, saying obscene things about her. Tendulkar confessed he was shattered by this sort of attack. The matter went to court when bans were suggested at the literary conferences held annually in Maharashtra. There were people there who got up and made speeches against Tendulkar and *Ghashiram* and *Sakharam Binder*. So the atmosphere was extremely turbulent during those times.

GH: But you would say it's worse now?

SG: It is because everyone senses this. As I said, Tendulkar came up against this only with *Sakharam* and *Ghashiram Kotwal*. His play *Gidhade* (*Vultures*, 1961) was full of violence and the censors suggested thirty-five cuts. And they couldn't tolerate the language in the play. But this was between the censors and the playwright, the producer and the director. It wasn't happening on the street.

Also, with the plays *Sakharam* and *Ghashiram*, several people in theatre asked for a ban. Tendulkar had many enemies in theatre because people were practising nostalgic theatre, sentimental theatre, and he seemed to be a threat to them. So he was attacked from all sides. Ultimately, I think the director of *Sakharam*, Kamlakar Sarang, went to Balasaheb Thackeray. I think Thackeray came to see the play and gave it a clean chit and then it was produced.

But the whole case of *Sakharam* makes engrossing reading. And when you read it today, you see what kind of legal minds went into defending it, what procedures. The Chief Justice of the Bombay High Court asked to see the play because he said, 'People are talking about this play. Now I want to see what's wrong with it.' So Kamlakar had underlined all the cuts that had been demanded, and it was proposed that each time one of those lines was said, a blue light should come on so the judge would know that this was banned or sought to be banned. The judge had come with his family. Lots of other people wanted to see the play, so they too came. And every two or three lines down the blue light came on. The Chief Justice finally said, 'What's this blue light? I don't want it. I want to see the play as it is. Please stop the blue.' And he saw the play.

GH: The people who wanted a ban—what were they against?

SG: In *Sakharam*, right from the start, there's a lot of cursing because that's who the man is. Sriram Lagoo[194] said, when he was defending *Vultures*, or *Gidhade*, to the censors, 'Our play is titled *Vultures*, it is not titled Sparrows. Vultures speak this kind of language and we will do the play as it is.' And they did.

GH: There is a different kind of censorship—a censorship through intimidation—that we are facing today.

SG: Yes.

GH: And so there is a certain self-censorship at work as well. Would you say this has altered our whole idea of freedom of speech?

SG: But I wonder how deep this urge to speak freely is among all of us? In my kind of family circle or acquaintances, the idea is, usually, not to speak.

GH: But if you have access to certain spaces, certain ideas and certain mentors, you may gain an ethos that encourages you to rebel. Which is of course how we started. It's not that we were

---

[194] Shriram Lagoo (1927–2019) acted in both Marathi and Hindi films and theatre, and also directed numerous Marathi plays. He was a rationalist, and was associated with the anti-superstition movement in Maharashtra.

extraordinary, but we started asking questions. Why? Because we had exposure to those ideas.

SG: Exactly. So if you happen to belong to that class, that group, and you are exposed to these ideas …

I was talking once with a young alumnus of the FTII Film Institute. He wanted to write a script based on my novel, *Tya Varshi* (2008). He came over and we talked for two hours. Finally, he said, 'What fascinates me about this novel is the freedom in it. I can't believe there are people who live so freely, and none of your protagonists is a rebel in any sense.' He also said, 'For me, it's been a very liberating experience just reading this novel and becoming aware that friendships like this are possible, that life like this is possible.'

What he said came as a revelation to me because it's something I take for granted. So this is a very real part of our world [and true for the young as well]. So how do we reach these young people? I've heard teachers talk so communally in class, and children end up speaking the same language. When a teacher is awarded her Bachelor of Education degree, is her ideology examined? And if it isn't, what is she passing on along with geography and history?

GH: That is a huge challenge.

SG: Yes. It's huge. Immense.

In 2023, I read Shanta's translation of Shridhar V. Ketkar's Kalindi *(2022) from Marathi to English. The novel is set in the early 1900s in Mumbai. Educated and financially independent, Kalindi Dagge dreams of living in a casteless and equitable society as a single mother—a life far removed from the one she had in the stifling world she's left behind.*

Kalindi, *originally published as* Brahmankanya *in 1930, has been hailed as brave and ahead of its time. Shanta's translation brings the classic alive for the contemporary reader, and we see how relevant it remains almost a century later. In her conversation with me in 2023, Shanta spoke about the impact Ketkar's* Kalindi *had on her as a reader and a translator. In Shanta's take on the novel, 'Caste is not merely a layer in this story. It is the driving theme …'*

18 February 2023

GH: *Brahmankanya* was first published in 1930. The challenge the text presents to the contemporary reader is constructing a context by peeling off one layer after another: that this is a novel of ideas by a sociologist; that its time is the earlier half of the twentieth century, with nationalism driving debates on Hindu reform; that a man takes up the issue of women's education and marriage choices; and that a man born a Chitpavan brahmin takes up caste inequalities, but with an awareness of class contradictions and transactions. Suppose we begin with the most important layer, that of caste. Would you comment on the continuity and/or change of caste discrimination between Ketkar's time and ours?

SG: For me, *Brahmankanya* is, first and foremost, a story, told in a direct narrative style, with snappy dialogue, great attention to characterisation, and to the contemporary circumstances that trap its characters—drawn from a wide cross-section of society, ranging from outcasts to upper castes, from educated young women to merchants to members of minorities to leaders of workers' unions. Each of these characters pushes the boundaries of custom, tradition and religion to find a modicum of personal freedom to be who they are. The reader is engaged throughout in following the detailed unfolding of their trajectories, wondering how they will resolve their several problems. The greatness of the novel lies in the sociological concerns of the author not being allowed, for the most part, to turn the story into a thesis. Its flesh-and-blood characters and their journeys make up the vehicle Ketkar has fashioned to carry his preoccupation with caste which, he believes, has done untold harm to Indian society. If we do not fight caste, it will do even more harm to the country. Caste is not merely a layer in this story. It is the driving theme.

Caste was very much part of the political discourse in Maharashtra. And in the second half of the nineteenth century, when the movement for the country's independence was gathering force, the sharpest debates took place between two passionate nationalists, Bal Gangadhar Tilak (1856–1920) and Gopal Ganesh Agarkar (1856–1895). Born within a few days of each other, these two towering personalities were fellow students and friends at school, and colleagues at Fergusson College in Pune, before they fell out over their opposing approaches to the country's independence. Tilak contended that independence had to be won first, before social problems were addressed. Agarkar took the longer view, arguing that social reforms were of prime importance if the Hindu was to become a fit citizen of a confident, modern, independent nation. Caste and women's education were the main axes on which these debates revolved.

Ketkar was a vital link in the history of this discourse. With sociology as his discipline, he had an academic interest in the problem of caste. At Cornell University where he had done his graduate and post-graduate degrees, he had become acutely aware of the flaws in the Western understanding of caste. He was equally conscious of the flaws in the conservative Hindu view of caste. His doctoral thesis [published in 1909 as *The History of Caste and Race in India*] was aimed at addressing both …

Ketkar's argument was that change was inevitable. It had to happen. But he confessed to not being sure how it could be brought about. 'To effect change in a society so complex and so highly organised, a tremendous force is needed, and where is it?' The upper castes, he asserted, had no interest in changing a system which worked so well for them. And so, 'When individuals cannot remove an evil, it is the duty of the community or government to do it.' Neither having done their duty, he relies on the knowledge of history to disabuse people of the notion that caste is divinely ordained and cannot be tampered with. Fully conscious of the apparent impossibility of the task, he says, 'All attempts made by previous workers to break caste have failed, but it should not be thought that all possible remedies have been exhausted … It is a critical moment, a question of life and death and there is no way to escape.'

Ketkar's conviction, shared by Jyotiba Phule (1827–1890), that the government had a role to play in correcting the injustice of the caste system, was to become reality when the country became independent. Has that made the difference Ketkar and Phule had hoped for? Legally, yes. On the ground, no. In fact, what government intervention seems to have done is to make individual action redundant. In the public mind, the problem of caste discrimination has been taken care of. Where is caste these days, people blithely ask. And yet news comes in every day of the worst caste atrocities happening across the country. We still have thriving caste organisations with their annual get-togethers and caste-driven projects. People still marry within their caste or even their sub-caste. Honour killings happen when these lines are transgressed. While the upper castes eat together, there is still very little socialising between the upper and lower castes. Roti-beti transactions remain more or less where they were in Ketkar's time. Ketkar's hope that change would happen has so far been belied.

But in his time, Ketkar still hoped and pushed. The existence of caste was, as he said, a cancer that had to be removed. Knowing that *The History of Race and Caste in India* was likely to have been read only by fellow scholars, Ketkar was evidently compelled to address the problem in another, more accessible form. *Brahmankanya* was the result.

GH: There is also the complex situation of a person born into an upper caste talking about possible solutions to caste inequality. Would you help us contextualise this 'reformist' intention and consequent plan for action in Ketkar's times, especially in the context of nationalism?

SG: Ketkar's argument in *Brahmankanya* is precisely that if anyone can change caste hierarchies as the organising principle of society, it is brahmins, the original authors and highest beneficiaries of the system. Brahmins have the social power to stand up against the system which their ancient forefathers instituted.

There was no concerted plan of action in Ketkar's times. The big initiatives were the Prarthana[195] and Arya Samaj.[196]

[195] Founded in 1867 by Atmaram Pandurang, the Prarthana Samaj was active in proposing social and educational reform, such as promoting inter-caste gatherings and encouraging education for girls, widow remarriage and the ending of purdah. Mahadev Govind Ranade and R.G. Bhandarkar, a judge and a historian, respectively, were among its leading figures.

[196] Founded in 1875 by Dayanand Saraswati, an ascetic who sought the consolidation of Hinduism by uniting religious practice under the Vedas. Dayanand Saraswati pioneered the conversion of non-Hindus as

These are examined in the novel as pushbacks against the system. Then there is the fictional Vaijnath Shastri (he could be Ketkar himself), who attempts to write a Smriti to rival the Manusmriti, but dies before he can complete it. The protagonists of the novel arrive, heuristically, at the realisation that an all-inclusive movement for dismantling the caste system must be left to the future. Meanwhile, such difference to the status quo as could be made in Ketkar's time could only come from individual action. The novel begins with an individual action—an inter-caste, inter-class marriage—which has been taken in the naïve hope that it would serve as an example that such a thing was possible. The fact that what he had hoped for did not happen comes as a shock to the idealist. He and his children now begin to explore possibilities that go beyond individual action. None of them answer the need that they feel for change. With this knowledge gained, they return to individual action. This is not a case of returning to where they began. This is not a circle, but the first curve of a spiral. The individual choices they make which go against social norms are now made in the full knowledge that they will have little or no effect on society in general, rather than on the naïve hope on which the initial action was based. The hope is that more such individual actions might, in the long run, dent social norms. In that sense, there is progress.

GH: Ketkar's novel has been hailed as a classic that is ahead of its times. Yes, the discussion of a more equitable society, in terms of caste or gender, is brave; Ketkar takes risks, as do his

---

a means of 'restoring' their ancestral faith—services that the Arya Samaj continues to offer today (https://theprint.in/theprint-essential/purification-ritual-chants-and-caste-by-choice-different-ways-one-converts-to-hinduism/782083/).

characters. But is it not very much of his times, rather than 'ahead'? Is it not a part of the debate on women's rights in general, and women's education in particular, that was going on in the larger movement for Hindu reform at the time?

SG: In one sense *Brahmankanya* is of its times. But in another very important sense, it can be said to be ahead of its times. The novel is of its times because reformist movements which addressed a range of social issues, including caste and women's education, were part of the public discourse that held centre stage. However, while the discourse was dominated by the educated and the articulate who wielded powerful pens and were entitled to public fora, there was a massive undertow of orthodox belief opposed to change, and this surged up at critical times. We have seen its resurgence in our times. Tilak was of his times and continues to be of our times. He is revered in Maharashtra even today. Agarkar has been totally forgotten. Ketkar himself was not a popular novelist of his times because he swam against the stream. He was also a victim of the orthodoxy in his personal life—he suffered because he chose to marry a German Jew,[197] deemed mlechcha or vratya by the orthodox citizens of Pune. His family severed all ties with him.

The orthodox undertow came into its own when the British government in India did what it did not generally do: it intervened in Hindu social customs through acts like the Hindu Widows Remarriage Act of 1856 and the Age of Consent Act of 1891, which raised the age of consent for sexual intercourse for all girls, married or unmarried, from ten

[197] Edith Kohn (1886–1979) first met Ketkar during his stay in London after completing his PhD at Cornell University, around 1912. She later joined him in Poona where they were married in 1920, upon which she took on the name Sheelavati.

to twelve years. Reformists who supported the new laws were ostracised and excommunicated. Many of them have recorded the terrible effects this had on their social and economic lives. Who then was of the times? The orthodoxy, not reformists …

GH: You said, apropos your translation of Lakshmibai Tilak's *Smritichitre*, that you found an affinity between her 'homely' language and your own. What was the translator's relationship you established with *Brahmankanya*?

SG: I first read *Brahmankanya* in the late sixties. I felt impelled to read it again a decade or so later. What drew me to the novel at first was the easy, natural friendship between Kalindi, the chief protagonist, and Esther, her Bene Israel friend. This was a breath of fresh air in a literary world which stuck closemindedly to the Hindu middle class. A very close friend of mine had been Bene Israel, a community that found no representation in Marathi fiction. Then suddenly I discovered Esther.

In my second reading of the novel, I was taken with Ketkar's direct narrative style, the freedom with which he coined new words that became current in the spoken language of my times. To my great relief, his language was free of the punditry of Sanskritised Marathi, as well as the sloppy vagueness of sentimental expression that had come to dominate the fiction of the fifties and early sixties. Although Ketkar's knowledge of Sanskrit was apparent through some of his coinages, it was seamlessly melded with a modern language that had its roots in a sensibility moulded by European thought.

Most importantly, *Brahmankanya* unlocked the world of the textile mills and the relationship between owners and workers. Although textile workers lived in a large swathe of the city I inhabited, they were once again absent from Marathi literature. The only exception was dramatist B.V.

Warerkar's (1883–1964) novel published in the same year as *Brahmankanya*. Warerkar's novel [*Dhvata Dhota* (Running Spindle)][198] centred on the relationship between mill owners and mill workers. The novel was not much read then and has been forgotten since. But Warerkar later wrote a play based on the novel which did well precisely because it did not confront reality with the toughness of Ketkar's novel. It submitted to the audience's taste in the naïve sentimentality of its denouement.

After my first novel *Rita Welinkar* was published, a couple of critics observed that it carried shades of *Brahmankanya*. I had not realised it, but once it was pointed out, I saw how true the observation was, and how deeply I had responded to Ketkar's novel.

---

[198] See *Notes from the Archive*, Alkazi Theatre Archives (https://alkazifoundation.org/alkazi-theatre-archives/).

ASHOK VAJPEYI

The Moral Stature of Cultural Institutions

Ashok Vajpeyi is a major Hindi poet. This sentence is true but it is not complete. Ashok is also a former civil servant, a cultural and arts administrator, and an institution builder. He has written numerous volumes of literary criticism; he has written extensively on art and music. But I would like to think of him as, first and foremost, a poet; a poet who has always been very much in the public realm, speaking up on issues of concern—not only to cultural practitioners, but to all citizens.

How do you write about a poet without bringing a poem into it? How else do you look into the poet's soul, what he is when he is writing poetry; but even more so, what he is when he is not writing poetry?

I heard Ashok recite his poem 'Chhote Muhn Badi Baat' and chased him to translate it into English. The poem sums up what Ashok would like to be as a poet and a citizen:

'What do you do?'
I write poetry—I'm a poet.

Anyone else consider you a poet?
Not many know my poetry. Some do—and they think I'm
a poet.

'Then why leave poetry and talk politics?'
I haven't left poetry: I do what I can as a poet.
When politics trespasses on poetry, on life,
Why can't the poet trespass a little on politics?

'You know where you will end up?'
Yes—but I also know where dictators end up …

The poem goes on to send a call to all of us, in times unfriendly to writers. It asks us to look at ourselves, at what we do, and summon the courage to say, simply, 'Yes, I am just a writer, just a "little mouth".' But what is this little mouth capable of, what sort of words does it let loose into the world?

'So you're used to talking big out of a small mouth?'
That's what poetry does. A poem becomes a poem when it
speaks
of big things out of a little mouth.

'The days left to you: What will you do with them?'
Live with dignity. Let my poetry talk big; let it hold its head
high.
Never let my poetry or my head bend for anybody.[199]

---

[199] Ashok Vajpeyi, 'Out of Little Mouths', *Battling for India, A Citizen's Reader*, eds Githa Hariharan and Salim Yusufji, Speaking Tiger, 2019.

Ashok has spoken through words, but also gestures of protest and solidarity. On 7 October 2015, Ashok returned his Sahitya Akademi award saying 'This is in solidarity with writers and intellectuals being murdered in broad daylight …'[200] In January 2016, after Rohith Vemula's suicide, Ashok returned the honorary D.Litt. awarded to him by the University of Hyderabad to protest institutional discrimination against dalit students. Moments like these remain alive—hopefully for posterity, bearing witness to the times as powerfully as the poet's words.

When we spoke in May 2019, the context was the general elections of 2019 and its aftermath. Four years had passed since the spontaneous protest of writers through a return of state awards. But, said Ashok, 'The return of awards in 2015 still rattles those in power.' He revisited the significance of writers returning their Sahitya Akademi awards in 2015, the assassination of scholar and social critic M.M. Kalburgi and the lynching of Mohammad Akhlaq. Ashok spoke about the role of writers in standing up to intolerance and hate politics, in contributing to a larger political churning, and the way ahead, post-elections, for writers and citizens.

6 May 2019

Githa Hariharan (GH): Before we talk about the present moment, I thought we could revisit 2015—a very fine moment for the writing community, when so many of you returned your state awards to protest against the political murders of

[200] 'Dissent in October, 2015 and Now', *Indian Cultural Forum*, 10 October 2020 (https://indianculturalforum.in/2020/10/10/dissent-in-october-2015-and-now/).

people like M.M. Kalburgi,[201] but also the lynching of citizens like Mohammed Akhlaq.[202]

Ashok Vajpeyi (AV): Some of us, quite independently and without being in conversation with each other, did this. It was one of the most spontaneous moments ever. In fact, in my own case, a young writer who used to work with *The Indian Express* called me and said, 'Nayantara Sahgal has returned her Sahitya Akademi award. What is your comment?'

I replied, 'My comment is that I join her! I will also return mine, because I am equally agitated by what is happening.' We were the first three then, but by evening, there was a fourth, an Urdu writer who joined us.[203]

GH: It was as if there was something simmering, and this particular gesture spoke to such a range of writers who couldn't even actually speak to each other because of …

AV: Half of them I didn't even know! They were from all kinds of languages. It was important in another sense—one,

---

[201] Malleshappa Madivalappa Kalburgi, a leading scholar and writer working in Kannada, who was shot outside his home at Dharwad in August 2015. See footnote in the conversation with Nayantara Sahgal.

[202] See footnote in the conversation with Nayantara Sahgal.

[203] In September 2015, a month after Kalburgi's assassination, writer Uday Prakash returned his Sahitya Akademi award in protest against the Akademi's silence at the killing of a writer it had honoured in 2006. In the first week of October, six writers—Veeranna Madiwalar, T. Satish Javare Gowda, Sangamesh Menasinakai, Hanumantha Haligeri, Shridevi V. Aloor, and Chidananda Sali—returned their Kannada Sahitya Parishat awards to protest against the state's delay in investigating the murder of Kalburgi. They were joined on 6 October by Nayantara Sahgal and by Ashok Vajpeyi the next day. Urdu novelist Rahman Abbas returned his state Akademi award on 9 October. In the largest such protest in the country's history, within weeks forty writers and artists had returned their awards. Many others resigned from posts in state bodies and returned awards received from state governments.

that the writers, without being in some kind of an organised movement, felt the way they did, and spontaneously acted the way they did. Two, the murder of writers took place south of the Vindhyas in Maharashtra and Karnataka, and [after the first response within Karnataka], the initiative to raise our voices came from North India. I think that was important because, all of a sudden, the writing community across the country felt that we were one, and that we could raise our voice for what it is worth. Also important, for the first time in the Republic of India's history, writers were on the front page of newspapers! Narendra Modi recently gave a two-page interview to *The Times of India* in which he mentions the 'Award Wapsi' and, of course, he alleges that we were moved by a foreign hand.[204]

GH: The fact is those in power keep going back to the return of awards, which is evidence of how important it was.

AV: The day they accused us of having created some kind of a manufactured intolerance, luckily for us and unluckily for them, the president of India talked about intolerance. So did the Reserve Bank governor and the major industrialist Narayana Murthy.[205] When I was confronted with this allegation, I asked them, if we have manufactured intolerance, were they

[204] See PM Modi exclusive interview to *The Times of India*, 18 April 2019 (https://www.narendramodi.in/mar/pm-modi-exclusive-interview-to-the-times-of-india-544548).

[205] See, for instance, the coverage in the *Hindustan Times* (https://www.hindustantimes.com/india-news/country-passing-through-rising-intolerance-says-former-president-pranab-mukherjee/story-NIP7mem9WyxbODmWlgp5yN.html) and (https://www.hindustantimes.com/india/there-is-considerable-fear-among-minorities-narayana-murthy/story-okX3mRCXpXPtMnwYpDURyN.html) and *Mint* (https://www.livemint.com/Politics/U5WVi6toiDJdmmL6vy68KJ/Raghuram-Rajan-says-India-cant-afford-to-become-an-intolera.html).

suggesting that the president of India, the RBI governor and one of the top industrialists of the country were also part of it? The fact of the matter is that we were heard, although some of us continued to be attacked for it, being called the 'Award Wapsi gang'. That moment created the realisation that issues of wider significance should be addressed by writers, once in a while, as citizens.

GH: I think as far as writers are concerned, it also gave us a sense of connection. What would you suggest to individual writers, artists, filmmakers—also institutions—as a possible 'action plan'?

AV: I don't know whether I'm in a position to suggest an action plan. Individual writers and artists will have to find ways to express, embody and disseminate their dissent. We will have to keep our vigil. Nobody has appointed us the keepers of conscience, but sometimes you have to assume it is your job to raise the voice of conscience. Quite simply, I would say a larger community of people who practise creativity, courage and conscience—the three C's, if you like—should work individually and, when required, in unison. We may be marginalised, our voices may not be heard, we may not get the response we expect. But, apart from the state, we are also addressing society. It would be a moral failure if we gave up this role. I think it's unusual that the writing, creative community have to be adversaries of power, but there is no other way to retain the moral fibre and the human vision that the arts and literature ultimately create.

In the second part of our conversation, Ashok and I went on to discuss the nature of doubt, debate and dissent, not just in abstract terms, but also as praxis in work as well as engagement with what is happening around us, and the institutions that are supposed to promote culture and knowledge …

GH: You edited a fascinating anthology called *India Dissents* [2017]. I loved its subtitle, *3000 Years of Difference, Doubt and Argument*, which points to the fact that dissent involves more than debate and argument. It also involves difference, which is a fact of life and certainly a fact of life in India, and then doubt, which is very much part of the thinking process.

AV: If you recall, the anthology starts from the Nasadiya Sukta of the *Rig Veda*, where the rishi, after having described the wonderful universe and this, that and the other, says, 'But what was there when there was no absence and no presence, no light, no darkness, no being, no non-being? What was there?'

And then he says maybe he who has created this universe, the vidhaata, may know. And then creeps in what Amartya Sen has famously described as the beginning of Indian scepticism: maybe even the vidhaata doesn't know.

GH: Absolutely.

AV: We have to remind ourselves of two or three things. Dissent has been a part of Indian tradition as much as affirmation has been, and it has been there right from the Vedic period. That's one. Two, I argue that if Hinduism, for instance, had been all that much of a self-satisfying and all-satisfying religion, why did we have three more religions?

Buddhism, Jainism and Sikhism are all religions of dissent from Hinduism. And mind you, two of these religions, Buddhism and Jainism, do not have a concept of god. That they make Mahavir or Buddha into god is another matter but theologically, they don't have this concept. All this is part of Indian tradition, and you need to remind people of that. One of the jobs of the writer is to keep memory alive and not allow people to lapse into amnesia.

GH: Yes, many of us have continued to do that in our different, and often modest, ways. But the other side, if I may call it that, has continued in different ways to intimidate, to hound, to harass. We have a laundry list of people being hounded on social media, or their families being threatened, cases ranging from Perumal Murugan[206] to S. Hareesh.[207] How do we insist that the writer—or any cultural practitioner—is also a political creature? We have seen how often T.M. Krishna is told, 'Don't politicise your art.'[208] Now, when did the word 'political' become a bad word, a term of abuse? Those of us who write deal with power structures all the time.

AV: In fact, it is very strange that the word 'political' should be used as abuse. The fact of the matter is that democracy makes every citizen political, because democracy requires you to choose. And that choice is a political decision. However, the notion that writers have nothing to do with politics has also been a trend, which is not recent. It has always been there.

---

[206] In January 2015, Perumal Murugan announced in a Facebook post that his inner novelist was dead and only the professor survived. The previous month, a novel that he had published in 2010, *Madhorubagan*—translated into English as *One-Part Woman* in 2013—suddenly became the object of violent protest, and he received death threats (https://www.bbc.com/news/blogs-trending-30785930).

[207] In July 2018, S. Hareesh was forced to withdraw his first novel, *Meesha* (*Moustache*) when his life was threatened by right-wing outfits (https://thewire.in/books/kerala-author-s-harish-withdraws-book-due-to-sang-parivar-threat).

[208] 'Silencing T.M. Krishna is an act of pure disgrace', *Hindustan Times*, November 2018 (https://www.hindustantimes.com/editorials/silencing-tm-krishna-is-an-act-of-pure-disgrace/story-KTQaeVdpW0cBlc2bOVSWJL.html).

GH: Yes, you had those aesthetic sorts even earlier, the kind whom we used to call ivory tower intellectuals …

AV: Even those who are accused of being ivory tower creatures had to contend with reality, and reality consists of the mud and dust of everyday life, of politics. After all, one of the unfortunate things that has happened is that politics has become an overriding, overpowering, overarching phenomenon. And the other ways of looking at the world, organising the world, or changing the world, have been pushed aside. This is unfortunate. However, the fact remains that if politics has come to occupy such a crucial position in human affairs, then the writer cannot possibly, not only as a citizen but as a writer, keep away from politics, because not taking an interest in politics is also a political decision.

GH: Ashok, I want to underline that writers have always overtly or indirectly dealt with power structures—whether those of caste or gender or region. I just want to say all art is political.

AV: If you look at post-Independence Indian literature, most of it, in most languages, is anti-establishment. Whether the establishment is that of social morality, of politics, gender, caste, religion or whatever. Now, anti-establishment is an element which questions tyrannies of all kinds—a tyranny of uniformity, a tyranny of 'unity'; the tyranny of a sort of consonance, the tyranny of consent, [even the tyranny of] consensus. These are all forms of tyranny and writers have questioned them. Murugan, for instance, was not doing something overtly political. He was writing about a community [the landowning gounder community] which he knew, and it was the same community which decided to curb him. So it is not merely the state; sometimes it is the community. And now, of course, we have the phenomenon of the Hurt Feelings group.

GH: Yes. Increasingly, censorship is by forces which have nothing to do with the state. Of course, the state might look the other way …

AV: The state might look the other way, and sometimes it falls a prey. Salman Rushdie's novel [*The Satanic Verses*, 1988] for instance, was banned—by whom? Whose feelings were hurt? Most of the Muslims who spoke about the novel had never read it. So how do you get hurt without reading the novel? But this has now become a recurrent phenomenon.

The complicity of the state shows, whether in saying that people are getting hurt so we'll take some action, which is censorial; or, two, by keeping quiet, not acting against those who are the culprits; or, three, by sort of rejecting the artist and the work in the name of patriotism, nationalism, tradition. Incidentally, the nation, tradition, India, plurality—everything that makes up the complex that we are living in—has been completely misinterpreted by these power structures. These are people who just don't understand that our tradition was a tradition of shastrarth, and a Shankaracharya could not win over a Mandana Misra by just his spiritual glow or philosophical insights. He had to engage him in debate and that debate was mostly a public event. It used to take place before others, with others watching and hearing you. In a country where such an intellectual tradition existed …

Also, if you want to come up with a new idea. Let's say Githa Hariharan has a new idea about the world. Now, your duty in the Indian tradition was, first, you honestly describe what has been said about this issue earlier. You have to give the poorva paksha. Then you propose what you do now. These are intellectual traditions that should have been strengthened. In fact, they have the seeds of a democratic mind and a democratic ethos. They should have been strengthened, but ours is a democracy which is trying to forget all this.

GH: I would suggest that it's precisely because the powers that be know how powerful culture is. And that this diverse culture includes collisions, transactions and so on. So by using diversity to divide, they have turned culture into a battlefield.

Ashok, I want to move from the individual practitioner to the institution. I want to recall what Nehru had to say about the relationship between the writer and the state in the context of the Sahitya Akademi.

AV: He said, 'Prime Minister Nehru cannot and should not interfere with the President of the Sahitya Akademi.'

There was an occasion when Rahul Sankrityayan [1893–1963], a major Hindi figure, was recommended for a Sahitya Akademi Award, for his *Madhya Asia ka Itihas* [1959]. He was perhaps the first Indian ever to attempt a history of Central Asia. Now, he was a communist, a cardholder. So there was something of a stir in the Akademi echelons, and it was decided that the matter should go to the president for the final decision. And Nehru seems to have written or said that if the jury had recommended him, the fact that he has an ideology should not come in the way. And Sankrityayan got the award. The idea of these academies and institutions was that, one, they should work as autonomous institutions without interference, political or bureaucratic. Two, their autonomy would mean that they would have the courage and, once in a while, the occasion to speak. To speak up. Three, they should be representative but they should care for excellence. Now, between excellence and representation, there was always a tension, and that tension never got resolved. Mostly the representational pull took over.

GH: A mechanical kind of representation ...

AV: Yes, everybody has to be represented, so there have to be awards in every language. And part of that autonomous nature of the Sahitya Akademi is that the Akademi acknowledges more languages than the Eighth Schedule of the Constitution.[209] It was possible for the Sahitya Akademi to take a decision about languages with literature the Akademi thought was worth looking at, even if the languages were not listed in the Eighth Schedule.

GH: Beyond the Sahitya Akademi, you've been involved in institution building. What went wrong with so many of our cultural institutions over time?

AV: There are, I think, three issues. These institutions created their own bureaucracies, and the bureaucracies began exploiting the facilities and the notions of autonomy to their own advantage. This is one. Today, in the academies you have people whom nobody knows. Inside the Sahitya Akademi is somebody who's a nice fellow otherwise, but it's someone who …

GH: But you don't know what his link with literature is …

AV: This is one problem. The second one is that the notion that politics would not interfere did not hold for long. Although Indira Gandhi interfered in many institutions, she did not interfere in the cultural institutions. They were allowed to … be.

Three, mediocrity is the most organised entity. You see, greatness is also accompanied by loneliness, by isolation. Geniuses are sort of not concerned. In the initial stages,

---

[209] The Eighth Schedule to the Constitution of India, in Articles 344(1) and 351, lists twenty-two official languages. The Sahitya Akademi recognises twenty-four.

if you look at the list of people who were office bearers in these academies, if you look at the list of members, it was an absolute galaxy of the Indian scene, whether in literature, or the performing arts, or the visual arts. They gradually receded, with age, or other preoccupations, and organised mediocrity took over. If you look at the concern for excellence, it was completely undermined. And mind you, the government of India was aware of these difficulties.

GH: Because time and again …

AV: They would appoint a committee. There was the Haksar committee. There was a Khanna committee and then there was another committee.

GH: The second time I was asked to give my views, I looked at the old file and copy pasted. This has been going on for quite a while but nothing has happened.

AV: There's another aspect to consider. During the Nehru era, and to a certain extent in the Indira Gandhi era, culture—as creativity, as music, theatre, visual arts, literature—had mattered to politics, to the state. Increasingly, this attention to culture began to recede, for whatever reason. Now you have politics without ideas. You have politics without any ideological concerns. You have politics which is pure management.

How do you manage without being concerned about values? If you notice, the decline in the education system and the decline in these institutions is more or less concurrent. This happened, and I think another aspect to remember is that you had people like Lohia, Narendra Deva, E.M.S. Namboodiripad, Hiren Mukherjee, Madhu Limaye …

GH: People with some vision.

AV: Some vision, and they were all concerned about culture … but now, culture has been reduced to spectacles, to the daily life rituals …

GH: Or norms, to control people, to exclude people.

AV: Yes, this, that and the other. The whole problem, I think, has been that as a nation, we have also lagged in professionalising these institutions.

GH: People might think of that as the bureaucracy.

AV: The bureaucracy is already there. People don't understand that these academies have been destroyed, most importantly and crucially, by the mediocrity of their bureaucracies. And they have substantial bureaucracies. You know, when I took over as chairman of the Lalit Kala Akademi, one day I asked how many people we had. It was 180. I was shocked. It was such a lazy, slow-moving institution—180 people, I thought, what do they do?

The other thing is that alternative forums appeared. For instance, in the visual arts today, the Lalit Kala Akademi counts for nothing. One major failing of these institutions was that they never worked as guilds, taking up [relevant] issues, issues of copyright and royalties for instance …

GH: So it is not surprising that when Kalburgi, one of their own awardees, is murdered, they don't even speak up. And apparently the president of the Sahitya Akademi then said to Nayantara Sahgal, 'We never protest. We didn't protest during the Emergency.' They were proud that they'd never taken a political stand.

AV: That's how it was. The point is, there's nothing to stop them. The Sahitya Akademi enjoys a kind of autonomy which the other two akademies don't enjoy. The presidents of the other two akademies are appointed by the president of India, whereas the president of the Sahitya Akademi is elected by the Sahitya Akademi itself. They are not constrained by the governing party. And I can tell you, it all depends on who you are. If you are a non-entity, as unfortunately most of them have been, then the government will interfere at the bureaucratic level and at the political level. I had four years, I was let down by my own bureaucracy, but neither the bureaucratic system in the government nor the ministers interfered with me.

To go back to your question [about the Akademi's silence after Kalburgi's murder] … How can you not be concerned when three of your own, three writers, are killed? What stops you from making a statement? I think it means that the moral stature of the institutions has gone down. And you cannot blame only the state for it, because you never stood up.

SAMIK BANDYOPADHYAY

Contested Spaces, Contested Texts

I think of Samik Bandyopadhyay as a repository of large chunks of literary and cultural history—whether that history is in the past or in the making; whether it comes in the form of theory, movement or individual practice. Samik is also the sort of cultural curator who has interviewed everyone from Satyajit Ray to Nathalie Sarraute, introduced major Indian plays and reconstructed film scripts for publication, and worked with a range of institutions, from the Sangeet Natak Akademi to the National School of Drama.

I wish we had a good Indian equivalent for a 'Renaissance man' because Samik cannot be just the one thing; he is as shape-shifting as the culture he writes about. He is a teacher, beginning with school, then colleges, then universities. He is a scholar; a scholarly critic, whether of theatre, film or literature. He is a writer who has commented on art, theatre, literature and politics. He is an editor and a publisher. Many of us discovered writers and texts in Bangla, fiction and drama, through his translations. And as if this were not dizzying enough, he is a lexicographer and a bibliophile. In more recent times, Samik the avid reader donated his collection of more than 40,000 books—from first editions of Rabindranath's books to Marxist texts from the Soviet Union of the fifties and early sixties—to create a library in Kolkata.

All this talk of scholar and curator and encyclopaedic knowledge makes Samik sound a bit like a textbook, but that is exactly what he is not. His stories (and lectures) humanise cultural movements and institutions and make them come alive. Indeed a conversation with him is a study in how to connect this thing called culture with real life, as lived by real people, in many places and at different times. Not surprisingly, his view of culture cannot be separated from his political framework. (And not surprisingly, he readily agreed to be an advisor to the *Indian Cultural Forum*.)

Many years before I got to know him, I came across Samik's work via Mahasweta Devi. I read his translations of plays and fiction, one after the other, hungry for more. I read the translations of Badal Sarkar's plays, but it was Mahasweta who took my breath away, from *Bashai Tudu* to *Mother of 1084*. In 1994, I was on the jury of the Neustadt Prize, which has a unique process. Each member of the jury has a 'literary candidate' for the prize, and mine was Mahasweta Devi. At this time I revisited Samik's translations, along with those by Gayatri Spivak and Ella Datta.

Years later, Samik would speak to me about Mahasweta, and I would learn more about her, her life and work. And it was Mahasweta's story 'Draupadi' which brought us together in conversation for the *Indian Cultural Forum* in November 2016.

Just two months before, in September 2016, the Akhil Bharatiya Vidyarthi Parishad (ABVP), the student arm of the RSS, targeted the Central University of Haryana for holding an event to commemorate the life of Mahasweta Devi. Their particular target was a stage adaptation of her short story, 'Draupadi' (1978), in which the protagonist, the adivasi activist Dopdi Mejhen, is a survivor of custodial gang rape. Angry protests against the in-house university function took place in the town of Mahendragarh, twelve kilometres away, presumably because it was the location nearest the university where crowds could be rustled up. Despite having given clearance to the function and stage performance, the university agreed to launch a formal probe into the event.

My conversation with Samik began with Mahasweta—to take on attacks on the space for debate, discussion and imagination in Indian universities, as well as possibilities for collective resistance to such attacks.

1 November 2016

Githa Hariharan (GH): Samik, we're in the midst of a time when anything can be censored, and it can be done through intimidation, the new form of censorship. Could you talk about the Mahasweta Devi example at the University of Haryana first?

Samik Bandyopadhyay (SB): As we know, this story is about the movement in Bengal and in Jharkhand, set in the Naxalite period. At the same time, the question, which is still central, is how the Army has been violent, cruel, barbaric, whenever they've come into confrontation with the tribals all over India. And this had happened also in Naxalbari.

GH: The army as an instrument of the state?

SB: Yes, an instrument of the state; and Mahasweta was a target when she wrote 'Draupadi'. I remember her reading out the story to me in Bangla immediately after she had written it in the 1970s. It's one of her early stories. And it was really about the state, the state challenging the marginal. That was its setting, the battleground on which the battle of 'Draupadi' is fought. And, as you know, the novella *Bashai Tudu* (1990) is the longer work, of which 'Draupadi' is, in a way, a sequel. Both the central characters appear there at greater length.

I remember how this story works in other settings, and how it travels—nothing was planned. For example, I remember my recently departed friend [the theatre person] Heisnam Kanhailal (1941–2016) in Manipur. I recall a very, very moving experience one day, when he sat in the courtyard of his parents' home. He was showing me all the other houses around his place. He could identify the families in those houses, and he told me very quietly, sombrely, how every family had a victim. A victim to this battle between the state and the marginals in Manipur. One by one, he told me these separate stories. He then said he was going to make a play out of that. I was completely silenced by the burden of that experience, the horror of it.

A few months later, he told me that he couldn't bring all the experiences together because they were so varied, so different and so charged, every one of them. And I gave him the translation[210] of 'Draupadi' to read. In 2000, as you know, he staged 'Draupadi'. We do not know whether there was a direct connection or not. But in 2004, there was this massive

---

[210] In collaboration with Bandyopadhyay, Mahasweta Devi had adapted her novel, *Mother of 1084*, and some of her short stories into plays, which he translated into English (1986). The short story 'Draupadi' was translated by Gayatri Chakravorty Spivak (1981), and reprinted in a version slightly revised by Bandyopadhyay in *Bashai Tudu* (Thema, 1990).

movement against the state and the army, with twelve very, very tradition-bound Manipuri women demonstrating before the Assam Rifles, the camp of the Assam Rifles. They bared their bodies and they said, 'Rape Us, Indian Army.' That is what the banner they carried said.

GH: Samik, there is a very interesting textual question about 'Draupadi'. The most powerful aspect of the story is that her naked body is both the sign of her 'victimisation', of the violence, as well as of her strength, her assertion. The astonishing thing is that this new intimidation in Haryana is unable to see this complexity. So our question then would be whether it is possible to write about these realities if you don't ask complicated questions, if you won't name the instruments of the state who might not be making decisions individually, but who are the perpetrators of violence?

SB: I think you're absolutely right, Githa. But what is also coming into play is that the story is a text in the portals of academia. But the moment it steps out in performance it is embodied. It becomes more dangerous for the authorities, for the powers that be, and it is then that the attack, the assault, happens.

What happened in Manipur was that the people rallied around the work. And from 'Draupadi' they took the next step. I've been going to Manipur for years, and one of the signs of this power of the state trampling the rights of the people, the indigenous people, the people of the place itself, was the fact that the old palace, which is the old seat of the pre-Vaishnava gods and the Vaishnava gods at the same time; the site of the first confrontation of the British and the Manipuris in the 1890s, where the first great Manipuri fighters against British colonial rule were hanged; and before that, they had hanged the British on the same site—that entire site of history, of mythology, the site of memory, the site of religion, all this had been turned into an army camp where the Manipuris were not allowed to enter without passes. That very site becomes the site of this protest. And when I go to Manipur four years after that, I find, for the first time after all these years—I've been travelling to Manipur for over three decades—I find that the camp has at last been removed.

GH: Let me move back to Haryana but continue with sites being turned into disputed sites literally or metaphorically. What is the whole idea of the educational site, the campus? One of the most shocking things about the Haryana University incident is that it was actually a response to the teachers saying, 'Let's look at the story, let's try and understand it, let's do a play, so we understand it even better by performing it, and then let's link it to the India we live in now.' Theoretically, that seems to me the agenda of any good teacher. So, the fact that those teachers are being victimised—what does this sort of attitude do to the educational space?

SB: Obviously we are going into a kind of fascism. Think of how it started in Germany. The first sites occupied by Hitler's state were the universities, the academe. Because these are sites where you raise questions, you dispute and you study, then understand. Majoritarian power politics can only take off if your understanding is closed down. As long as you are critiquing, questioning, raising doubts, that majoritarian engine can't rev up. So it's perfectly understandable that these are the sites of confrontation. And it's not just the enactment of one play. It happens systematically, in various forms. What happened in Haryana has to be seen in the context of what happened in Hyderabad,[211] then in JNU,[212] then in Jadavpur,[213] or BHU.[214] We are looking at an entire chain of such activities and incidents.

GH: Let me ask the hardest question of all, the hardest question for all of us. Given this narrative, it's very clear where the sites of conflict are. What is the narrative of resistance that has been built up? And what should we continue to build, as cultural practitioners, readers, writers, teachers and students?

SB: At one level, these attacks, these assaults, have served to consolidate the line of resistance, the force of resistance in the academies. There was a feeling of a comfort zone—that we will not be affected here, we are safe and we can get away with anything. But once that safety zone has been threatened, even

---

[211] When Rohith Vemula was driven to suicide by officials at the University of Hyderabad in January 2016, the officials, as also ministers of the central (BJP) government, sought to absolve themselves of blame for his persecution by attacking his record and reputation, even claiming that he was not a dalit. A large student protest flared up across major cities in the succeeding months. Supported by rights groups and large sections of civil society, the protesters set the record straight, reclaiming Vemula as a nationally admired figure of Ambedkarite resistance.

[212] See the interview with Romila Thapar.

[213] The 'let there be polyphony' movement at Jadavpur University was a four-month-long student protest that began in September 2014. Students protesting at the sexual assault of a woman on campus were attacked by police (called in by the vice-chancellor, Abhijit Chakrabarti), and this led to demonstrations in solidarity with the student protesters across Kolkata, West Bengal, and on university campuses in the rest of India.

[214] In September 2017, the authorities at Banaras Hindu University took no action when a woman student complained of sexual assault, and even blamed her for being out late. When a large body of students protested outside the vice-chancellor, Girish Chandra Tripathi's home, they were lathi-charged by police. The protest immediately spread to students in Delhi and other cities.

taken away, there is a stronger build-up of resistance within academia. That, I think, is an extremely positive sign. Beyond that, there are small hubs where people are meeting to talk about these things seriously, and making a concerted attempt to understand what is going on and what can be done. And this is happening at various levels. Sometimes it is a small theatre group, sometimes a group of teachers coming together, getting a section of the students together … In the 1950s and sixties we used to call them study circles. They have come back. And these groups are coming up all over the country.

GH: What is the central issue that brings them together?

SB: The central issue is that the state is trampling almost every oppositionist critical voice, at every point. And being supported in this by goons. So, there isn't any discursive confrontation at all. It is a confrontation of brawn.

GH: The youth may be showing us the way. When you spoke about the comfort zone, it occurred to me that it's also a time when those who were never in the comfort zone, such as those discriminated against in campuses because of their caste, suddenly find exposure and access to a larger public space.

SB: They find a constituency where they can come and join in rather than being separated and kept at the margins.

GH: So something is brewing …

SB: Protest is growing slowly but quite determinedly. There are risks, and people are taking the risks.

Postscript: In August 2021, during the BJP government's second term, Delhi University's Academic Council dropped

Mahasweta Devi's 'Draupadi' from its syllabus of reading for the undergraduate honours course in English literature. 'Draupadi' was cast aside along with works by two dalit authors, Bama and Sukirtharini.[215]

[215] 'DU drops Mahasweta Devi's "Draupadi" from English syllabus; here's what the short story is all about', *The Indian Express*, 26 August 2021 (https://indianexpress.com/article/books-and-literature/du-drops-mahasweta-devis-draupadi-from-english-syllabus-heres-what-the-short-story-is-all-about-7471619/).

SANJNA KAPOOR

'Artists Need to Think Strategically'

Sanjna Kapoor began her career in films but then shifted her attention to her real love, the theatre. Between 1990 and 2011, she built Prithvi Theatre, in Mumbai, into one of India's premier cultural hubs. Sanjna is convinced that 'all the arts need to be under one roof' if an arts centre or theatre is to be vibrant. And so Prithvi had more than plays; it had, for instance, touring festivals, theatre exhibitions, children's workshops, an art gallery, partnership programmes, and a monthly newsletter.

In 2011, she left Prithvi and, along with Sameera Iyengar, set up the theatre company Junoon in 2012. Junoon was to take theatre to small towns and city suburbs, and make theatre and the arts accessible in every possible way to more people. Sanjna told the press, 'It's sad that the same places my grandfathers[216] travelled to with their theatre companies still don't have access to the performing arts and culture. We will be the connector

[216] Prithviraj Kapoor (1906–1972), who started Prithvi Theatres in 1944 and Geoffrey Kendal (1909–1998), who led Shakespeareana on tour throughout India in the 1940s and 1950s.

between theatre companies and these areas.'[217] And indeed, till it closed down in 2020, Junoon served as a lively platform, and as a bridge linking the arts, artists and audiences.

Sanjna has always said that the role of theatre in schools holds a special place in her heart. It is not surprising then that she now works in education, through a teacher training programme she has founded, at select schools across India.

Sanjna and I have mutual friends but I met her first through the *Indian Cultural Forum*. In 2017, she visited our studio for a conversation with me. Kapoor discussed her own experience, and that of others, producing and acting in plays in the face of censorship, threats and occasional reasonableness. She was down to earth: 'Artists,' she said, 'need to think strategically.'

31 August 2017

Githa Hariharan (GH): Suppose we go straightaway to where we are now with Indian Culture—capital I, capital C—and the various people who want to tell us what it is, and how to practise it. I'd love to hear what you have to say about the experiences you've had through Prithvi, or any other situation in cultural practice when you have faced either direct censorship, or censorship through intimidation.

Sanjna Kapoor (SK): For years we've had a censor board for theatre in Bombay and Gujarat, and so we have to get every script censored. In a strange way that seems to work, dare I say it, as a sort of protective measure in a weird way, given all these

---

[217] *The Hindustan Times*, 14 November 2011 (https://www.hindustantimes.com/art-and-culture/no-feud-at-prithvi-sanjna-kapoor/story-6El27SIjgvT1L4o9hrosGO.html).

new forces that are getting more and more volatile in our field. Once you can say that my script has been censored, it gives you some standing to go to the cops and say, 'Well, tell me what's wrong in what I'm doing, and all that [the censorship] has already happened.' I have experienced these situations where I've actually had their backing. What we've very cleverly managed to do over many, many years is have at least two 'theatrewalas' on the censor board. They get in there and keep a watch on what's going on. This has been the practice, in Maharashtra at least.

GH: How exactly does that work?

SK: Once you have a script, you have to send a copy to the censor board. It usually takes them at least a month to get back to you. In a festival situation, at Prithvi for instance, when we're inviting shows from outside the state, we have to get the scripts [pre]censored.

GH: You're saying the word 'censored', but you're really saying 'approved'.

SK: Yeah, there's no certification. They have to just see that there's nothing offensive there. I'll give you a few instances. (There are the other stories of course, of social censorship as well, one has faced both.)

I'm just reading a beautiful book by Shanta Gokhale on Satyadev Dubey and how he used to really play around with the playwright's work and turn the meanings upside-down and change characters. He did treacherous things but still playwrights, most of them, adored him, except for one, who took great umbrage at what Dubey did to his play. He actually got one character, the main character, to be played by three people. And so—this was in the sixties and seventies—the playwright went and produced the play himself. Simultaneously, in Bombay, you had these two shows going on of the same play. Ironically enough, Dubey actually made this statement once when he was accosted by a person saying, 'How could you do this? How could you mutilate the playwright's play?' And Dubey, without ranting or raving—which was unlike him, he did rant and rave a lot, actually—said quietly, 'You know, the censor board has asked me to make cuts in this play and I'm fighting them. I haven't made a single cut, haven't changed a single word. But I've changed, you know, how I present it. The playwright has made all the changes that the censor board asked him to make and yet he's doing the play.'

I had a very different experience. This one time—I'm not even going to mention these people by name because I refuse to mention them—I had this Hindutva organisation come and try to ban a play on M.F. Husain's life by Nadira Babbar's company Ekjute, and I think it was called *Pencil se Brush Tak*. It was actually quite a lovely play about his life, in the autobiographical style, and this organisation claimed it was on a mission to stop anything that ever claimed that M.F. Husain was a great artist. They wanted to chalk this up as Yet Another Bad Thing Stopped by Them. And it was a moment of glory for them that a play would be stopped at the Prithvi Theatre.

It was the most horrendous two days of my life: a weekend that I had to spend in a police station talking to the cops, and my own cops back in the locality wouldn't speak to me, my local police station were too busy. I had to go to the area district, the area superintendent, and he finally did meet us, us and the producers together, and had a one-hour conversation and finally said, 'Listen, you can do it, all right.' The producers had decided to change the play ever so slightly with one or two scenes. Of course, they hadn't seen the play, this Hindutva outfit, but they came to watch it.

The only thing the cops asked me to do was to get two members of the censor board to watch it again, because I said, 'You tell me what I'm doing that's illegal, and I'll stop if I am doing something illegal, but you've got to back me up if I'm not.' So, he just said get two members of the censor board to see and okay it again. This is not the norm. Actually, the norm in Bombay is you have to have two seats reserved for the censor board. If they should ever want to come and see your show they can. Any day, anywhere, all over the state. It's supposed to be the norm but it never really happens. I got two of my friends on the censor board to come and see the play—two playwrights—and they came and of course I rustled up all my theatrewalas to come and be my bouncers in case there was any ruckus on the big day. And the cops came, so we were allowed to do the show.

The show happened and the Hindutva organisation had nothing to say. They sat there with their pen and paper and their phones and I had the great thrill of being able to tell them to switch off their phones during the show because that wasn't allowed. But there was nothing offensive about the show.

Postscript: Sanjna had the right idea in not dignifying the Hindu Janajagruti Samiti by naming them, but they were back at it two years later, in 2011. When the Nehru Centre staged the Ekjute production—this time under Juhi Babbar's direction—the Samiti decided they wanted to protest all over again, even though this was the version with cuts, which they had sat through earlier. By this time, the Samiti had lodged 1,250 complaints against Husain all over the country.[218]

---

[218] 'Hindu outfit now protests against play on M.F. Husain', *The Indian Express*, 20 September 2011 (https://indianexpress.com/article/mumbai/hindu-outfit-now-protests-against-play-on-m-f-husain/).

SUNIL SHANBAG

Words Have Been Spoken

For more than four decades, theatre producer and director Sunil Shanbag has embraced the formal performance space and worked beyond it. He has grappled with ideas critical to our time through text and performance. He has involved the larger community in exploring the political terrain of theatre, and its possibilities for a country as diverse as India.

Just a few examples: *Sex, Morality, and Censorship,* written by Shanta Gokhale and Irawati Karnik, dealt with the censorship of Vijay Tendulkar's play *Sakharam Binder* in 1972. 'As a director,' says Sunil, 'I was very aware that we were constructing an argument about censorship of a play in the context of its times.' *Loretta*, a musical in the Konkani form known as Tiatr, spoke of identity by probing parochialism as well as linguistic 'purity' and hybridity, 'at a time when we were being asked to prove our "Indian-ness" by the rapidly growing ranks of right-wing *bhakts*.' Ramu Ramanathan's play *Cotton 56, Polyester 84* told the story of the textile mill workers of Mumbai. The play was based on interviews with mill workers and their families, as well as the history of the confrontation between textile trade unions and mill owners. The play, 'brought to light the suppressed history, subculture and marginalisation of the mill workers of Mumbai, whose plight was largely ignored in the raging public debate on the development of the mill lands.'[219]

The choice of text and, of course, the performative mode, says a great deal about Sunil's theatre. On the one hand, his work looks at authoritarianism, censorship (including self-censorship), and the tyranny of 'morality', squarely in the eye. On the other, his work struggles to define and map cultural resistance—dissent. Indeed dissent is the idea, the metaphor, the object of the quest, in a play such as *Words Have Been Uttered*. This is how the play unfolds: eight actors and a musician sit with papers and books and musical instruments onstage. They read, recite, sing or perform texts that may be poetic or satirical, and that may be in different languages or from different cultures. What all the texts do is probe, highlight nuance and, above all, question. From caste, gender, religion and superstition to majoritarianism and notions of nationalism—everything that bears upon the world we live in is liable to this performative process of unravelling.

Sunil reflects on the dilemmas he and his colleagues face today:

> The space available for alternatives views, ideologies, and thoughts has always been limited, but in more recent times the situation has become much more fraught. It doesn't take much for someone to take objection to a piece of work, or a thought, and for the authorities to slap rather serious charges on the hapless 'offender'.

---

[219] All the quotations are from Sunil Shanbag, 'Breaking Silences Makes Civilizations Heal', *Indian Cultural Forum*, 9 July 2023 (https://indianculturalforum.in/2023/07/09/breaking-silences-makes-civilisations-heal-theatre-director-sunil-shanbag/).

> We are not activists, so are we psychologically and otherwise prepared for this kind of an eventuality?
>
> On the other hand, today more than ever before, the need for alternative narratives is critical.
>
> Why do artists have an added responsibility? Can art provide the nuances that journalism cannot? Even the best of journalism? Can art resist the numbing influence of the mainstream? We believe the answer to both is yes.[220]

In August 2022, Sunil spoke to me about the nature of politically engaged theatre practice in India—the many risks it must take, and how its interaction with a live audience has been disrupted by the vetoes of the state, social morality and mob censorship. In recent years, says Sunil, the ruling party, its ideology, (and lately, COVID), have imposed new restrictions on live performance and collective engagement. The challenge theatre faces, he says, is figuring out how to keep alive the spirit of dissent. And indeed, this a challenge for the entire cultural community …

8 August 2022

Githa Hariharan (GH): I think we agree that our artistic practice is political, but in all sorts of complicated ways that are not always obvious. What is your take on this truism that all of us experience, but also relearn every day?

Sunil Shanbag (SS): I think what has happened is that the definition of what constitutes the political has widened considerably in the last fifteen years. The earlier understanding of politics in the arts was restricted to what was obvious at the

[220] Ibid.

time, for instance, the relationship between the individual and the state, or with the institutions of state power. I remember someone expressing disappointment about a play I did, which, among other things, looked at the cultural politics of music-making in the Indian tradition, and I was told that it lacked the 'politics' of my earlier plays. Again, in another instance, a play that looked at identity and language was not accepted as being political. People still construct and find comfort in categories, and that's a disappointment.

I think it also has to do with the growing anti-intellectual environment in the country, supported so aggressively by mainstream art—whether it is cinema or music, or even theatre—which then brings us to how radically political it is today to create and nurture safe spaces for ideas and the intellect. Spaces where there can be reflection, thoughtfulness, respect for different ideas, and discussion and debate without the terror of being shouted down, even attacked physically. I believe we have slid backwards in these times. I remember, not long ago, our aim was to occupy a part of the mainstream space in theatre with our idea of theatre. In the present circumstances, that seems almost impossible—foolhardy even. So, you're right … it is a process of continuous learning and relearning.

GH: Theatre and film are among the most powerful forms to communicate with the audience, not just as individuals but as a community. Theatre, arguably, is even more direct, with the actors and their bodies present before the audience. What advantages does this give your performance as a political act? What challenges?

SS: Undoubtedly theatre has that power to provoke, to subvert. There is a certain charged atmosphere during a live performance, in that anything can happen. It's something happening in the moment, and that's a very special quality. Which is why the pre-censorship of live performance, to which we're still subjected in Maharashtra, is absurd.

The subversive quality of live performance makes people wary and it often makes them over-react. But I want to use this observation to present another view, questioning something that we assume, take for granted, often to our own detriment.

One of the important debates that the COVID period threw up was about what constitutes 'live-ness'. This debate was sparked when live performers, like theatre-makers, had to go digital and found themselves having to perform to an imagined audience, and within a pre-fixed visual frame (usually provided by Zoom). Very discomfiting, as you can imagine. There was a strong purist position that theatre performed in the digital domain was not theatre at all. There was also the counterview; we saw how quickly so many theatre-makers in India found all kinds of innovative ways to deal with the challenge of not being live. However, what was disappointing was the lost opportunity to re-look at the whole idea of live-ness. A lot of live theatre is in fact 'dead' theatre, or 'deadly' theatre as Peter Brook put it. Theatre that just does not work, does nothing for anyone. And yet it is played live. So, what is live-ness? And do we work hard enough to make it happen? This is a problem, especially when theatre is being done for a larger idea—for instance, in activist theatre.

GH: I have spoken of the community—but of course, the 'accidental community' of an audience in a theatre hall is quite different from the neighbourhood community. Do you feel street theatre or the adaptation of 'traditional'/'folk' forms have greater potential as 'people's theatre'?

SS: There are two distinct ideas in the question but they are connected. I think different spaces allow for different possibilities in communication. The kind of communication possible in an enclosed space, and further, in a space designed for performance, might be very difficult 'out on the street' and vice versa. There is also a difference of accessibility to the two kinds of space. The street is more democratic—anyone can be there. But it also means that there is a shifting audience and varying degrees of commitment to the performance. When we were performing *Cotton 56, Polyester 84*,[221] in our eagerness to perform for worker audiences, we offered to work in small community centres or even out in the open. But the workers very firmly let us know that they preferred to see it in a formal auditorium because they would enjoy that experience!

I think when we speak about street theatre, or the adaptation of folk forms as being suitable for 'people's' theatre, perhaps what we are referring to, apart from what the plays are about, are some of the special theatrical qualities these forms have. I have always loved and played with some of these theatrical elements in my own 'formal' work. For instance, the possibility of breaking the conventional 'fourth wall', and including the audience in the performance; the possibility of moving back and forth in time and space; and the possibility of using different language registers.

GH: Just as poets are essential (although prose may arguably be easier to write, publish and sell), the documentary film, with its imaginative use of reportage, could be seen as necessary to chronicle ideas, people and the times. What do you think?

[221] Ramu Ramanathan's play from 2006, about the textile mill workers of Mumbai, was originally in English. At Shanbag's instance, it was translated into Hindi by Chetan Datar and also came to include songs in Marathi.

SS: It's so interesting that you use the idea of a poet in your question! Documentary filmmaking practice has evolved significantly in the past couple of decades, and has produced some beautiful poetic work which also serves as a valuable chronicle of the time. In many ways, independent documentary filmmakers have not just pushed forward the language of film, but have also been the last bastion of that independent thought which resists and challenges the narratives of both the state and the mainstream. Again, like theatre, the documentary has tremendous subversive possibilities, and attracts a pushback from power, which often seems wildly out of proportion to the number of people it reaches! I remember we were once screening a film that looked at the resistance movement in Kashmir with a degree of empathy. This was at a small informal space in Mumbai and no more than fifty to sixty people had showed up for the film. But suddenly twenty police personnel from the local police station, among them senior inspectors, arrived to shut down the screening. The reaction was completely out of proportion to the occasion, but I think it demonstrates the power of independent thought.

GH: Whether as writer, actor or director, how do you use the past to make fresh meaning for the present? And how do you do this while resisting the increasingly chauvinistic narrative of the fabricated past?

SS: Our understanding of both the present and the past gain from referring to them. In *Sex, Morality, and Censorship* [developed from primary sources by Shanta Gokhale and Irawati Karnik, 2009], we had researched the history and context of the 1972 attack by the state and civil society on the [Vijay Tendulkar] play *Sakharam Binder*. This was to understand the idea of censorship in our times. But in our re-imagining of

Prithviraj Kapoor's iconic play, *Deewar*, we used our present understanding of colonialism and nationalism to understand the argument presented by the play in 1945.[222] In *Words Have Been Uttered* [a collection of songs, poems, narrations and play-extracts curated by Shanbag, Karnik and Sapan Saran], which is an exploration of the idea of dissent, we move seamlessly between time, space, geography and language, to emphasise how dissent is an inevitable part of human civilisation. In my experience, this kind of juxtaposition leads to the making of very exciting and illuminating meaning.

GH: What, to your mind, is dissent? And how does it bridge your life as theatre person, filmmaker and citizen?

SS: Dissent is a creative force, a powerful force of transformation and, to my mind, very difficult to separate from life itself. Art requires you to question, from the banal to the profound. I don't think I can say this in any other way.

GH: How does the dissent expressed by a particular play performance get tempered by the collective involved—from the playwright (or text) to the director to the actors?

SS: Yes, theatre is collective work, and all such work depends on a series of negotiations. In an ideal situation, everyone involved is pulling in the same direction, and this adds to the richness and diversity of the ideas being expressed. Sometimes the situation is not so smooth, but negotiation can often lead to interesting outcomes which were not imagined at the beginning of the process.

---

[222] An allegorical work staged two years before Independence, *Deewar* had attracted the attention of the colonial censor. The play encouraged its audience to imagine the kind of India they wished to see. Shanbag's adaptation was staged in 2018.

When we work with a pre-written text, the ideas are laid out before the process begins. So everyone has to have bought into the text at the very beginning. But in a process which involves devising in some form, not everyone in the room is able or willing to be as open or outspoken as someone else. How does one respond to this? Do we see the unwillingness or inability as an obstacle? Do we see it as a challenge to find creative and mutually respectful solutions?

I am familiar with such situations both in our work and in the work of others, and different people respond differently. As long as there is good faith, creative solutions can be found. Also, we have to keep reminding ourselves as artists that a specific piece of work is not our last one. There will be an opportunity to do another, and then another. We have to learn to relax … it's never the end of the world.

GH: Does our multilingual condition hinder the travel of 'local' theatre within the country? Or do we have instances of adaptation that actually enrich the local?

SS: The awareness of a pan-Indian theatre practice in the sixties and the early seventies was mostly built on the strength of translations of plays written in different languages. Translations led to productions, and productions brought different regional sensibilities and ideas to audiences. This happened because of the passion and initiative of individuals, of those who saw themselves as part of a contemporary Indian theatre community. Playwrights translated each other's plays, and these translations circulated, and readings were done. I think this kind of a sense of ownership, and of responsibility and generosity, is critical. The works of the major playwrights of that time are known in translation across the country. When I began doing theatre in 1974, my first play as an actor was a translation of a Marathi play into Hindi. In the next few years, I worked with translations of plays from Kannada and Bengali.

But returning to your question, language does play a major part in how easily a play travels across a vastly multi-lingual country. It sometimes leads to having to make a choice which is not in sync with the cultural specificity of a play. For instance, the 'natural' language for *Cotton 56, Polyester 84* was Marathi, but because my theatre work travels a lot, it was strategic to do the play in a language that was more widely understood. The challenge then was how to retain the essence of Marathi while doing the play in Hindi.

Even in a city like Mumbai where so many languages co-exist, our theatre audiences and performance spaces, are ghettoised. For instance, there is a distinct audience for Marathi plays, and one for Gujarati, and there are dedicated theatre spaces for plays in these languages. At the same time, plays from either language do get translated and produced in the other, so eventually some plays do reach a larger audience.

But translations do need to be published in some manner, shared, and made widely and easily available. That remains a critical task.

GH: You have developed the theme of experiencing and living with censorship in your work. Would you unravel some of the layers of censorship we are subject to today? Also, what may be some strategies of resistance?

SS: When we were researching the idea of censorship for *Sex, Morality and Censorship*, we had a long conversation with the playwright G.P. Deshpande,[223] and he, in his erudite and deeply

[223] Govind Purushottam Deshpande (GPD) (1938–2013), the Marathi playwright and columnist of the *Economic and Political Weekly*, edited

thoughtful way, opened up the idea for us. Among the many things he said, one that stood out for us as practitioners was about the difference between censorship by formal institutions of the state, and informal censorship by society and the mob. In the former, there is the possibility of recourse to appeal against an act of censorship. In the latter there is no such possibility. The (moral) censorship of society is insidious, and can only be addressed by a long and consistent process of education and awareness building.

But how does one deal with the censorship of the mob? There is no space for rational discussion. Often there are threats of violence, and the law bends easily in the name of averting a 'law and order situation', strengthening the attackers rather than the artist. This form of censorship is our biggest challenge today. It is actively encouraged and supported with a view to dismantle the processes of law and justice. Then there is the murkiness inherent in this form of attack. Often there are other agenda at play. The attack on a piece of art is not about offended sensibilities, it is a simple case of extortion. Money changes hands and the attack is withdrawn. This kind of cynicism is extremely damaging to the fabric of society, and no words can be too harsh to condemn it. Again, the reality is that many artists support the idea of censorship. We face this situation in Maharashtra. The theatre scrutiny board is projected as some kind of enlightened and benevolent protector of public morality!

Modern Indian Drama (Sahitya Akademi, 2004), an anthology of plays in English translation. His critical writings were published under the title *Dialectics of Defeat: Problems of Culture in Post-colonial India* (Seagull, 2006). In 1996 he received the Sangeet Natak Akademi Award for his work as a dramatist. GPD was also Professor of International Studies at the Centre of East Asian Studies, Jawaharlal Nehru University, New Delhi.

Historically, theatre practitioners have employed many strategies to get around censorship. Some have to do with their negotiations and engagement with formal institutions. Some are artistic strategies. Some have to do with how they scale their work, to stay below the radar.

In my own practice, I have seen a relatively liberal phase when it was possible to engage in a public discourse on artistic freedom. I now see a deeply cynical and intolerant phase in which such an idea has been completely side-lined and the artistic community is in a state of siege. We have to believe things will change, but this can only happen if we survive the moment, and find ways to continue working without losing our integrity.

GH: The COVID pandemic has shown us how important it is to build a sense of community, of solidarity, among cultural practitioners. How do we sustain the efforts that people like you have been involved in? Is there some way we can pressure state institutions to be more supportive?

SS: The pandemic confirmed our worst fears that state institutions have no real interest in the arts or artists. Their insensitivity to the terrible difficulties faced by artists during the pandemic period was unimaginable. Where some support was given, artists were subject to the worst kind of humiliation and disrespect. One of our premier cultural institutions exhorted artists to celebrate and participate in state-sponsored events like Surgical Strike Diwas![224] All this during the pandemic.

---

[224] On 28 September 2016, the BJP government claimed it had ordered the Indian Army to launch strikes within Pakistan. The government has since encouraged public celebrations on every anniversary of Modi's 'surgical strike'. In 2018, the University Grants Commission asked universities to join in, even suggesting that students pledge their support to the armed

Unless there is space for artists, especially artists who are able to see larger issues beyond their own practice, to participate in formal institutions, I think it's a waste of time trying to work with the state. I understand the argument that these institutions are, by their very public character, obliged to do their duty. But our personal experience of dealing with them has been very poor. Honestly, our time is better spent finding ways to form communities and support each other. We have to find, individually and collectively, ways to resist the state's appropriation of the cultural capital we have built.

forces (https://indianexpress.com/article/india/ugc-asks-varsities-to-celebrate-september-29-as-surgical-strike-day-5366706/).

Contributors

Section I

NAYANTARA SAHGAL has written fiction and non-fiction over the years. Her first book, the autobiographical *Prison and Chocolate Cake*, was published in 1954. Since then, she has written numerous novels, including *This Time of Morning* (1965), *The Day in Shadow* (1972), *A Situation in New Delhi* (1977), *Rich Like Us* (1985), *Lesser Breeds* (2003) and *The Fate of Butterflies* (2019).

Her non-fiction includes memoirs, such as her first book and, subsequently, *From Fear Set Free* (1962) and *Relationship* (1994); political commentary and history, such as *Indira Gandhi: Her Road to Power* (1982) and *Jawaharlal Nehru: Civilising a Savage World* (2010); and edited work that combines personal and political history, such as *Before Freedom: Nehru's Letters to His Sister, 1909–1947* (2000).

Sahgal has won several awards, including the Sahitya Akademi Award (which she returned in 2015 as a gesture of protest) and the Sinclair Prize. She has been Vice President of the PUCL (People's Union for Civil Liberties) as well as Vice President of PEN International.

Author, activist and parliamentarian Anis Kidwai (1906–1982) was born in Barabanki, Uttar Pradesh. She was a member of the Rajya Sabha (1956–68) and a social activist, committed to secularism and the rights of minorities and women. Kidwai had a six-decade long literary career as an essayist, and is perhaps best known for her two collections of essays—*Nazre Khush Guzre* (1975) and *Ab Jin ke Dekhne Ko* (1978), as well as her sombre Urdu memoir of Delhi during Partition, *Āzādi Ki Chhaon Mein*. A prolific contributor to Urdu women's journals and literary periodicals, Anis Kidwai perfected a highly individual style in which wit and sarcasm combined with perspicacious observation, literary allusion and progressive politics. In 1981, she was awarded the Sahitya Kala Parishad Award. The site https://aniskidwai.hcommons.org/ is both a repository of her literary work and political interventions in Urdu and in translation, and critical responses to it.

Ayesha Kidwai is a linguist, a translator and an activist. She is Professor at the Centre for Linguistics in the School of Language Literature and Culture Studies, Jawaharlal Nehru University, New Delhi. Her areas of interest include field linguistics, the politics of language, translation and partition studies. She published *Xp-Adjunction in Universal Grammar, Scrambling and Binding in Hindi-Urdu* in 2000. She won the Infosys Prize for Humanities-Linguistics in 2013, and has been Visiting Professor in a number of institutions in the US and Europe. In addition to *In Freedom's Shade*, she has translated a selection of Anis Kidwai's writings from Urdu to English, *Dust of the Caravan* (2020).

Romila Thapar received her PhD in 1958 and her thesis was published in 1961 as *Aśoka and the Decline of the Mauryas.* Since then, she has written more than twenty books of historical research and on the politics of history in India, including *A History of India: Volume 1* (1966); *The Past and Prejudice* (2010); *Ancient Indian Social History: Some Interpretations* (1978); *Cultural Pasts: Essays in Early Indian History* (2000); and *The Past Before Us: Historical Traditions of Early North India* (2013).

In her own words: 'My research into early Indian history has been part of the shift from treating ancient history as Indology to establishing it as a social science. The two themes on which I have worked are: the social and cultural history of early India which involved asking new questions of textual data and integrating some archaeological sources as well, in attempting to understand the correlation of society, economy, and religion; the second theme has been historiography, both the modern perspective of writing the history of early India, as well as the manner in which history was recorded in the early past.'[225]

Awarded honorary doctorates by nearly a dozen universities from across India and the world, and a recipient of the US Library of Congress' Kluge Prize in 2008 for 'lifetime achievement in the humanities and the social sciences', Thapar is equally known for turning down honours from non-academic sources, such as state awards.

[225] See https://www.jnu.ac.in/sites/default/files/RomilaThapar.pdf.

Section II

Bama is the pen name of Bama Faustina Soosairaj, a writer and feminist giving voice to the dalit experience of discrimination as well as resistance. She has been a dedicated school teacher all her life.

Her first book, the autobiographical *Karukku* (1992), brought her considerable attention. Some of this attention was initially negative, but subsequently, the pathbreaking memoir achieved recognition for its honest and powerful chronicle of dalit lives, especially those of women. *Karukku* won the Crossword Book Award in 2000. Her response to the award was typical: 'Winning prizes … does not mean anything to me. It does not satisfy me. One thing that gives me most satisfaction is that I used the language of my people—a language that was not recognised by the pundits of literature …'[226]

In addition to *Karukku*, Bama's work includes novels and short story collections. *Sangati* (1994) was translated into English in 2005, and *Vanmam* (2002) was translated into English as *Vendetta* (2008). Other works include *Kusumbukkaran* (1996), *Oru Thathavum Erumaiyum* (2003), *Kondattam* (2009), *Manushi* (2011), *Thavittu Kuruvigal* (2015) and a novel based on her experiences as a teacher, *Virutchangalagum Vithaigal* (2022). Her stories have been translated and published in English in collections such as *Harum-Scarum Saar and Other Stories* (2006), *Just One Word* (2018) and *The Ichi Tree Monkey, New and Selected Stories* (2021).

---

[226] Gopinath S., 'Recognition for The Language of My People Is the Biggest Award I Can Win', *Outlook Magazine*, 3 February 2022 (https://www.outlookindia.com/website/story/recognition-for-the-language-of-my-people-is-the-biggest-award-i-can-win/211431).

Considered the first modern dalit poet in Telugu, GURRAM JASHUVA (1895–1971) was born in Vinukonda, Guntur district, Andhra Pradesh, in a community of leather workers. Whether in school, college or in his professional life, he experienced caste discrimination, exacerbated by the inter-caste marriage of his parents, as well as poverty. Jashuva worked as a primary school teacher, then as a Telugu producer in All India Radio from 1946 to 1960.

Protests against untouchability and segregation have been common themes in all his works; he was also a significant literary voice in the anti-colonial movement. In addition to *Gabbilam* (1941) (Bat), his work includes *Firdausi* (1932) (Rebel), *Kandiseekudu* (1945) (Refugee) and *Baapoojee* (1948) (Bapuji). He was appointed Member of the Andhra Pradesh Legislative Council in 1964. He received the Sahitya Akademi award in 1964 for *Christhu Charitra* (1958), and the Padma Bhushan in 1970.

CHINNAIAH JANGAM is an Associate Professor in the Department of History, Carleton University, Ottawa, Canada. He holds an MA in History from the University of Hyderabad; an MPhil in Modern Indian History from Jawaharlal Nehru University, and a PhD from the School of Oriental and African Studies, University of London. He was awarded the Felix Fellowship and Harry Frank Guggenheim Dissertation Fellowship for Doctoral Studies. Jangam was a Postdoctoral Fellow at the International Centre for Advanced Studies, New York University (2005–2006). He is the author of *Dalits and the Making of Modern India* (2017).

In 2024, Chinnaiah Jangam's English translation of *Gabbilam* was awarded the A.K. Ramanujan Book Prize for Translation by the Association for Asian Studies.

Eknath Awad (1956–2015), known with affectionate respect as Jija, was a prominent dalit activist involved in several social movements to change the lives of oppressed communities, whether dalit, adivasi or poor peasant.

He was born in Beed district and grew up suffering from the twin miseries of caste and poverty. Despite it all, he got an education and, quite early in life, got involved with the Namantar movement. He was also an active member of the Dalit Panthers. After a Masters in Social Work, he joined the Vidhayak Sansad in 1981, and organised the adivasi groups in Thane, especially on the issue of bonded labour. He joined the Church's Auxiliary for Social Action (CASA) in 1983, and in addition to working against bonded labour, helped establish programmes against caste-based practices, and for literacy and women's empowerment. He founded the Rural Development Centre (RDC) in 1985 and the Manavi Haq Abhiyaan (Human Rights Campaign) in 1990.

Milind Awad did his undergraduate studies at Fergusson College, Pune, and his MA at the University of Pune, followed by an MPhil and PhD in English Studies from Jawaharlal Nehru University (JNU), New Delhi. He has taught at Zakir Husain College, University of Delhi, and Jamia Millia Islamia. He is, at present, Associate Professor at the Centre for English Studies in the School of Language Literature and Culture Studies in JNU. His areas of interest include modern dalit writing, caste and gender studies, literary theory, and studying caste in humanities.

He was Charles Wallace India Trust SOAS Fellow at the SOAS South Asian Institute, 2012–2013. He is the author of *The Life and Work of Annabhau Sathe: A Marxist-Ambedkarite*

Mosaic (2010). He has also participated, over the years, in campaigns and fact-finding committees related to dalit studies.

—∞—

Aravind Malagatti has taught in Mangalore Government College, Mangalore University and Mysore University. He has been director of institutions such as the Kuvempu Kannada Adhyayana Samsthe, Prasaranga (the publishing wing of Mysore University) and the Folklore Museum and served as the President of the Karnataka Sahitya Akademi, Bengaluru.

Malagatti has published more than fifty books—he has written poetry, fiction, drama, essays and literary criticism. His autobiography, *Government Brahmana* (1994) is the first by a dalit in Kannada; it was published in English translation with the same title in 2007. His numerous works include *Karya* (1988) published in English translation with the same title (2021); a collection of short stories, *Mugiyada Kategalu* [Unending Stories] (2000); the poetry collections, *Mookanige Baayi Bandaaga* [When the Mute Opens his Mouth] (1980), *Chandaal Swargaarohanam* [The Untouchable Ascends to Heaven] (2003) and *Masthakaabhisheka* [The Ablution] (1983).

He has received numerous awards, including the Karnataka Sahitya Akademi Award in 1996 for his autobiography, the Honorary Award of the Karnataka Sahitya Akademi in 2002 and the state government's Rajyotsava award for contribution to literature in 2011.

—∞—

Martin Macwan has been an activist over four decades, combatting untouchability and caste-based prejudices in Gujarat and other parts of India.

Macwan was born in a dalit family in Nadiad, Gujarat; he financed his education through labour in the fields. He received a degree in psychology from the Gujarat University and a law degree from the Sardar Patel University. As part of the Behavioural Science Centre (BSC) in Ahmedabad, he was a lecturer and also worked in the field with dalits and adivasis. In 1988, he founded the Navsarjan Trust and was its director till 2004. He is also the founder of the Dalit Shakti Kendra (1999) and a trustee of the Indian Institute of Dalit Studies, New Delhi.

As national convener of the National Campaign for Dalit Human Rights (NCDHR) between 1999 and 2001, he led the Indian Dalit contingent to the World Conference against Racism, Racial Discrimination, Xenophobia and Related Intolerance (WCAR) in Durban. He has received several awards for his work, including the Robert F. Kennedy Human Rights Award and the Gleitsman Foundation's Activist of the Year Award. He is the author, along with Sukhadeo Thorat and Gail Omvedt, of *Social Justice Philanthropy: Approaches and Strategies of Funding Organizations* (2019).

Section III

Shashi Deshpande was born in Dharwad, Karnataka, in 1938. She was educated in Dharwad, Bombay and Bangalore. She has degrees in Economics and Law and also studied Journalism.

She has written short stories, novels and essays for over more than four decades. Her thirteen novels include *The Dark Holds No Terrors* (1980); *That Long Silence* (1990), which won the Sahitya Akademi Award; *Small Remedies* (2000); *Moving*

On (2004); *In the Country of Deceit* (2008) and *Shadow Play* (2013). Her essay collection titled *Writing from the Margin and Other Essays* was published in 2003 and her memoir, *Listen to Me*, in 2018. She has also written for children, and translated from Kannada and Marathi into English.

Shashi Deshpande won the Padma Shri award in 2009. In 2015, she resigned from the Sahitya Akademi's General Council and returned her Sahitya Akademi award to protest the Akademi's silence over the assassination of M.M. Kalburgi.

INQUILAB (Inkulab, Ingulab), (1944–2016) was born Shahul Hameed in Ramanathapuram district, Tamil Nadu. He was part of the Vanambadi movement of modern Tamil poetry that addressed contemporary social and political issues. Inquilab was popularly known as 'Makkal Kavignar' or the people's poet. He was also a dramatist whose plays, including *Avvai* and *Manimegalai*, challenged patriarchal norms. He retired as Professor of Tamil from New College in Chennai.

Inquilab's work was informed by his activism, first with the Dravidian movement, and then, after the Kilvenmani massacre of dalit agricultural workers in 1968, the left. His song *'Manusangada, naanga manusangada'* (Humans, we are humans) on the Kilvenmani massacre became a powerful expression of progressive movements. In 2006 he returned the Kalaimamani award to protest at the Tamil Nadu government's failure to protect Sri Lankan Tamils.

A. MANGAI is the pen name of V. Padma (b. 1960), who retired from teaching English at Stella Maris College, Chennai. A scholar and activist who combines feminism with theatre practice, she has been a great force for increasing women's participation in theatre across Tamil Nadu. She has been involved with several theatre groups as a founder and/or a member, from the Chennai Kalai Kuzhu to Voicing Silence and Marappachi. Her rich career of direction includes the highly acclaimed *Pacha Mannu* (The New Born), a play about female infanticide; *Pani Thee* (Frozen Fire), a re-reading of the ancient myth of Ambai-Shikhandi, an ambivalent male-female figure in the Mahabharata, presenting the epic from the point of view of a marginal character; and *Kaala Kanavu* (Dreams of the Times), about the feminist history of Tamil Nadu.

Mangai writes in both English and Tamil, and translates between them. She is the author of *Acting Up: Gender and Theatre in India, 1979 Onwards* (2015). Her translations include *Our Lives, Our Words* (2011), a collection of first-person accounts by transgender communities around Tamil Nadu; *Theri Gatha*, a canonical Pali text of Elder Nuns' Verses translated into Tamil (2007); and also the Tamil translation (2023) of Githa Hariharan's novel *I Have Become the Tide*. She has co-edited, with Tapan Basu and Indranil Acharya, a collection of writings by Dalit authors titled *Listen to the Flames: Texts and Readings from the Margins* (2016).

VAASANTHI (Vaasanthi Sundaram) writes in both Tamil and English. Her work from over forty years includes novels, short story collections and travelogues. Her numerous novels include *Aakasa Veedugal* (1981, translated into English as *A Home in the Sky*, 2007), *Sirai* (2014), *Mouna Puyal* (1985, translated into English as *The Silent Storm,* 1990), *Kadaisi Varai* (1996, translated into English as *Birthright*, 2005), *Yuga Sandhi* (2000, translated into English as *At the Cusp of Ages*, 2008) and *Vittu Viduthalaiyagi* (2012, translated into English as *Breaking*

Free, 2022). Her stories have been translated into English and published in collections such as *The Guilty and Other Stories* (2002) and *Ganga's Choice and Other Stories* (2021).

In addition to English, her works in Tamil have been translated into Malayalam, Hindi, Telugu, Kannada, Norwegian, Czech and Dutch. She has won numerous awards for her writing, including the Gyana Bharati Award, the UP Sahitya Sansthan Award and the Punjab Sahitya Akademi Award for the Hindi and English translations of her novels.

Vaasanthi's books in English include *Cut-outs, Caste and Cine Stars: The World of Tamil Politics* (2008); and the popular biographies *Amma: Jayalalithaa's Journey from Movie Star to Political Queen* (2016), *The Lone Empress: A Portrait of Jayalalithaa* (2019), *Karunanidhi: The Definitive Biography* (2020), and *Rajinikanth: A Life* (2021).

She was editor of the Tamil edition of *India Today* in Chennai for nearly ten years.

Popuri Lalitha Kumari writes under the pen name Volga. She has a large body of work that includes novels, short stories, poetry, plays, essays, translations and literary criticism.

Starting with her early novels *Sahaja* (1986) and *Svechcha* (1987), her work examines and questions the demands of custom, especially as imposed on women, and the theme of liberation. Her publications include the short story collection *Rajakeeya Kathalu* (Political Stories, 1992); the anthology of feminist poems, *Neeli Meghalu* (Blue Clouds, 1993); the volume of feminist essays, *Maaku Godalu Levu* (We Have No Walls, 1989); and the play *Charitra Swaralu* (Voices of History, 2001).

Volga has won numerous awards, including the Lok Nayak Foundation Award in 2014, the Sahitya Akademi Prize for her short story collection *Vimuktha* in 2015 and the South Asia Ladli Media and Advertising Award for Gender Sensitivity in 2017.

She is a founding member and chairperson of the Asmita Resource Centre for Women in Hyderabad.

RITU MENON is a feminist publisher and writer who has been active in the South Asian women's movement for several decades. She is co-founder of Kali for Women, India's first feminist press, and founder of Women Unlimited, an associate of Kali for Women.

Besides her biographies of Nayantara Sahgal and Zohra Sehgal, Menon is the author or co-author of several works of non-fiction, including *Borders & Boundaries: Women in India's Partition* (1998), co-authored with Kamla Bhasin; *Unequal Citizens: A Study of Muslim Women in India* (2004) and *Educating Muslim Girls: A Comparison of Five Indian Cities* (2005), both co-authored with Zoya Hasan; and *From Mathura to Manorama: Resisting Violence Against Women in India* (2007), co-authored with Kalpana Kannabiran. Besides *India on Their Minds,* more recent works include *Loitering with Intent: Diary of a Happy Traveller* (2016) and *Address Book: A Publishing Memoir in the Time of Covid* (2021).

She has edited a number of anthologies of prose, poetry and memoirs, including *No Woman's Land: Women from Pakistan, India & Bangladesh Write about the Partition of India* (2004); and co-edited, with Zoya Hasan, *In a Minority: Essays on Muslim Women in India* (2005).

Section IV

Seema Chishti is currently editor, *The Wire*. She has worked for over three decades as a reporter, author, researcher, educator, broadcaster and editor. She worked with Karan Thapar in Eyewitness, Hindustan Times TV, then with BBC World Service in London and was later Editor, Delhi, with BBC India. She was a senior editor with *The Indian Express* for fourteen years. She is one of the co-founders of *The India Cable* newsletter.

Besides writing *Sumitra and Anees*, she has co-written *Note by Note: The India Story (1947–2017)*, a history of independent India, told alongside the sound of Hindi film music for each of the years.

Besides being an innovative vocalist in the Karnatik tradition, T.M. Krishna is known as an articulate examiner of cultural history. His books include *A Southern Music, The Karnatik Story* (2013), *Reshaping Art* (2018), *Sebastian and Sons: A Brief History of Mrdangam Makers* (2020), *The Spirit of Enquiry: Notes on Dissent* (2021). The inter-relatedness of aesthetics and politics is a hallmark of his writing, whether in books or articles featured across the spectrum of print and digital media.

In August 2018, T.M. Krishna received threats from Hindutva groups for singing Christian hymns. He went on to support the anti-CAA-NRC public protests of 2019–20. The Edict Project, launched in 2020, expresses his virtuoso fusion of political engagement and musical innovation, at once infusing music with ancient Prakrit texts and leading it towards a democratic concern with justice, non-violence and inclusion. With the second edition of the Project, launched in October

2022, he has continued to recite and sing from the Maurya emperor Ashoka's inscriptions on ethical conduct.[227]

Krishna is actively involved in 'alternative' festivals such as the Chennai Kalai Theru Vizha (formerly Urur Olcott Kuppam Vizha) and Svanubhava festival, and the Sumanasa Foundation that fosters connections between the arts and the community.

Krishna has won numerous awards including the Ramon Magsaysay Award, Manila (2016), the Isai Perarignar (2017) from the Tamil Isai Sangam, the Indira Gandhi Award for National Integration (2017) and the Swathi Sangeetha Puraskaram (2019) from the Kerala State Government. The announcement that Krishna will be the recipient of the Sangita Kalanidhi award from the Madras Music Academy in 2024 led to a storm of sorts among the self-appointed guardians of Karnatik music. Much of the noisy indignation came from those who identified as upper caste—to be precise, brahmin—and also with the political right-wing. The 'controversy' illustrated several challenges individuals and institutions face in creating a more inclusive artistic practice.

SHANTA GOKHALE has worked as a lecturer at Elphinstone College and H.R. College of Commerce, as a sub-editor with *Femina*, and arts editor with *The Times of India*. She has been a culture columnist for *The Sunday Times of India*, *Mid-Day* and *Mumbai Mirror*.

She also spent some years in the corporate world. It was while working as a PR professional for Glaxo Laboratories that she began what became her first novel, *Rita Welinkar*, published in Marathi in 1992, and in English three years later.

[227] See https://www.youtube.com/watch?v=l6cMA1JTT_w

Her second novel, *Tya Varshi*, was published in 2008. Both novels won the Maharashtra State Award for the best novel of the year, and both were translated by the author into English.

She has translated plays by a long list of major playwrights in Marathi. Between 1972 and 1975, Gokhale translated Vijay Tendulkar's *Ghashiram Kotwal* and *Sakharam Binder*, along with Mahesh Elkunchwar's *Vasanakand*. She has since edited the *Collected Plays of Elkunchwar* (2008), translated the autobiography of Durga Khote, as also *Smritichitre*, the memoirs of Laxmibai Tilak. She, along with Jerry Pinto, translated his novel *Em and the Big Hoom* into Marathi. The two have also translated selected abhangs of Tukaram in *Behold! The Word is God, Hymns of Tukaram* (2023).

Her literary work on theatre includes *Playwright at the Centre: Marathi Drama from 1843 to the Present* and the edited volumes *The Scenes We Made: An Oral History of Experimental Theatre in Mumbai* and *Satyadev Dubey: A Fifty-Year Journey Through Theatre*. Gokhale's autobiography, *One Foot on the Ground: A Life Told Through the Body*, and a biography of her Bombay habitat, *Shivaji Park: Dadar 28: History, Places, People*, were published in 2018, along with an edition of her selected writings, *The Engaged Observer*, edited by Jerry Pinto.

Shanta Gokhale has won several awards including the Sahitya Akademi Award for translation and the Sangeet Natak Akademi Award for overall contribution to the performing arts.

Both as a poet and bureaucrat, ASHOK VAJPEYI has had a memorable impact on cultural life. A force behind the foundation in 1981 of the Dhrupad Kendra in Bhopal, and in 1982 of the arts and museum complex of Bharat Bhavan, he has, since retiring from the civil service, held numerous other posts in educational and cultural institutions.

His writings in English and Hindi run to over forty titles of verse, translation, art and literary criticism. He has won numerous awards and honours, including the Sahitya Akademi award (1994) which he returned as a gesture of protest in 2015; the Dayavati Kavi Shekhar Samman (1994) and the Kabir Samman (2006). In 2016, he returned his honorary D.Litt. degree to the University of Hyderabad in protest at the institution's role in driving Rohith Vemula to end his life.

He is currently the managing trustee of the Delhi-based Raza Foundation, a non-profit organisation devoted to arts, literature and ideas.

—w—

SAMIK BANDYOPADHYAY is a critic of art, theatre and film, a translator and editor. He has held various positions in universities, including Rabindra Bharati University, Kolkata, the School for Arts and Aesthetics, JNU, New Delhi, and the Freie Universität, Berlin. He was the Vice-Chairman of the National School of Drama from 2006 to 2010.

He was also regional editor, Oxford University Press, Kolkata (1973–82), founder-editor, Seagull Books (1982–88), and founder-editor of Thema (1988).

His numerous published works include a reconstruction of the script for Shyam Benegal's film on Satyajit Ray, translations from Mahasweta Devi, the introduction to the collected plays of Vijay Tendulkar, and a wide range of articles and interviews.

—w—

Sanjna Kapoor is well known for her passionate work in theatre over two decades, in the Prithvi Theatre in Mumbai (1990–2011) and Junoon (2012–2020). She now works in the field of education.

She is responsible for having brought to Indian audiences some of the finest of world and Indian theatre, as well as introducing a touring theatre festival into the Indian scene. She has also played a key role as catalyst for theatre for children. She co-founded Junoon and spearheaded its school programme. She has, since then, developed The Artful Teacher Workshop Programme and conducts workshops in schools across the country.

Sanjna has also been responsible for initiating the India Theatre Forum network for theatre practitioners. She was involved in building an all India theatre alliance that developed the first theatre management training programme, and she was one of the core team members and facilitators of SMART India (Strategic Management in the Art of Theatre).

In 2020 Sanjna was awarded the Chevalier dans l'Ordre des Arts et des Lettres by the Ministry of Culture, the Government of France, in recognition of significant contributions to the arts, literature and the propagation of these fields.

Sunil Shanbag counts among his formative theatrical influences Satyadev Dubey and Samuel Beckett. Over the past forty-five years, Shanbag's work has spanned themes and issues that concern modern Indian society, across class, caste, gender and other inequalities.

Shanbag is the co-founder and artistic director of the theatre companies Arpana and Tamaasha Theatre. Arpana, founded in 1985, specialises in staging contemporary Indian works and has since put on a string of productions in a variety of theatrical forms, such as *Stories in a Song*, a musical staged in 2011. His Gujarati production of Shakespeare's *All's Well That Ends Well* was staged at The Globe Theatre in 2012 and was invited back for another run in 2014.

Shanbag's involvement with film and television has included collaborations with Shyam Benegal, and the film *Maihar Raag* (1993), produced by him and directed by Arunabh Bhattacherjee, which won the National Film Award for best non-feature film in 1994.

Acknowledgements

The achingly resonant lines by Lal Singh Dil are from his poem 'Words', translated from Punjabi by Chaman Lal. See 'The Colour of Pain: Five Punjabi Poets', *Guftugu*, 2016 (https://guftugu.in/2016/07/15/the-colour-of-pain-five-punjabi-poets/). Also *Battling for India, A Citizen's Reader*, eds. Githa Hariharan and Salim Yusufji, Speaking Tiger, 2019.

The lines by Eduardo Galeano are from *The Book of Embraces*, W.W. Norton & Company, 1992.

The line by James Baldwin is from his essay 'As Much Truth as One Can Bear', published in *The New York Times Book Review*, 14 January 1962.

All the conversations in this book are edited versions of videotaped interviews or lengthy exchanges on email. Most of them were published in their original form on the *Indian Cultural Forum* site, www.indianculturalforum.in.

That Glittering Aspiration Called India

'Making and Unmaking India' is based on a Facebook Live interview with Nayantara Sahgal conducted by the *Indian*

Cultural Forum, on 18 September 2017. An earlier version was included in *Battling for India, A Citizen's Reader*, ed. Githa Hariharan and Salim Yusufji, Speaking Tiger, 2019.

'Revisiting Freedom's Shade with Anis Kidwai' is based on a two-part videotaped conversation for *Newsclick*, 'Revisiting Freedom', 24 February 2012 (https://www.newsclick.in/revisiting-freedom-part-i and https://www.newsclick.in/revisiting-freedom-part-ii).

'Battling for the Future' is based on several conversations between 2016 and 2020, all of which were published as videos in the *Indian Cultural Forum*:

https://indianculturalforum.in/2016/02/15/romila-thapar-the-protests-by-jnu-students-and-teachers-have-been-remarkable/

https://indianculturalforum.in/2016/02/21/romila-thapar-the-battle-now-is-between-religious-nationalism-and-secular-nationalism/

https://indianculturalforum.in/2020/03/07/universities-are-spaces-for-free-thinking-romila-thapar/

https://indianculturalforum.in/2020/03/19/romila-thapar-on-the-evolution-of-citizenship/https://indianculturalforum.in/2020/07/20/nrc-is-against-the-nation-says-romila-thapar/

https://indianculturalforum.in/2020/03/28/romila-thapar-we-are-marching-towards-a-surveillance-state/

https://indianculturalforum.in/2022/07/25/learning-from-the-past-lessons-for-the-future/, originally published by the Kerala Literary Festival, 2018 (https://youtu.be/GqnL8viYJ9k)

Annihilating Caste

'Cutting Through the System' is based on private conversations with Bama; a piece I wrote for *The Telegraph*, Kolkata, 'The Hard Business of Life', 28 December 2003 (https://www.telegraphindia.com/opinion/the-hard-business-of-life-writer-teacher-woman-christian-tamil-and-dalit/cid/1016925); and a conversation for the *Indian Cultural Forum*, 29 January 2016 (https://www.youtube.com/watch?v=pnqfyazZLsY).

'How Gurram Jashuva Turned the Literary Canon Upside Down' is based on an email conversation with Chinnaiah Jangam for the *Indian Cultural Forum*, 'Hanging like a bat, turning the literary canon upside down', 26 November 2022 (https://indianculturalforum.in/2022/11/26/gabbilam-hanging-like-a-bat-turning-the-literary-canon-upside-down/).

'Striking a Blow to Change the World with Eknath Awad' is based on a videotaped conversation for the *Indian Cultural Forum*, 'Eknath Awad and his Autobiography', 31 October 2018 (https://indianculturalforum.in/2018/10/31/strike-a-blow-to-change-the-world/).

'Ambedkar's Spectacles and Gandhi's Walking Stick' is based on an email interview for the *Indian Cultural Forum*, '*Karya* portrays the tragedy of dalit lives—their exploitation by landowners & ascetics' 12 April 2021 (https://indianculturalforum.in/2021/04/12/aravind-malagatti-and-susheela-punitha-on-karya/).

'You Cannot Kill Caste by Living Within the Caste System' is based on an email interview for the *Indian Cultural Forum*, 'There have been even more atrocities against dalits and adivasis since 2014', 28 April 2019 (https://indianculturalforum.in/2019/04/28/there-have-been-even-more-atrocities-against-dalits-and-adivasis-since-2014/).

Holding Up Many Skies

'Listening to the Woman's Voice' is based on several private and public exchanges over the years, as well as email conversations for the *Indian Cultural Forum* and *Guftugu*, published as 'Listening to the Woman's Voice', *Guftugu*, 2018 (https://guftugu.in/2018/12/31/listening-to-the-womans-voice/); 'Democracy means dialogue, debate, discussion …', *Indian Cultural Forum*, 8 November 2021 (https://indianculturalforum.in/2021/11/08/democracy-means-dialogue-debate-discussion/); and 'I am driven by the desire to tell women's stories', *Indian Cultural Forum*, 9 November 2021 (https://indianculturalforum.in/2021/11/09/i-am-driven-by-the-desire-to-tell-womens-stories/).

'Conscience-Keepers, from Avvai to Inquilab' is based on an email interview for the *Indian Cultural Forum*, 'Inquilab led a secular life until the end', 8 April 2022 (https://indianculturalforum.in/2022/04/08/inquilab-led-a-secular-life-until-the-end/).

'I Continue to Write Because I Dare to Hope' is based on an email interview for the *Indian Cultural Forum*, 18 May 2022 (https://indianculturalforum.in/2022/05/18/i-continue-to-write-because-i-dare-to-hope/).

'Building Solidarity through Sisterhood' is based on an email interview for the *Indian Cultural Forum*, 'We have to build solidarity and sisterhood on an urgent basis', 23 February 2023 (https://indianculturalforum.in/2023/02/23/we-have-to-build-solidarity-and-sisterhood-on-an-urgent-basis/).

'Do Women Have a Country?' is based on email interviews for the *Indian Cultural Forum*, 'I'm trying something new—a feminist biography …', 2 August 2021 (https://indianculturalforum.in/2021/08/02/in-conversation-with-ritu-menon-on-zohra/) and 'Do women have a country?'—Eight ideas of India from eight women', 9 July 2023 (https://indianculturalforum.in/2023/07/09/do-women-have-a-country-eight-ideas-of-india-from-eight-women/), 'Translating Creativity', an event organised by the English Department of Jamia Millia Islamia, New Delhi, 27 August 2010, and numerous informal conversations over the years.

Diversity and Dissent: The Body and Soul of Culture

'Bringing Home the Big Promise of India' is based on an email interview, 'Bringing the big promise of India into a modest home', 18 June 2022 (https://indianculturalforum.in/2022/06/18/bringing-the-big-promise-of-india-into-a-modest-home/).

'Unravelling Tradition and Practice' is based on several conversations with T.M. Krishna, including 'Githa Hariharan in Conversation with T.M. Krishna', *Guftugu*, 2015 (https://guftugu.in/2015/10/20/githa-hariharan-interviews/).

'Culture and Conflict' is based on a video interview of the same title, 2 January 2020 (https://indianculturalforum.in/2020/01/02/culture-and-conflict/), and an email conversation, 'Caste is not merely a layer in this story. It is the driving theme ....', 18 February 2023 (https://indianculturalforum.in/2023/02/18/caste-is-not-merely-a-layer-in-this-story-it-is-the-driving-theme/).

'The Moral Stature of Cultural Institutions' is based on a two-part video interview, 6 May 2019 (https://indianculturalforum.in/2019/05/06/the-return-of-awards-in-2015-still-rattles-those-in-power/ and https://indianculturalforum.in/2019/05/13/the-moral-stature-of-the-institutions-has-gone-down/).

'Contested Spaces, Contested Texts' is based on a video interview, 'The Fascists, in Germany too, first came after the universities', 1 November 2016 (https://indianculturalforum.in/2016/11/01/githa-hariharan-in-conversation-with-samik-bandyopadhyay/).

'Artists Need to Think Strategically' is based on a video interview, 31 August 2017 (https://indianculturalforum.in/2016/08/31/artists-need-to-think-strategically/).

'Words Have Been Spoken' is based on a two-part email interview, 'Dissent is a creative force, a powerful force of transformation', 8–9 August 2022 (https://indianculturalforum.in/2022/08/31/theatre-has-the-power-to-provoke-to-subvert/ and https://indianculturalforum.in/2022/09/08/dissent-is-a-creative-force-a-powerful-force-of-transformation/).

To acknowledge the two sites *Indian Cultural Forum* and *Guftugu* means acknowledging a very large number of people. First, there are those who set up the Indian Writers Forum Trust with me, starting with K. Satchidanandan, Romila Thapar and Indira Jaising; the Trustees who got on board later, Shyam B. Menon and Anuradha Kapur; and our populous and distinguished advisory panels over the years, including Nayantara Sahgal, T.M. Krishna, Gulammohammed Sheikh, Shubha Mudgal, Pushpamala N., Samik Bandyopadhyay, Chandrakant Patil, Nandini Sundar, Paul Zacharia, Sambhaji Bhagat, Satyajit Rath, Sumangala Damodaran and Sabitha Satchi. Then there was the even larger network of fellow travellers, including individuals, groups and organisations. And most of all, the young people who worked on the two sites over the years.

This book owes a great deal to Abhilasha Chattopadhyay, Ishita Mehta and Rajesh Kalithody, who helped with transcripts. V.K. Karthika helped by being the kind of friend, editor and publisher all writers should have. And, as always, my trio of argumentative supporters kept me going through both good and bad times: Prabir, Rishab, Nishad.